W9-BWG-043

VOICES OF FREEDOM
A Documentary History

Second Edition

Volume 2

VOICES OF FREEDOM

A Documentary History

Second Edition

EDITED BY

ERIC FONER

Volume 2

W.W. NORTON & COMPANY · NEW YORK · LONDON

W. W. Norton & Company has been independent since its founding in 1923, when William Warder Norton and Mary D. Herter Norton first published lectures delivered at the People's Institute, the adult education division of New York City's Cooper Union. The Nortons soon expanded their program beyond the Institute, publishing books by celebrated academics from America and abroad. By mid-century, the two major pillars of Norton's publishing program—trade books and college texts—were firmly established. In the 1950s, the Norton family transferred control of the company to its employees, and today—with a staff of four hundred and a comparable number of trade, college, and professional titles published each year—W. W. Norton & Company stands as the largest and oldest publishing house owned wholly by its employees.

Manufactured by Victor Graphics, Inc.
Book design by Antonina Krass
Composition by Binghamton Valley Composition

ISBN 13: 978-0-393-93108-2 (pbk.)

W. W. Norton & Company, Inc., 500 Fifth Avenue, New York, NY 10110
   www.wwnorton.com
W. W. Norton & Company Ltd., Castle House, 75/76 Wells Street, London W1T 3QT
   1 2 3 4 5 6 7 8 9 0

ERIC FONER is DeWitt Clinton Professor of History at Columbia University, where he earned his B.A. and Ph.D. In his teaching and scholarship, he focuses on the Civil War and Reconstruction, slavery, and nineteenth-century America. Professor Foner's publications include *Free Soil, Free Labor, Free Men: The Ideology of the Republican Party Before the Civil War; Tom Paine and Revolutionary America: Politics and Ideology in the Age of the Civil War; Nothing But Freedom: Emancipation and Its Legacy; Reconstruction: America's Unfinished Revolution, 1863– 1877; Freedom's Lawmakers: A Directory of Black Officeholders During Reconstruction; The Story of American Freedom; Who Owns History? Rethinking the Past in a Changing World;* and *Forever Free: The Story of Emancipation and Reconstruction.* His history of Reconstruction won the *Los Angeles Times* Book Award for History, the Bancroft Prize, and the Parkman Prize. He has been co-curator for two historical exhibits, "A House Divided" at the Chicago Historical Society, and "America's Reconstruction" at the Virginia Historical Society. He served as president of the Organization of American Historians (1993–1994), the American Historical Association (2000) and the Society of American Historians (2006–2007).

Contents

Preface   *xv*

15

"What Is Freedom?": Reconstruction, 1865–1877

92. *"Colloquy with Colored Ministers" (1865)*   *1*
93. *Petition of Committee on Behalf of the Freedmen to Andrew
    Johnson (1865)*   *4*
94. *The Mississippi Black Code (1865)*   *7*
95. *Sidney Andrews on the White South and Black Freedom (1866)*   *12*
96. *Elizabeth Cady Stanton, "Home Life" (ca. 1875)*   *16*
97. *Frederick Douglass, "The Composite Nation" (1869)*   *20*
98. *Robert B. Elliott on Civil Rights (1874)*   *26*

16

America's Gilded Age, 1870–1890

99. *Chief Joseph, "An Indian's View of Indian Affairs" (1879)*   *30*
100. *William Graham Sumner on Social Darwinism (ca. 1880)*   *34*

101. *George E. McNeill on the Labor Movement in the*
     Gilded Age (1887)   39
102. *Henry George,* Progress and Poverty *(1879)*   42
103. *Edward Bellamy,* Looking Backward *(1888)*   46
104. *Walter Rauschenbusch and the Social Gospel (1912)*   49

17

Freedom's Boundaries, at Home and Abroad, 1890–1900

105. *The Populist Platform (1892)*   52
106. *John Marshall Harlan, Dissent in* Plessy v. Ferguson *(1986)*   57
107. *Ida B. Wells,* Crusade for Justice *(ca. 1892)*   62
108. *Saum Song Bo, Chinese-American Protest, from*
     American Missionary *(1885)*   68
109. *Frances E. Willard,* Women and Temperance *(1883)*   70
110. *Rev. Charles G. Ames on the Anti-Imperialist*
     Movement (1898)   72
111. *Albert Beveridge, a Defense of Imperialism (1900)*   77

18

The Progressive Era, 1900–1916

112. *Manuel Gamio on a Mexican-American Family*
     and American Freedom (ca. 1926)   82
113. *Charlotte Perkins Gilman,* Women and Economics *(1898)*   86
114. *John Mitchell, "The Workingman's Conception*
     of Industrial Labor" (1910)   89

115. *The Industrial Workers of the World and the Free*
     Speech Fights (1909)   *93*

116. *Margaret Sanger on "Free Motherhood," from*
     Women and the New Race *(1920)*   *98*

117. *Carlos Montezuma, "What Indians Must Do" (1914)*   *102*

118. *Woodrow Wilson and the New Freedom (1912)*   *105*

119. *The Progressive Party Platform (1912)*   *109*

19

Safe for Democracy: The United States and World War I, 1916–1920

120. *Woodrow Wilson on America and the World (1916)*   *117*

121. *Carrie Chapman Catt, Address to Congress*
     on Women's Suffrage (1917)   *121*

122. *Eugene V. Debs, Speech to the Jury (1918)*   *126*

123. *Randolph Bourne, "Trans-National America" (1916)*   *130*

124. *W. E. B. Du Bois, "Returning Soldiers" (1919)*   *135*

125. *Marcus Garvey on Africa for the Africans (1921)*   *137*

126. *John A. Fitch on the Great Steel Strike (1919)*   *140*

20

From Business Culture to Great Depression: The Twenties, 1920–1932

127. *André Siegfried on the "New Society," from the* Atlantic
     Monthly *(1928)*   *147*

128. *The Fight for Civil Liberties (1921)*   *151*

129. *Clarence Darrow at the Scopes Trial (1924)*   *156*

130. *Congress Debates Immigration (1921)*   *160*

131. Meyer v. Nebraska *and the Meaning of Liberty (1923)*   *164*

132. *Alain Locke,* The New Negro *(1925)*   *168*

133. *Freedom and the Modern World (1928)*   *173*

21

The New Deal, 1932–1940

134. *Letter to Secretary of Labor Frances Perkins (1937)*   *177*

135. *John Steinbeck,* The Harvest Gypsies *(1936)*   *180*

136. *Labor's Great Upheaval (1936)*   *182*

137. *Franklin D. Roosevelt on Economic Freedom (1936)*   *186*

138. *Herbert Hoover on the New Deal and Liberty (1936)*   *190*

139. *Norman Cousins, "Will Women Lose Their Jobs?" (1939)*   *194*

140. *Frank H. Hill on the Indian New Deal (1935)*   *198*

141. *W. E. B. Du Bois, "A Negro Nation within a Nation" (1935)*   *202*

22

Fighting for the Four Freedoms: World War II, 1941–1945

142. *Franklin D. Roosevelt on the Four Freedoms (1941)*   *207*

143. *Henry R. Luce,* The American Century *(1941)*   *209*

144. *Henry A. Wallace on "The Century of the Common
     Man" (1942)*   *212*

145. *F. A. Hayek,* The Road to Serfdom *(1944)*   *214*

146. *World War II and Mexican-Americans (1945)*   218
147. *A. Philip Randolph, "Why We Should March" (1942)*   221
148. *Justice Robert A. Jackson, Dissent in* Korematsu v. United States *(1944)*   224

23

The United States and the Cold War, 1945–1953

149. *The Truman Doctrine (1947)*   228
150. *NSC 68 and the Ideological Cold War (1950)*   231
151. *Walter Lippmann, a Critique of Containment (1947)*   235
152. *The Universal Declaration of Human Rights (1948)*   238
153. *President's Commission on Civil Rights,* To Secure These Rights *(1947)*   244
154. *Joseph R. McCarthy on the Attack (1950)*   249
155. *Henry Steele Commager, "Who Is Loyal to America?" (1947)*   252

24

An Affluent Society, 1953–1960

156. *Richard M. Nixon, "What Freedom Means to Us" (1959)*   256
157. *Clark Kerr,* Industrialism and the Industrial Man *(1960)*   261
158. *David E. Lilienthal on Big Business and American Freedom (1952)*   266
159. *Milton Friedman,* Capitalism and Freedom *(1962)*   269
160. *C. Wright Mills on "Cheerful Robots" (1959)*   273
161. *Allen Ginsberg, "Howl" (1955)*   275
162. *Martin Luther King Jr. and the Montgomery Bus Boycott (1955)*   277

25

The Sixties, 1960-1968

163. *James Baldwin on Student Radicals (1960)*   282
164. *The Sharon Statement (1960)*   284
165. *Barry Goldwater on "Extremism in the Defense
     of Liberty" (1964)*   287
166. *Lyndon B. Johnson, Commencement Address at Howard
     University (1965)*   291
167. *The Port Huron Statement (1962)*   294
168. *Paul Potter on the Antiwar Movement (1965)*   301
169. *Betty Friedan,* The Feminine Mystique *(1963)*   303
170. *César Chavez, "Letter from Delano" (1969)*   307

26

The Triumph of Conservatism, 1969-1988

171. *Redstockings Manifesto (1969)*   312
172. *Barry Commoner,* The Closing Circle *(1971)*   315
173. *Jimmy Carter on Human Rights (1977)*   319
174. *Jerry Falwell,* Listen America *(1980)*   323
175. *Phyllis Schlafly, "The Fraud of the Equal
     Rights Amendment" (1972)*   327
176. *James Watt, "Environmentalists: A Threat
     to the Ecology of the West" (1978)*   330
177. *Ronald Reagan, Inaugural Address (1981)*   332

27

Globalization and Its Discontents, 1989–2000

178. *Declaration for Global Democracy (1999)*   *336*

179. The Freedom Revolution *(1995)*   *338*

180. *The Beijing Declaration on Women (1995)*   *341*

181. Puwat Chaukamnoetkanok, *"Triple Identity: My*
     Experience as an Immigrant in America" (1990)   *346*

182. Bill Clinton, *Remarks at the "America's Millennium"*
     Celebration (1999)   *351*

28

September 11 and the Next American Century

183. *The National Security Strategy of the United States (2002)*   *356*

184. *Robert Byrd on the War in Iraq (2003)*   *359*

185. *Second Inaugural Address of George W. Bush (2005)*   *363*

186. *Archbishop Roger Mahoney, "Called by God to Help" (2006)*   *366*

187. *Anthony Kennedy, Opinion of the Court in* Lawrence v.
     Texas *(2003)*   *369*

188. *Sandra Day O'Connor, Opinion of the Court in* Hamdi v.
     Rumsfeld *(2004)*   *371*

Preface

Voices of Freedom is a documentary history of American freedom from the earliest days of European exploration and settlement of the Western Hemisphere to the present. It was prepared as a companion volume to *Give Me Liberty!*, my survey textbook of the history of the United States centered on the theme of freedom. But it can also stand independently as a documentary introduction to the history of American freedom. This second edition of *Voices of Freedom* is organized in chapters that correspond to those in the second edition of *Give Me Liberty!*. It has been expanded to include more than fifty documents not available in the first edition. Many of the new documents reflect revisions that were made in the textbook, in whose second edition considerable material was added strengthening discussions of the history of Native Americans, immigration and the controversies surrounding it, and the American West.

Thus, this edition of *Voices of Freedom* includes such new documents as Father Jean de Brêbeuf's account of the customs and beliefs of the Hurons in New France and Carlos Montezuma's 1914 critique of federal Indian policy; Gottlieb Mittelberger's description of the arrival of Geman indentured servants in eighteenth-century Philadelphia and Archbishop Roger Mahoney's explanation in 2006 of why he would refuse to obey a proposed law making it illegal to aid illegal immigrants; John L. O'Sullivan's 1845 defense of territorial expansion in the name of "manifest destiny" and James Watts's 1978 attack on the environmentalist movement and call for the development of western energy resources. I have also taken the opportunity to add documents reflecting the diversity of the American experience, and of American ideals of freedom, including Frederick Douglass's plea for acceptance of Chinese immigrants in his "Composite Nation" speech of 1869, Carrie Chapman Catt's address to Congress calling for women's suffrage in 1917, and a condemnation of prejudice against Mexican-Americans from 1945.

No idea is more fundamental to Americans' sense of themselves as individuals and as a nation than freedom, or liberty, with which it is almost always used interchangeably. The Declaration of Independence lists liberty among humanity's inalienable rights; the Constitution announces as its purpose to secure liberty's blessings. "Every man in the street, white, black, red or yellow," wrote the educator and statesman Ralph Bunche in 1940, "knows that this is 'the land of the free'... 'the cradle of liberty.' "

The very universality of the idea of freedom, however, can be misleading. Freedom is not a fixed, timeless category with a single unchanging definition. Rather, the history of the United States is, in part, a story of debates, disagreements, and struggles over freedom. Crises like the American Revolution, the Civil War, and the Cold War have permanently transformed the idea of freedom. So too have demands by various groups of Americans for greater freedom as they understood it.

In choosing the documents for *Voices of Freedom*, I attempted to convey the multifaceted history of this compelling and contested idea. The documents reflect how Americans at different points in our history have defined freedom as an overarching idea or have understood its many dimensions, including political, religious, economic, and personal freedom. For each chapter, I tried to select documents that highlight the specific discussions of freedom that occurred during that time period. I hope that students will gain an appreciation of how the idea of freedom has expanded over time, and how it has been extended into more and more areas of Americans' lives. But, at the same time, the documents suggest how freedom for some Americans, at various times in our history, rested on lack of freedom—slavery, indentured servitude, the subordinate position of women—for others.

The documents that follow reflect the kinds of historical developments that have shaped and reshaped the idea of freedom, including war, economic change, territorial expansion, and international involvement. The selections try to convey a sense of the rich cast of characters who contributed to the history of American freedom. They include presidential proclamations and letters by runaway slaves, famous court cases and obscure manifestos, ideas dominant in a particular era and those of radicals and dissenters. They range from the John Peter Zenger case in colonial New York, which helped to establish the principle of freedom of the press, to Frederick Douglass's account of how he learned to cherish the idea of freedom while in slavery, Charlotte Perkins Gilman's discussion at the turn of the twentieth century of how expanding employment opportunities instilled a new spirit of freedom in American women, and Franklin D. Roosevelt's Four Freedom's speech of 1941, outlining Allied aims in World War II. I have been particularly attentive to how battles at the boundaries of freedom—the efforts of racial minorities, women, and others to secure greater freedom—deepened and transformed the concept of freedom and extended it into new realms.

All of the documents in this collection are "primary sources"; that is, they were written or spoken by men and women enmeshed in the events of the past rather than by later historians. They therefore offer students the opportunity to encounter ideas about freedom in the actual words of participants in the drama of American history. Some of the documents are reproduced in their entirety. Most are excerpts from longer articles or books. In editing the documents, I tried to remain faithful to the original purpose of the author, while highlighting the portion of a text that deals directly with one or another aspect of freedom. In most cases, I reproduced the wording of the original texts exactly, but I modernized the spelling and punctuation of some early documents to make them more understandable to the modern reader. Each document is preceded by a brief introduction that places it in historical context and is followed by two questions that highlight key elements of the argument and may help to focus students' thinking about the issues raised by the author.

A number of these documents were suggested by students in a U. S. history class at Juniata College in Huntingdon, Pennsylvania, taught by Professor David Hsiung. I am very grateful to these students, who responded enthusiastically to an assignment by Professor Hsiung asking them to locate documents that might be included in this second edition of *Voices of Freedom* and to justify their choices with historical arguments. I also wish to thank Professor Barbara Y. Welke of the University of Minnesota, who offered valuable suggestions for documents to be included.

Taken together, the documents suggest the ways in which American freedom has changed and expanded over time. But they also remind us that American history is not simply a narrative of continual progress toward greater and greater freedom. While freedom can be achieved, it may also be reduced or rescinded. It can never be taken for granted.

Eric Foner

VOICES OF FREEDOM
A Documentary History

Second Edition

Volume 2

CHAPTER 15

"What Is Freedom?": Reconstruction, 1865–1877

92. "Colloquy with Colored Ministers" (1865)

Source: Journal of Negro History, *Vol. 16, January 1931, pp. 88–92. Reprinted with permission of the Association for the Study of African-American Life.*

On the evening of January 12, 1865, twenty leaders of the local black community met in Savannah with General William T. Sherman and Secretary of War Edwin M. Stanton. Less than a month had passed since Sherman's army had captured the city, at the end of the March to the Sea. The group chose as its spokesman Garrison Frazier, a Baptist minister who had purchased the freedom of himself and his wife in 1856.

One of the most remarkable interchanges of those momentous years, the "Colloquy" offered a rare insight into African-Americans' ideas and aspirations at the dawn of freedom. Four days after the meeting, Sherman issued Special Field Order 15, which set aside the Sea Islands and a large area along the South Carolina and Georgia coasts for the settlement of black families on forty-acre plots of land. He also offered them broken-down mules that the army could no longer use. In Sherman's order lay the origins of the phrase, "forty acres and a mule," that would reverberate across the South in the next few years.

ON THE EVENING of Thursday, the 12th day of January, 1865, the following persons of African descent met, by appointment, to hold an interview with EDWIN M. STANTON, Secretary of War, and Major-General SHERMAN, to have a conference upon matters relating to the freedmen of the State of Georgia....

• • •

Garrison Frazier being chosen by the persons present to express their common sentiments upon the matters of inquiry, makes answers to inquiries as follows:

1. State what your understanding is in regard to the acts of Congress, and President Lincoln's proclamation, touching the condition of the colored people in the rebel States.

Answer. So far as I understand President Lincoln's proclamation to the rebellious States, it is, that if they would lay down their arms and submit to the laws of the United States before the 1st of January, 1863, all should be well; but if they did not, then all the slaves in the rebel States should be free, henceforth and forever; that is what I understood.

2. State what you understand by slavery, and the freedom that was to be given by the President's Proclamation.

Answer. Slavery is receiving by irresistible power the work of another man, and not by his consent. The freedom, as I understand it, promised by the proclamation, is taking us from under the yoke of bondage and placing us where we could reap the fruit of our own labor, and take care of ourselves, and assist the Government in maintaining our freedom.

3. State in what manner you think you can take care of yourselves, and how can you best assist the Government in maintaining your freedom.

Answer. The way we can best take care of ourselves is to have land, and turn in and till it by our labor—that is, by the labor of the women, and children, and old men—and we can soon maintain ourselves and have something to spare; and to assist the Government, the young men should enlist in the service of the Government, and serve in such manner as they may be wanted (the rebels told us that they piled them up and made batteries of them, and sold them to Cuba, but we don't believe that). We want to be placed on land until we are able to buy it and make it our own.

4. State in what manner you would rather live, whether scattered among the whites, or in colonies by yourselves.

Answer. I would prefer to live by ourselves, for there is a prejudice against us in the South that will take years to get over; but I do not know that I can answer for my brethren.

[*Mr.* [James] *Lynch* says he thinks they should not be separated, but live together. All the other persons present being questioned, one by one, answer that they agree with "brother *Frazier.*"]

5. Do you think that there is intelligence enough among the slaves of the South to maintain themselves under the Government of the United States, and the equal protection of its laws, and maintain good and peaceable relations among yourselves and with your neighbors?

Answer. I think there is sufficient intelligence among us to do so.

6. State what is the feeling of the black population of the South toward the Government of the United States; what is the understanding in respect to the present war, its causes and object, and their disposition to aid either side; state fully your views.

Answer. I think you will find there is thousands that are willing to make any sacrifice to assist the Government of the United States, while there is also many that are not willing to take up arms. I do not suppose there is a dozen men that is opposed to the Government. I understand as to the war that the South is the aggressor. President Lincoln was elected President by a majority of the United States, which guaranteed him the right of holding the office and exercising that right over the whole United States. The South, without knowing what he would do, rebelled. The war was commenced by the rebels before he came into the office. The object of the war was not, at first, to give the slaves their freedom, but the sole object of the war was, at first to bring the rebellious States back into the Union, and their loyalty to the laws of the

United States. Afterwards, knowing the value that was set on the slaves by the rebels, the President thought that his proclamation would stimulate them to lay down their arms, reduce them to obedience, and help to bring back the rebel States; and their not doing so has now made the freedom of the slaves a part of the war. It is my opinion that there is not a man in this city that could be started to help the rebels one inch, for that would be suicide. There was two black men left with the rebels, because they had taken an active part for the rebels, and thought something might befall them if they staid behind, but there is not another man. If the prayers that have gone up for the Union army could be read out, you would not get through them these two weeks.

Questions

1. Why do the black leaders believe that owning land is essential to freedom?

2. How do blacks understand their relationship to the national government as the Civil War draws to a close?

━━━━━

93. Petition of Committee on Behalf of the Freedmen to Andrew Johnson (1865)

Source: Henry Bram et al. to the President of the United States, October 28, 1865, P-27, 1865, Letters Received (series 15), Washington Headquarters, Freedmen's Bureau Papers, National Archives.

By June 1865, some 40,000 freedpeople had been settled on "Sherman land" in South Carolina and Georgia, in accordance with Special Field Order 15. That summer, however, President Andrew Johnson, who had succeeded Lincoln, ordered nearly all land in federal hands returned to its former owners. In October, O. O. Howard, head of the Freedmen's Bureau, traveled to the Sea Islands to inform blacks of the new policy.

Howard was greeted with disbelief and protest. A committee drew up petitions to Howard and President Johnson. Their petition to the president pointed out that the government had encouraged them to occupy the land and affirmed that they were ready to purchase it if given the opportunity. Johnson rejected the former slaves' plea. And, throughout the South, because no land distribution took place, the vast majority of rural freedpeople remained poor and without property during Reconstruction.

▬▬▬▬▬▬▬

EDISTO ISLAND S.C. Oct 28th, 1865.

To the President of these United States. We the freedmen of Edisto Island South Carolina have learned From you through Major General O O Howard commissioner of the Freedmans Bureau. with deep sorrow and Painful hearts of the possibility of government restoring These lands to the former owners. We are well aware Of the many perplexing and trying questions that burden Your mind. and do therefore pray to god (the preserver of all and who has through our Late and beloved President (Lincoln) proclamation and the war made Us A free people) that he may guide you in making Your decisions. and give you that wisdom that Cometh from above to settle these great and Important Questions for the best interests of the country and the Colored race: Here is where secession was born and Nurtured Here is were we have toiled nearly all Our lives as slaves and were treated like dumb Driven cattle, This is our home, we have made These lands what they are. we were the only true and Loyal people that were found in posession of these Lands. we have been always ready to strike for Liberty and humanity yea to fight if needs be To preserve this glorious union. Shall not we who Are freedman and have been always true to this Union have the same rights as are enjoyed by Others? Have we broken any Law of these United States? Have we forfieted our rights of property In Land?—If not then! are not our rights as A free people and good citizens of these United States To be considered before the rights of those who were Found in rebellion against this good and just Government (and now being conquered) come (as they Seem) with penitent hearts and beg forgiveness For past offences and also ask if their lands Cannot be restored to them are these rebellious Spirits to be reinstated in their *possessions* And we who have been abused and oppressed For many long years not to be allowed the Privilege of purchasing land But be subject To the will of these large Land owners? God forbid, Land monopoly is injurious to the advancement of the course of freedom, and if Government Does not make some provision by which we as Freedmen can obtain A Homestead, we have Not bettered our condition.

We have been encouraged by Government to take Up these lands in small tracts, receiving Certificates of the same—we have thus far Taken Sixteen thousand (16000) acres of Land here on This Island. We are ready to pay for this land When Government calls for it. and now after What has been done will the good and just government take from us all this right and make us Subject to the will of those who have cheated and Oppressed us for many years God Forbid!

We the freedmen of this Island and of the State of South Carolina— Do therefore petition to you as the President of these United States, that some provisions be made by which Every colored man can purchase land. and Hold it as his own. We wish to have A home if It be but A few acres. without some provision is Made our future is sad to look upon. yess our Situation is dangerous. we therefore look to you In this trying hour as A true friend of the poor and Neglected race. for protection and Equal Rights. with the privilege of purchasing A Homestead—A Homestead right here in the Heart of South Carolina.

We pray that God will direct your heart in Making such provision for us as freedmen which Will tend to united these states together stronger Than ever before—May God bless you in the Administration of your duties as the President Of these United States is the humble prayer Of us all.—

In behalf of the Freedmen
                  Henry Bram
Committee   Ishmael Moultrie.
                  yates. Sampson

Questions

1. How important is it for the petitioners to obtain land on Edisto Island, as opposed to land elsewhere in the country?

2. What do they think is the relationship between owning land and freedom?

94. The Mississippi Black Code (1865)

Source: Walter L. Fleming, ed., **Documentary History of Reconstruction** *(Cleveland, 1906–07), Vol. 1, pp. 281–90.*

During 1865, Andrew Johnson put into effect his own plan of Reconstruction, establishing procedures whereby new governments, elected by white voters only, would be created in the South. Among the first laws passed by the new governments were the Black Codes, which attempted to regulate the lives of the former slaves. These laws granted the freedpeople certain rights, such as legalized marriage, ownership of property, and limited access to the courts. But they denied them the right to testify against whites, serve on juries or in state militias, or to vote. And in response to planters' demands that the freedpeople be required to work on the plantations, the Black Codes declared that those who failed to sign yearly labor contracts could be arrested and hired out to white landowners. The Black Codes indicated how the white South would regulate black freedom if given a free hand by the federal government. But they so completely violated free labor principles that they discredited Johnson's Reconstruction policy among northern Republicans.

VAGRANT LAW

Sec. 2. . . . All freedmen, free negroes and mulattoes in this State, over the age of eighteen years, found on the second Monday in January, 1866, or thereafter, with no lawful employment or business, or found unlawfully assembling themselves together, either in the day or night time, and all white persons so assembling themselves with freedmen, free negroes or mulattoes, or usually associating with freedmen, free negroes or mulattoes, on terms of equality, or living in adultery or fornication with a freed woman, free negro or mulatto, shall be deemed vagrants, and on conviction thereof shall be fined in a sum not exceeding, in the case of a freedman, free negro, or mulatto, fifty dollars, and a white man two hundred dollars, and imprisoned at the discretion of the court, the free negro not exceeding ten days, and the white man not exceeding six months. . . .

Sec. 7. . . . If any freedman, free negro, or mulatto shall fail or refuse to pay any tax levied according to the provisions of the sixth section of this act, it shall be *prima facie* evidence of vagrancy, and it shall be the duty of the sheriff to arrest such freedman, free negro, or mulatto or such person refusing or neglecting to pay such tax, and proceed at once to hire for the shortest time such delinquent tax-payer to any one who will pay the said tax, with accruing costs, giving preference to the employer, if there be one.

CIVIL RIGHTS OF FREEDMEN

Sec. 1. . . . That all freedmen, free negroes, and mulattoes may sue and be sued, implead and be impleaded, in all the courts of law and equity of this State, and may acquire personal property, and choses in action, by descent or purchase, and may dispose of the same in the same manner and to the same extent that white persons may: *Provided*, That the provisions of this section shall not be so construed as to allow any freedman, free negro, or mulatto to rent or lease any lands or tenements except in incorporated cities or towns. . . .

Sec. 2.... All freedmen, free negroes, and mulattoes may inter-marry with each other, in the same manner and under the same reg-ulations that are provided by law for white persons: *Provided,* That the clerk of probate shall keep separate records of the same.

Sec. 3.... All freedmen, free negroes, or mulattoes who do now and have herebefore lived and cohabited together as husband and wife shall be taken and held in law as legally married, and the issue shall be taken and held as legitimate for all purposes; that it shall not be lawful for any freedman, free negro, or mulatto to intermarry with any white person; nor for any white person to intermarry with any freedman, free negro, or mulatto; and any person who shall so intermarry, shall be deemed guilty of felony, and on conviction thereof shall be confined in the State penitentiary for life; and those shall be deemed freedmen, free negroes, and mulattoes who are of pure negro blood, and those descended from a negro to the third gen-eration, inclusive, though one ancestor in each generation may have been a white person.

Sec. 4.... In addition to cases in which freedmen, free negroes, and mulattoes are now by law competent witnesses, freedmen, free ne-groes, or mulattoes shall be competent in civil cases, when a party or parties to the suit, either plaintiff or plaintiffs, defendant or defen-dants; also in cases where freedmen, free negroes, and mulattoes is or are either plaintiff or plaintiffs, defendant or defendants, and a white person or white persons, is or are the opposing party or parties, plaintiff or plaintiffs, defendant or defendants. They shall also be competent witnesses in all criminal prosecutions where the crime charged is alleged to have been committed by a white person upon or against the person or property of a freedman, free negro, or mu-latto: *Provided,* that in all cases said witnesses shall be examined in open court, on the stand; except, however, they may be examined be-fore the grand jury, and shall in all cases be subject to the rules and tests of the common law as to competency and credibility.

Sec. 5.... Every freedman, free negro, and mulatto shall, on the second Monday of January, one thousand eight hundred and sixty-six and annually thereafter, have a lawful home or employment, and shall have written evidence thereof....

Sec. 6.... All contracts for labor made with freedmen, free negroes, and mulattoes for a longer period than one month shall be in writing, and in duplicate, attested and read to said freedman, free negro, or mulatto by a beat, city or county officer, or two disinterested white persons of the county in which the labor is to be performed, of which each party shall have one; and said contracts shall be taken and held as entire contracts, and if the laborer shall quit the service of the employer before the expiration of his term of service, without good cause, he shall forfeit his wages for that year up to the time of quitting.

Sec. 7.... Every civil officer shall, and every person may, arrest and carry back to his or her legal employer any freedman, free negro, or mulatto who shall have quit the service of his or her employer before the expiration of his or her term of service without good cause.... *Provided*, that said arrested party, after being so returned, may appeal to the justice of the peace or member of the board of police of the county, who, on notice to the alleged employer, shall try summarily whether said appellant is legally employed by the alleged employer, and has good cause to quit said employer; either party shall have the right of appeal to the county court, pending which the alleged deserter shall be remanded to the alleged employer or otherwise disposed of, as shall be right and just; and the decision of the county court shall be final.

CERTAIN OFFENSES OF FREEDMEN

Sec. 1.... That no freedman, free negro or mulatto, not in the military service of the United States government, and not licensed so to do by the board of police of his or her county, shall keep or carry firearms of any kind, or any ammunition, dirk or bowie knife, and on conviction thereof in the county court shall be punished by fine, not exceeding ten dollars, and pay the costs of such proceedings, and all such arms or ammunition shall be forfeited to the informer....

Sec. 2.... Any freedman, free negro, or mulatto committing riots, routs, affrays, trespasses, malicious mischief, cruel treatment to animals, seditious speeches, insulting gestures, language, or acts, or assaults on any person, disturbance of the peace, exercising the function of a minister of the Gospel without a license from some regularly organized church, vending spirituous or intoxicating liquors, or committing any other misdemeanor, the punishment of which is not specifically provided for by law, shall, upon conviction thereof in the county court, be fined not less than ten dollars, and not more than one hundred dollars, and may be imprisoned at the discretion of the court, not exceeding thirty days.

Sec. 3.... If any white person shall sell, lend, or give to any freedman, free negro, or mulatto any fire-arms, dirk or bowie knife, or ammunition, or any spirituous or intoxicating liquors, such person or persons so offending, upon conviction thereof in the county court of his or her county, shall be fined not exceeding fifty dollars, and may be imprisoned, at the discretion of the court, not exceeding thirty days....

Sec. 5.... If any freedman, free negro, or mulatto, convicted of any of the misdemeanors provided against in this act, shall fail or refuse for the space of five days, after conviction, to pay the fine and costs imposed, such person shall be hired out by the sheriff or other officer, at public outcry, to any white person who will pay said fine and all costs, and take said convict for the shortest time.

Questions

1. Why do you think the state of Mississippi required all black persons to sign yearly labor contracts but not white citizens?

2. What basic rights are granted to the former slaves and which are denied to them by the Black Code?

95. Sidney Andrews on the White South and Black Freedom (1866)

Source: Sidney Andrews, "Three Months among the Reconstructionists," Atlantic Monthly, *Vol. 17 (February 1866), pp. 237–45.*

Many northern journalists visited the South after the end of the Civil War to report on conditions there. One of the most influential was Sidney Andrews, who toured the Southeast late in 1865. Andrews offered a vivid description of how white southerners defined black freedom. Most, he reported, were convinced that the emancipated slaves equated freedom with idleness; they would not work except if compelled to do so. Andrews considered this a "cruel slander." The attitudes he encountered help explain the motives for the enactment of the Black Codes.

I SPENT THE months of September, October, and November, 1865, in the States of North Carolina, South Carolina, and Georgia. I travelled over more than half the stage and railway routes therein, visited a considerable number of towns and cities in each State, attended the so-called reconstruction conventions at Raleigh, Columbia, and Milledgeville, and had much conversation with many individuals of nearly all classes.

• • •

Going into the States where I went—and perhaps the fact is true also of the other Southern states—going into Georgia and the Carolinas, and not keeping in mind the facts of yesterday, any man would almost be justified in concluding that the end and purpose in respect to this poor negro was his extermination.... It is proclaimed everywhere that he will not work, that he cannot take care of himself, that he is a nuisance to society, that he lives by stealing, and that he is sure to die in a few months; and, truth to tell, the great body of the people, though one must not say intentionally, are doing all they well can to make these assertions true. If it is not said that any considerable number wantonly abuse and outrage him, it must be said that they manifest a barbarous indifference to his fate, which just as surely drives him on to destruction as open cruelty would.

There are some men and a few women—and perhaps the number of these is greater than we of the North generally suppose—who really desire that the negro should now have his full rights as a human being. With the same proportion of this class of persons in a community of Northern constitution, it might be justly concluded that the whole community would soon join or acquiesce in the effort to secure for him at least a fair share of those rights.... Unfortunately, however, in these Southern communities the opinion of such persons cannot have such weight as it would in ours. The spirit of the caste, of which I have already spoken, is an element figuring largely against them in any contest involving principle—an element of whose practical workings we here know very little. The walls between individuals and classes are so high and broad, that the men and women who recognize the negro's rights and privileges as a freeman are almost as far from the masses as we of the North are. Moreover, that any opinion savors of the "Yankee"—in other words, is new to the South—is a fact that even prevents its consideration by the great body of the people. Their inherent antagonism to everything from the North—an antagonism fostered and cunningly cultivated for half a century by the politicians in the interest of Slavery—is something that no traveller can photograph, that no Northern man can understand, till he sees it with his own eyes, hears it with his own ears, and feels it by his own consciousness. That the full freedom of the negroes would be acknowledged at once is something we had no warrant for expecting. The old masters grant them nothing, except at the requirement of the nation—as a military and political necessity; and any plan for reconstruction is wrong which proposes at once or in the immediate future to substitute free-will for this necessity.

Three fourths of the people assume that the negro will not labor, except on compulsion; and the whole struggle between the whites on the one hand and the blacks on the other hand is a struggle for and against compulsion. The negro insists, very blindly perhaps, that he shall be free to come and go as he pleases; the white insists that he shall come and go only at the pleasure of his employer. The whites seem wholly unable to comprehend that freedom for the negro means the same thing as freedom for them. They readily enough admit that the Government has made him free, but appear to believe that they still have the right to exercise over him the old control. It is partly their misfortune, and not wholly their fault, that they cannot understand the national intent, as expressed in the Emancipation Proclamation and the [Thirteenth] Constitutional Amendment. I did not anywhere find a man who could see that laws should be applicable to all persons alike; and hence even the best men hold that each State must have a negro code. They acknowledge the overthrow of the special servitude of man to man, but seek through these codes to establish the general servitude of man to the commonwealth. I had much talk with intelligent gentlemen in various sections, and particularly with such as I met during the conventions at Columbia and Milledgeville, upon this subject, and found such a state of feeling as warrants little hope that the present generation of negroes will see the day in which their race shall be amenable only to such laws as apply to the whites.

I think the freedmen divide themselves into four classes: one fourth recognizing, very clearly, the necessity of work, and going about it with cheerful diligence and wise forethought; one fourth comprehending that there must be labor, but needing considerable encouragement to follow it steadily; one fourth preferring idleness, but not specially averse to doing some job-work about the towns and cities; and one fourth avoiding work as much as possible, and living by voluntary charity, persistent begging, or systematic pilfering. It is true, that thousands of the aggregate body of this people appear to have hoped, and perhaps believed, that freedom meant idleness; true, too, that thousands are drifting about the country or loafing about the centres of population in a state of vagabondage.

Yet of the hundreds with whom I talked, I found less than a score who seemed beyond hope of reformation. It is a cruel slander to say that the race will not work, except on compulsion. I made much inquiry, wherever I went, of great numbers of planters and other employers, and found but very few cases in which it appeared that they had refused to labor reasonably well, when fairly treated and justly paid. Grudgingly admitted to any of the natural rights of man, despised alike by Unionists and Secessionists, wantonly outraged by many and meanly cheated by more of the old planters, receiving a hundred cuffs for one helping hand and a thousand curses for one kindly word—they bear themselves toward their former masters very much as white men and women would under the same circumstances. True, by such deportment they unquestionably harm themselves; but consider of how little value life is from their stand-point. They grope in the darkness of this transition period, and rarely find any sure stay for the weary arm and the fainting heart. Their souls are filled with a great, but vague longing for freedom; they battle blindly with fate and circumstance for the unseen and uncomprehended, and seem to find every man's hand raised against them. What wonder that they fill the land with restlessness!

Questions

1. Given that blacks had done all the work on plantations under slavery, how do you explain the widespread belief among whites that they would not work in freedom?

2. How do white understandings of freedom differ from those of the former slaves?

96. Elizabeth Cady Stanton, "Home Life" (ca. 1875)

Source: "Home Life," manuscript, ca. 1875, Elizabeth Cady Stanton Papers, Library of Congress.

Women activists saw Reconstruction as the moment for women to claim their own emancipation. With blacks guaranteed equality before the law by the Fourteenth Amendment and black men given the right to vote by the Fifteenth, women demanded that the boundaries of American democracy be expanded to include them as well. Other feminists debated how to achieve "liberty for married women." In 1875, Elizabeth Cady Stanton drafted an essay that demanded that the idea of equality, which had "revolutionized" American politics, be extended into private life. Genuine liberty for women, she insisted, required an overhaul of divorce laws (which generally required evidence of adultery, desertion, or extreme abuse to terminate a marriage) and an end to the authority men exercised over their wives.

Women's demand for the right to vote found few sympathetic male listeners. Even fewer supported liberalized divorce laws. But Stanton's extension of the idea of "liberty for women" into the most intimate areas of private life identified a question that would become a central concern of later generations of feminists.

WE ARE IN the midst of a social revolution, greater than any political or religious revolution, that the world has ever seen, because it goes deep down to the very foundations of society.... A question of magnitude presses on our consideration, whether man and woman are equal, joint heirs to all the richness and joy of earth and Heaven, or whether they were eternally ordained, one to be sovereign, the other slave.... Here is a question with half the human family, and that the stronger half, on one side, who are in possession of the citadel, hold the key to the treasury and make the laws and public sentiment to suit their own purposes. Can all this be made to change base without prolonged discussion, upheavings, heartburnings, violence and war? Will man yield what he considers to be his legitimate authority over woman with less struggle than have Popes and Kings their supposed rights over their subjects, or slaveholders over their slaves? No, no. John Stuart Mill says the generality of the male sex cannot yet tolerate the idea of living with an equal at the fireside; and here is the secret of the opposition to woman's equality in the state and the church—men are not ready to recognize it in the home. This is the real danger apprehended in giving woman the ballot, for as long as man makes, interprets, and executes the laws for himself, he holds the power under any system. Hence when he expresses the fear that liberty for woman would upset the family relation, he acknowledges that her present condition of subjection is not of her own choosing, and that if she had the power the whole relation would be essentially changed. And this is just what is coming to pass, the kernel of the struggle we witness to day.

This is woman's transition period from slavery to freedom and all these social upheavings, before which the wisest and bravest stand appalled, are but necessary incidents in her progress to equality. Conservatism cries out we are going to destroy the family. Timid reformers answer, the political equality of woman will not change it. They are both wrong. It will entirely revolutionize it. When woman is man's equal the marriage relation cannot stand on the basis it is to day. But this change will not destroy it; as state constitutions and statute laws did not create conjugal and maternal love, they cannot annul them.... We shall have the family, that great conservator of national strength and morals, after the present idea of man's headship is repudiated and woman set free. To establish a republican form of government [and] the right of individual judgment in the family must of necessity involve discussion, dissension, division, but the purer, higher, holier marriage will be evolved by the very evils we now see and deplore. This same law of equality that has revolutionized the state and the church is now knocking at the door of our homes and sooner or later there too it must do its work. Let us one and all wisely bring ourselves into line with this great law for man will gain as much as woman by

an equal companionship in the nearest and holiest relations of life....
So long as people marry from considerations of policy, from every possible motive but the true one, discord and division must be the result.
So long as the State provides no education for youth on the questions
and throws no safeguards around the formation of marriage ties, it is
in honor bound to open wide the door of escape. From a woman's
standpoint, I see that marriage as an indissoluble tie is slavery for
woman, because law, religion and public sentiment all combine under
this idea to hold her true to this relation, whatever it may be and there
is no other human slavery that knows such depths of degradations as a
wife chained to a man whom she neither loves nor respects, no other
slavery so disastrous in its consequences on the race, or to individual
respect, growth and development....

• • •

By the laws of several states in this republic made by Christian representatives of the people divorces are granted to day for ... seventeen reasons.... By this kind of legislation in the several states we
have practically decided two important points: 1st That marriage is a
dissoluble tie that may be sundered by a decree of the courts. 2nd
That it is a civil contract and not a sacrament of the church, and the
one involves the other....

A legal contract for a section of land requires that the parties be of
age, of sound mind, [and] that there be no flaw in the title.... But a legal
marriage in many states in the Union may be contracted between a boy
of fourteen and a girl of twelve without the consent of parents of
guardians, without publication of banns.... Now what person of common sense, or conscience, can endorse laws as wise or prudent that
sanction acts such as these. Let the state be logical: if marriage is a civil
contract, it should be subject to the laws of all other contracts, carefully
made, the parties of age, and all agreements faithfully observed....

Let us now glance at a few of the popular objections to liberal divorce laws. It is said that to make divorce respectable by law, gospel
and public sentiment is to break up all family relations. Which is to
say that human affections are the result and not the foundation of

the canons of the church and statutes of the state.... To open the doors of escape to those who dwell in continual antagonism, to the unhappy wives of drunkards, libertines, knaves, lunatics and tyrants, need not necessarily embitter the relations of those who *are* contented and happy, but on the contrary the very fact of freedom strengthens and purifies the bond of union. When husbands and wives do not own each other as property, but are bound together only by affection, marriage will be a life long friendship and not a heavy yoke, from which both may sometimes long for deliverance. The freer the relations are between human beings, the happier....

• • •

Home life to the best of us has its shadows and sorrows, and because of our ignorance this must needs be.... The day is breaking. It is something to know that life's ills are not showered upon us by the Good Father from a kind of Pandora's box, but are the results of causes that we have the power to control. By a knowledge and observance of law the road to health and happiness opens before [us]: a joy and peace that passeth all understanding shall yet be ours and Paradise regained on earth. When marriage results from a true union of intellect and spirit and when Mothers and Fathers give to their holy offices even that preparation of soul and body that the artist gives to the conception of his poem, statue or landscape, then will marriage, maternity and paternity acquire a new sacredness and dignity and a nobler type of manhood and womanhood will glorify the race!!

Questions

1. How does Stanton define the "social revolution" the United States underwent after the Civil War?

2. How does Stanton believe that individual freedom within the family can be established?

97. Frederick Douglass, "The Composite Nation" (1869)

Source: Philip S. Foner and Daniel Rosenberg, eds., Racism, Dissent, and Asian Americans from 1850 to the Present *(Westport, Conn., 1993), pp. 217–30.*

Another group that did not share fully in the expansion of rights inspired by the Civil War and Reconstruction was Asian-Americans. Prejudices against Asians was deeply entrenched, especially on the West Coast, where most immigrants from Asia lived. When the radical Republican Charles Sumner, senator from Massachusetts, moved to allow Asians to become naturalized citizens (a right that had been barred to them since 1790), senators from California and Oregon objected vociferously, and the proposal was defeated.

Another advocate of equal rights for Asian-Americans was Frederick Douglass. In his remarkable "Composite Nation" speech, delivered in Boston in 1869, Douglass condemned anti-Asian discrimination and called for giving them all the rights of other Americans, including the right to vote. Douglass's comprehensive vision of a country made up of people of all races and national origins and enjoying equal rights was too radical for the time, but it would win greater and greater acceptance during the twentieth century.

────

THERE WAS A time when even brave men might look fearfully at the destiny of the Republic. When our country was involved in a tangled network of contradictions; when vast and irreconcilable social forces fiercely disputed for ascendancy and control; when a heavy curse rested upon our very soil, defying alike the wisdom and the virtue of the people to remove it; when our professions were loudly mocked by our practice and our name was a reproach and a by word to a mocking earth; when our good ship of state, freighted with the best hopes of the oppressed of all nations, was furiously hurled against the hard and flinty rocks of derision, and every cord, bolt, beam and bend in her body quivered beneath the shock, there was some apology for doubt and despair. But that day has happily passed away. The storm has been weathered, and the portents are nearly all in our favor.

There are clouds, wind, smoke and dust and noise, over head and around, and there will always be; but no genuine thunder, with destructive bolt, menaces from any quarter of the sky.

The real trouble with us was never our system or form of Government, or the principles under lying it; but the peculiar composition of our people; the relations existing between them and the compromising spirit which controlled the ruling power of the country.

We have for a long time hesitated to adopt and may yet refuse to adopt, and carry out, the only principle which can solve that difficulty and give peace, strength and security to the Republic, *and that is* the principle of absolute *equality.*

We are a country of all extremes, ends and opposites; the most conspicuous example of composite nationality in the world. Our people defy all the ethnological and logical classifications. In races we range all the way from black to white, with intermediate shades which, as in the apocalyptic vision, no man can name a number.

In regard to creeds and faiths, the condition is no better, and no worse. Differences both as to race and to religion are evidently more likely to increase than to diminish.

We stand between the populous shores of two great oceans. Our land is capable of supporting one fifth of all the globe. Here, labor is abundant and here labor is better remunerated than any where else. All moral, social and geographical causes, conspire to bring to us the peoples of all other over populated countries.

Europe and Africa are already here, and the Indian was here before either. He stands to-day between the two extremes of black and white, too proud to claim fraternity with either, and yet too weak to with stand the power of either. Heretofore the policy of our government has been governed by race pride, rather than by wisdom. Until recently, neither the Indian nor the negro has been treated as a part of the body politic. No attempt has been made to inspire either with

a sentiment of patriotism, but the hearts of both races have been diligently sown with the dangerous seeds of discontent and hatred.

The policy of keeping the Indians to themselves, has kept the tom-
ahawk and scalping knife busy upon our borders, and has cost us
largely in blood and treasure. Our treatment of the negro has slacked
humanity, and filled the country with agitation and ill-feeling and
brought the nation to the verge of ruin.

Before the relations of these two races are satisfactorily settled,
and in spite of all opposition, a new race is making its appearance
within our borders, and claiming attention. It is estimated that not
less than one-hundred thousand Chinamen are now within the limits of the United States. Several years ago every vessel, large or small,
of steam or sail, bound to our Pacific coast and hailing from the Flowery kingdom, added to the number and strength of this element of
our population.

Men differ widely as to the magnitude of this potential Chinese
immigration. The fact that by the late treaty with China, we bind
ourselves to receive immigrants from that country only as the subjects of the Emperor, and by the construction, at least, are bound not
to naturalize them, and the further fact that Chinamen themselves
have a superstitious devotion to their country and an aversion to
permanent location in any other, contracting even to have their
bones carried back should they die abroad, and from the fact that
many have returned to China, and the still more stubborn that resistance to their coming has increased rather than diminished, it is
inferred that we shall never have a large Chinese population in
America. This however is not my opinion.

It may be admitted that these reasons, and others, may check and
moderate the tide of immigration; but it is absurd to think that they
will do more than this. Counting their number now, by the thousands, the time is not remote when they will count them by the millions. The Emperor's hold upon the Chinaman may be strong, but
the Chinaman's hold upon himself is stronger.

Treaties against naturalization, like all other treaties, are limited by circumstances. As to the superstitious attachment of the Chinese to China, that, like all other superstitions, will dissolve in the light and heat of truth and experience. The Chinaman may be a bigot, but it does not follow that he will continue to be one, tomorrow. He is a man, and will be very likely to act like a man. He will not be long in finding out that a country which is good enough to live in, is good enough to die in; and that a soil that was good enough to hold his body while alive, will be good enough to hold his bones when he is dead.

Those who doubt a large immigration, should remember that the past furnishes no criterion as a basis of calculation. We live under new and improved conditions of migration, and these conditions are constantly improving. America is no longer an obscure and inaccessible country. Our ships are in every sea, our commerce in every port, our language is heard all around the globe, steam and lightning have revolutionized the whole domain of human thought, changed all geographical relations, make a day of the present seem equal to a thousand years of the past, and the continent that Columbus only conjectured four centuries ago is now the center of the world.

• • •

I have said that the Chinese will come, and have given some reasons why we may expect them in very large numbers in no very distant future. Do you ask, if I favor such immigration, I answer *I would*. Would you have them naturalized, and have them invested with all the rights of American citizenship? *I would*. Would you allow them to vote? *I would*. Would you allow them to hold office? *I would*.

But are there not reasons against all this? Is there not such a law or principle as that of self preservation? Does not every race owe something to itself? Should it not attend to the dictates of common sense? Should not a superior race protect itself from contact with inferior ones? Are not the white people the owners of this continent? Have they not the right to say what kind of people shall be allowed to come here and settle? Is there not such a thing as being more generous than wise? In the effort to promote civilization may we not corrupt and destroy what we have? Is it best to take on board more passengers than the ship will carry?

To all this and more I have one among many answers, altogether satisfactory to me, though I cannot promise that it will be so to you.

I submit that this question of Chinese immigration should be settled upon higher principles than those of a cold and selfish expediency. There are such things in the world as human rights. They rest upon no conventional foundation, but are external, universal, and indestructible. Among these, is the right of locomotion; the right of migration; the right which belongs to no particular race, but belongs alike to all and to all alike. It is the right you assert by staying here, and your fathers asserted by coming here. It is this great right that I assert for the Chinese and the Japanese, and for all other varieties of men equally with yourselves, now and forever. I know of no rights of race superior to the rights of humanity, and when there is a supposed conflict between human and national rights, it is safe to go to the side of humanity. I have great respect for the blue eyes and light haired races of America. They are a mighty people. In any struggle for the good things of this world they need have no fear. They have no need to doubt that they will get their full share.

But I reject the arrogant and scornful theory by which they would limit migratory rights, or any other essential human rights to themselves, and which would make them the owners of this great continent to the exclusion of all other races of men.

I want a home here not only for the negro, the mulatto and the Latin races; but I want the Asiatic to find a home here in the United States, and feel at home here, both for his sake and for ours. Right wrongs no man. If respect is had to majorities, the fact that only one fifth of the population of the globe is white, the other four fifths are colored, ought to have some weight and influence in disposing of this and similar questions. It would be a sad reflection upon the laws of nature and upon the idea of justice, to say nothing of a common Creator, if four-fifths of mankind were deprived of the rights of migration to make room for the one fifth. If the white race may exclude all other races from this continent, it may rightfully do the same in respect to all other lands, islands, capes and continents, and thus have all the world to itself. Thus what would seem to belong to the whole, would become the property only of a part. So much for what is right, now let us see what is wise.

And here I hold that a liberal and brotherly welcome to all who are likely to come to the United States is the only wise policy which this nation can adopt.

• • •

I close these remarks as I began. If our action shall be in accordance with the principles of justice, liberty, and perfect human equality, no eloquence can adequately portray the greatness and grandeur of the future of the Republic.

We shall spread the network of our science and civilization over all who seek their shelter whether from Asia, Africa, or the Isles of the sea. We shall mold them all, each after his kind, into Americans; Indian and Celt, negro and Saxon, Latin and Teuton, Mongolian and Caucasian, Jew and Gentile, all shall here bow to the same law, speak the same language, support the same government, enjoy the same liberty, vibrate with the same national enthusiasm, and seek the same national ends.

Questions

1. What does Douglass mean by the term "composite nation"?

2. Why does he believe that people should be allowed to move freely from one country to another?

98. Robert B. Elliott on Civil Rights (1874)

Source: Civil Rights. Speech of Hon. Robert B. Elliott, of South Carolina,
in the House of Representatives, January 6, 1874 *(Washington, D.C.,
1874), pp. 1–8.*

One of the South's most prominent black politicians during Reconstruction, Robert B. Elliott appears to have been born in England and arrived in
Boston shortly before the Civil War. He came to South Carolina in 1867,
where he established a law office and was elected as a delegate to the state's
constitutional convention of 1868. During the 1870s, he served in the legislature and was twice elected to the United States House of Representatives.

In January 1874, Elliott delivered a celebrated speech in Congress in
support of the bill that became the Civil Rights Act of 1875. The measure
outlawed racial discrimination in transportation and places of public
accommodation like theaters and hotels. Thanks to the Civil War and
Reconstruction, Elliott proclaimed, "equality before the law" regardless of
race had been written into the laws and Constitution and had become an
essential element of American freedom. Reconstruction, he announced, had
"settled forever the political status of my race."

Elliott proved to be wrong. By the turn of the century, many of the rights
blacks had gained after the Civil War had been taken away. It would be left
to future generations to breathe new life into Elliott's dream of "equal, impartial, and universal liberty."

═══════════

SIR, IT IS scarcely twelve years since that gentleman [Alexander H.
Stephens] shocked the civilized world by announcing the birth of a
government which rested on human slavery as its corner-stone. The
progress of events has swept away that *pseudo*-government which
rested on greed, pride, and tyranny; and the race whom he then ruth-
lessly spurned and trampled on are here to meet him in debate, and
to demand that the rights which are enjoyed by their former
oppressors—who vainly sought to overthrow a Government which
they could not prostitute to the base uses of slavery—shall be accorded to those who even in the darkness of slavery kept their alle-

giance true to freedom and the Union. Sir, the gentleman from Georgia has learned much since 1861; but he is still a laggard. Let him put away entirely the false and fatal theories which have so greatly marred an otherwise enviable record. Let him accept, in its fullness and beneficence, the great doctrine that American citizenship carries with it every civil and political right which manhood can confer. Let him lend his influence, with all his masterly ability, to complete the proud structure of legislation which makes this nation worthy of the great declaration which heralded its birth, and he will have done that which will most nearly redeem his reputation in the eyes of the world, and best vindicate the wisdom of that policy which has permitted him to regain his seat upon this floor....

• • •

Sir, equality before the law is now the broad, universal, glorious rule and mandate of the Republic. No State can violate that. Kentucky and Georgia may crowd their statute-books with retrograde and barbarous legislation; they may rejoice in the odious eminence of their consistent hostility to all the great steps of human progress which have marked our national history since slavery tore down the stars and stripes on Fort Sumter; but, if Congress shall do its duty, if Congress shall enforce the great guarantees which the Supreme Court has declared to be the one pervading purpose of all the recent amendments, then their unwise and unenlightened conduct will fall with the same weight upon the gentlemen from those States who now lend their influence to defeat this bill, as upon the poorest slave who once had no rights which the honorable gentlemen were bound to respect....

No language could convey a more complete assertion of the power of Congress over the subject embraced in the present bill than is expressed [in the Fourteenth Amendment]. If the States do not conform to the requirements of this clause, if they continue to deny to any person within their jurisdiction the equal protection of the laws, or as the Supreme Court had said, "deny equal justice in its courts," then Congress is here said to have power to enforce the constitutional guarantee by appropriate legislation. That is the power which this bill now seeks to put in exercise. It proposes to enforce the constitutional guarantee against inequality and discrimination by appropriate legislation. It does not seek to confer new rights, nor to place rights conferred by State citizenship under the protection of the United States, but simply to prevent and forbid inequality and discrimination on account of race, color, or previous condition of servitude. Never was there a bill more completely within the constitutional power of Congress. Never was there a bill which appealed for support more strongly to that sense of justice and fair-play which has been said, and in the main with justice, to be a characteristic of the Anglo-Saxon race. The Constitution warrants it; the Supreme Court sanctions it; justice demands it.

Sir, I have replied to the extent of my ability to the arguments which have been presented by the opponents of this measure. I have replied also to some of the legal propositions advanced by gentlemen on the other side; and now that I am about to conclude, I am deeply sensible of the imperfect manner in which I have performed the task. Technically, this bill is to decide upon the civil status of the colored American citizen; a point disputed at the very formation of our present Government, when by a short-sighted policy, a policy repugnant to true republican government, one negro counted as three-fifths of a man. The logical result of this mistake of the framers of the Constitution strengthened the cancer of slavery, which finally spread its poisonous tentacles over the southern portion of the body-politic. To arrest its growth and save the nation we have passed through the harrowing operation of intestine war, dreaded at all times, resorted to at the last extremity, like the surgeon's knife, but absolutely necessary to extirpate the disease which threatened with the life of the nation the overthrow of civil and political liberty on this continent. In that dire extremity the members of the race which I have the honor in part to represent—the race which pleads for justice at your hands to-day, forgetful of their inhuman and brutalizing servitude at the South, their degradation and ostracism at the

North—flew willingly and gallantly to the support of the national Government. Their sufferings, assistance, privations, and trials in the swamps and in the rice-fields, their valor on the land and on the sea, is a part of the ever-glorious record which makes up the history of a nation preserved, and might, should I urge the claim, incline you to respect and guarantee their rights and privileges as citizens of our common Republic. But I remember that valor, devotion, and loyalty are not always rewarded according to their just deserts, and that after the battle some who have borne the brunt of the fray may, through neglect or contempt, be assigned to a subordinate place, while the enemies in war may be preferred to the sufferers.

The results of the war, as seen in reconstruction, have settled forever the political status of my race. The passage of this bill will determine the civil status, not only of the negro, but of any other class of citizens who may feel themselves discriminated against. It will form the cap-stone of that temple of liberty, begun on this continent under discouraging circumstances, carried on in spite of the sneers of monarchists and the cavils of pretended friends of freedom, until at last it stands in all its beautiful symmetry and proportions, a building the grandest which the world has ever seen, realizing the most sanguine expectations and the highest hopes of those who, in the name of equal, impartial, and universal liberty, laid the foundation stones.

Questions

1. How does Elliott defend the constitutionality of the Civil Rights Bill?

2. Why does Elliott refer to the "cornerstone speech" of Alexander H. Stephens in making his argument?

CHAPTER 16

America's Gilded Age, 1870–1890

99. Chief Joseph, "An Indian's View of Indian Affairs" (1879)

Source: "An Indian's View of Indian Affairs," **North American Review, No. 269 (April 1879), pp. 415–33.**

In 1879, Chief Joseph, leader of the Nez Percé Indians, delivered a speech in Lincoln Hall, Washington, D.C., to a distinguished audience including President Rutherford B. Hayes. Two years earlier, U.S. troops had tracked Joseph and his people on a 1,700-mile trek through the Far West as they sought to escape to Canada after fights with settlers who had encroached on tribal lands in Oregon and Idaho. After four months, the Indians were forced to surrender, and they were removed to Oklahoma.

The speech was delivered in the Nez Percé language and then translated by an interpreter. An unidentified reporter took down the interpreter's version and passed it along to an influential magazine, *North American Review*, for publication. Whether the words are exactly those delivered by Joseph may be open to question, but the sentiments are certainly his. Joseph condemned the policy of confining Indians to reservations. Speaking in a hall named for the Great Emancipator, he appealed to the ideals of freedom and equal rights before the law so powerfully reinforced by the Civil War and Reconstruction. Until his death in 1904, Joseph would unsuccessfully petition successive presidents for his people's right to return to their beloved Oregon homeland.

MY FRIENDS, I have been asked to show you my heart. I am glad to have a chance to do so. I want the white people to understand my people. Some of you think an Indian is like a wild animal. This is a great mistake. I will tell you all about our people, and then you can judge whether an Indian is a man or not. I believe much trouble and blood would be saved if we opened our hearts more. I will tell you in my way how the Indian sees things. The white man has more words to tell you how they look to him, but it does not require many words to speak the truth. What I have to say will come from my heart, and I will speak with a straight tongue.

• • •

For a short time we lived quietly. But this could not last. White men had found gold in the mountains around the land of winding water. They stole a great many horses from us, and we could not get them back because we were Indians. The white men told lies for each other. They drove off a great many of our cattle. Some white men branded our young cattle so they could claim them. We had no friend who would plead our cause before the law councils. It seemed to me that some of the white men in Wallowa were doing these things on purpose to get up a war. They knew that we were not strong enough to fight them. I labored hard to avoid trouble and bloodshed. We gave up some of our country to the white men, thinking that then we could have peace. We were mistaken. The white man would not let us alone. We could have avenged our wrongs many times, but we did not. Whenever the Government has asked us to help them against other Indians, we have never refused. When the white men were few and we were strong we could have killed them all off, but the Nez Percés wished to live at peace.

If we have not done so, we have not been to blame. I believe that the old treaty has never been correctly reported. If we ever owned the land we own it still, for we never sold it. In the treaty councils the commissioners have claimed that our country had been sold to the Government. Suppose a white man should come to me and say, "Joseph, I like your horses, and I want to buy them." I say to him, "No,

my horses suit me, I will not sell them." Then he goes to my neighbor, and says to him: "Joseph has some good horses. I want to buy
them, but he refuses to sell." My neighbor answers, "Pay me the
money, and I will sell you Joseph's horses." The white man returns to
me, and says, "Joseph, I have bought your horses, and you must let
me have them." If we sold our lands to the Government, this is the
way they were bought.

On account of the treaty made by the other bands of the Nez
Percés, the white men claimed my lands. We were troubled greatly
by white men crowding over the line. Some of these were good
men, and we lived on peaceful terms with them, but they were not
all good.

• • •

At last I was granted permission to come to Washington and bring
my friend Yellow Bull and our interpreter with me. I am glad we
came. I have shaken hands with a great many friends, but there are
some things I want to know which no one seems able to explain. I
can not understand how the Government sends a man out to fight
us, as it did General Miles, and then breaks his word. Such a Government has something wrong about it. I can not understand why so
many chiefs are allowed to talk so many different ways, and promise
so many different things. I have seen the Great Father Chief (the President), the next Great Chief (Secretary of the Interior), the Commissioner Chief (Hayt), the Law Chief (General Butler), and many other
law chiefs (Congressmen), and they all say they are my friends, and
that I shall have justice, but while their mouths all talk right I do not
understand why nothing is done for my people. I have heard talk and
talk, but nothing is done. Good words do not last long unless they
amount to something. Words do not pay for my dead people. They
do not pay for my country, now overrun by white men. They do not
protect my father's grave. They do not pay for all my horses and cattle. Good words will not give me back my children. Good words will
not make good the promise of your War Chief General Miles. Good
words will not give my people good health and stop them from

dying. Good words will not get my people a home where they can live in peace and take care of themselves. I am tired of talk that comes to nothing. It makes my heart sick when I remember all the good words and all the broken promises. There has been too much talking by men who had no right to talk. Too many misrepresentations have been made, too many misunderstandings have come up between the white men about the Indians. If the white man wants to live in peace with the Indian he can live in peace. There need be no trouble. Treat all men alike. Give them all the same law. Give them all an even chance to live and grow. All men were made by the same Great Spirit Chief. They are all brothers. The earth is the mother of all people, and all people should have equal rights upon it. You might as well expect the rivers to run backward as that any man who was born a free man should be contented when penned up and denied liberty to go where he pleases. If you tie a horse to a stake, do you expect he will grow fat? If you pen an Indian up on a small spot of earth, and compel him to stay there, he will not be contented, nor will he grow and prosper. I have asked some of the great white chiefs where they get their authority to say to the Indian that he shall stay in one place, while he sees white men going where they please. They can not tell me.

I only ask of the Government to be treated as all other men are treated.

• • •

When I think of our condition my heart is heavy. I see men of my race treated as outlaws and driven from country to country, or shot down like animals.

I know that my race must change. We can not hold our own with the white men as we are. We only ask an even chance to live as other men live. We ask to be recognized as men. We ask that the same law shall work alike on all men. If the Indian breaks the law, punish him by the law. If the white man breaks the law, punish him also.

Let me be a free man—free to travel, free to stop, free to work, free to trade where I choose, free to choose my own teachers, free to follow

the religion of my fathers, free to think and talk and act for myself—
and I will obey every law, or submit to the penalty.

Whenever the white man treats the Indian as they treat each
other, then we will have no more wars. We shall all be alike—
brothers of one father and one mother, with one sky above us and
one country around us, and one government for all. Then the Great
Spirit Chief who rules above will smile upon this land, and send rain
to wash out the bloody spots made by brothers' hands from the face
of the earth. For this time the Indian race are waiting and praying. I
hope that no more groans of wounded men and women will ever go
to the ear of the Great Spirit Chief above, and that all people may be
one people.

• • •

Questions

1. How does Chief Joseph define what it means to be a "free man"?

2. What are Joseph's main complaints about the treatment of his people?

100. William Graham Sumner on Social Darwinism (ca. 1880)

Source: Albert G. Keller, ed., The Challenge of Facts and Other Essays by
William Graham Sumner *(New Haven, Conn., 1914), pp. 17–27. Keller
concludes that the essay from which this excerpt is taken was written during
the 1880s.*

During the Gilded Age, large numbers of businessmen and middle-class
Americans adopted the social outlook known as Social Darwinism. Adherents of this viewpoint borrowed language from Charles Darwin's great
work *On the Origin of Species* (1859), which expounded the theory of evolution among plant and animal species, to explain the success and failure of

individual human beings and entire social classes. According to Social Darwinists, evolution was as natural a process in human society as in nature, and government must not interfere. Especially misguided, in this view, were efforts to uplift those at the bottom of the social order, such as laws regulating conditions of work or public assistance to the poor.

The era's most influential Social Darwinist was Yale professor William Graham Sumner. For Sumner, freedom required frank acceptance of inequality. The growing influence of Social Darwinism helped to popularize a "negative" definition of freedom as limited government and an unrestrained free market. It also helped to persuade courts, in the name of "liberty of contract," to overturn state laws regulating the behavior of corporations.

MAN IS BORN under the necessity of sustaining the existence he has received by an onerous struggle against nature, both to win what is essential to his life and to ward off what is prejudicial to it. He is born under a burden and a necessity. Nature holds what is essential to him, but she offers nothing gratuitously. He may win for his use what she holds, if he can. Only the most meager and inadequate supply for human needs can be obtained directly from nature. There are trees which may be used for fuel and for dwellings, but labor is required to fit them for this use. There are ores in the ground, but labor is necessary to get out the metals and make tools or weapons. For any real satisfaction, labor is necessary to fit the products of nature for human use. In this struggle every individual is under the pressure of the necessities for food, clothing, shelter, fuel, and every individual brings with him more or less energy for the conflict necessary to supply his needs. The relation, therefore, between each man's needs and each man's energy, or "individualism," is the first fact of human life.

It is not without reason, however, that we speak of a "man" as the individual in question, for women (mothers) and children have special disabilities for the struggle with nature, and these disabilities grow greater and last longer as civilization advances. The perpetuation of the race in health and vigor, and its success as a whole in its struggle to expand and develop human life on earth, therefore, require that the head of the family shall, by his energy, be able to supply not only his own needs, but those of the organisms which are dependent upon him. The history of the human race shows a great variety of experiments in the relation of the sexes and in the organization of the family. These experiments have been controlled by economic circumstances, but, as man has gained more and more control over economic circumstances, monogamy and the family education of children have been more and more sharply developed. If there is one thing in regard to which the student of history and sociology can affirm with confidence that social institutions have made "progress" or grown "better," it is in this arrangement of marriage and the family. All experience proves that monogamy, pure and strict, is the sex relation which conduces most to the vigor and intelligence of the race, and that the family education of children is the institution by which the race as a whole advances most rapidly, from generation to generation, in the struggle with nature.

• • •

The constant tendency of population to outstrip the means of subsistence is the force which has distributed population over the world, and produced all advance in civilization. To this day the two means of escape for an overpopulated country are emigration and an advance in the arts. The former wins more land for the same people; the latter makes the same land support more persons. If, however, either of these means opens a chance for an increase of population, it is evident that the advantage so won may be speedily exhausted if the increase takes place. The social difficulty has only undergone a temporary amelioration, and when the conditions of pressure and competition are renewed, misery and poverty reappear. The victims of them are those who have inherited disease and depraved appetites, or have been brought up in vice and ignorance, or have themselves yielded to vice, extravagance, idleness, and imprudence. In the last analysis, therefore, we come back to vice, in its original and hereditary forms, as the correlative of misery and poverty.

The condition for the complete and regular action of the force of competition is liberty. Liberty means the security given to each man that, if he employs his energies to sustain the struggle on behalf of himself and those he cares for, he shall dispose of the product exclusively as he chooses. It is impossible to know whence any definition or criterion of justice can be derived, if it is not deduced from this view of things; or if it is not the definition of justice that each shall enjoy the fruit of his own labor and self-denial, and of injustice that the idle and the industrious, the self-indulgent and the self-denying, shall share equally in the product.

• • •

Private property, also, which we have seen to be a feature of society organized in accordance with the natural conditions of the struggle for existence produces inequalities between men. The struggle for existence is aimed against nature. It is from her niggardly hand that we have to wrest the satisfactions for our needs, but our fellow-men are our competitors for the meager supply. Competition, therefore, is a law of nature. Nature is entirely neutral; she submits to him who most energetically and resolutely assails her. She grants her rewards to the fittest, therefore, without regard to other considerations of any kind. If, then, there be liberty, men get from her just in proportion to their works, and their having and enjoying are just in proportion to their being and their doing. Such is the system of nature. If we do not like it, and if we try to amend it, there is only one way in which we can do it. We can take from the better and give to the worse. We can deflect the penalties of those who have done ill and throw them on those who have done better. We can take the rewards from those who have done better and give them to those who have done worse. We shall thus lessen the inequalities. We shall favor the survival of the unfittest, and we shall accomplish this by destroying liberty. Let it be understood that we cannot go outside of this alternative: liberty, inequality, survival of the fittest; not-liberty, equality, survival of the unfittest. The former carries society forward and favors all its best members; the latter carries society downwards and favors all its worst members.

• • •

What we mean by liberty is civil liberty, or liberty under law; and this means the guarantees of law that a man shall not be interfered with while using his own powers for his own welfare. It is, therefore, a civil and political status; and that nation has the freest institutions in which the guarantees of peace for the laborer and security for the capitalist are the highest. Liberty, therefore, does not by any means do away with the struggle for existence. We might as well try to do away with the need of eating, for that would, in effect, be the same thing. What civil liberty does is to turn the competition of man with man from violence and brute force into an industrial competition under which men vie with one another for the acquisition of material goods by industry, energy, skill, frugality, prudence, temperance, and other industrial virtues. Under this changed order of things the inequalities are not done away with. Nature still grants her rewards of having and enjoying, according to our being and doing, but it is now the man of the highest training and not the man of the heaviest fist who gains the highest reward. It is impossible that the man with capital and the man without capital should be equal. To affirm that they are equal would be to say that a man who has no tool can get as much food out of the ground as the man who has a spade or a plough; or that the man who has no weapon can defend himself as well against hostile beasts or hostile men as the man who has a weapon. If that were so, none of us would work any more. We work and deny ourselves to get capital, just because, other things being equal, the man who has it is superior, for attaining all the ends of life, to the man who has it not.

• • •

Questions

1. How does Sumner differentiate between the "natural" roles of men and women in society?

2. How does he explain the existence of poverty and social inequality?

101. George E. McNeill on the Labor Movement in the Gilded Age (1887)

Source: George E. McNeill, ed., The Labor Movement: The Problem of Today *(Boston, 1887), pp. 454–62.*

Not all Americans accepted the Social Darwinist definition of liberty as frank acceptance of social inequality in an unregulated market. During the Gilded Age, the labor movement offered a very different understanding of freedom. The Knights of Labor put forward a wide array of programs, from the eight-hour workday to public employment in hard times, currency reform, anarchism, socialism, and the creation of a vaguely defined "cooperative commonwealth." All these ideas arose from the conviction that the social conditions of the 1880s needed drastic change. Reaching back across the divide of the Civil War, George E. McNeill, a shoemaker and factory worker who became one of the movement's most eloquent writers, warned that a new "irrepressible conflict" had arisen, between "the "wage-system of labor and the republican system of government." The remedy was for the government to guarantee a basic set of economic rights for all Americans.

THE PROBLEM OF to-day, as of yesterday and to-morrow, is, how to establish equity between men. The laborer who is forced to sell his day's labor to-day, or starve tomorrow, is not in equitable relations with the employer, who can wait to buy labor until starvation fixes the rates of wages and hours of time. The labor movement is the natural effort of readjustment,—an ever-continued attempt of organized laborers, so that they may withhold their labor until the diminished interest or profit or capital of the employer shall compel him to agree to such terms as shall be for the time measurably equitable. These are the forceful methods of all time, and may continue to develop manhood and womanhood by peaceful revolution, as laborers advance their line, or may cause a social earthquake, and become destructive by the organized repression of labor's right. Before the solution of the labor problem can be reached, the nature of the complaint must be understood.

• • •

These extremes of wealth and poverty are threatening the existence of the government. In the light of these facts, we declare that there is an inevitable and irresistible conflict between the wage-system of labor and the republican system of government,—the wage-laborer attempting to save the government, and the capitalist class ignorantly attempting to subvert it.

The strike of the trainmen on the Baltimore & Ohio Railroad was the serving of a notice upon the people of this nation that wages could not be further reduced,—a protest against robbery, a rebellion against starvation. The trainmen were under despotic control. To leave their employ was to become tramps, outlaws; to submit was to starve in serfdom. They knew that the power of the railroad oligarchy exceeded and superseded that of the national and State governments. The railroad president is a railroad king, whose whim is law. He collects tithes by reducing wages as remorselessly as the Shah of Persia or the Sultan of Turkey, and, like them, is not amenable to any human power. He can discharge (banish) any employee without cause. He can prevent laborers from following their usual vocations. He can withhold their lawful wages. He can delay trial on a suit at law, and postpone judgment indefinitely. He can control legislative bodies, dictate legislation, subsidize the press, and corrupt the moral sense of the community. He can fix the price of freights, and thus command the food and fuel-supplies of the nation. In his right hand he holds the government; in his left hand, the people. And this is called law and order,—from which there is no appeal. It is war,—war against the divine rights of humanity; war against the principles of our government. There is no mutuality of interests, no co-operative union of labor and capital. It is the iron heel of a soulless monopoly, crushing the manhood out of sovereign citizens.

• • •

The crisis that we are rapidly approaching is not local. No Mason and Dixon's line, no color-tests divide North, South, East and West; wherever laborers congregate, whether in the factories of New England, or the sunless mines of Pennsylvania, one chord of sympathy unites them all.

No demagogue's cant of race or creed will hold them from their purpose to be free. In that coming time, woman will teach her children the lesson of her hate and wrong. Already a generation has arisen, schooled in the great moral agitation for public good.

Justice demands that those who earn shall receive; that no one has a right to add cost without adding value.

Recognizing that the steps toward the attaining of the end must be slow, we demand, first, legislative interference between capital and labor; restraining capital in its usurpations, and enlarging the boundaries of labor's opportunity.

The Constitution of the United States demands that each of the sovereign States shall have a republican form of government. A greater power than that of the State has arisen—"a State within a State,"—a power that is quietly yet quickly sapping the foundations of the majority-rule. The law of self-protection is greater than constitutions, and legislative bodies are bound to interfere to protect the sovereign citizen against the insidious inroads of the usurping power.

Monarchal governments rest upon the ability of the ruler to maintain order by physical force. Republican institutions are sustained by the ability of the people to rule. The government has the right, and is bound in self-defence to protect the ability of the people to rule. It has the right to interfere against any organized or unorganized power that imperils or impairs this ability. Upon no other argument can the free-school system be maintained, institutions of learning, of science, and art be endowed by the State or exempt from taxation. It is the policy of the government to protect, not only her domain from monarchal interference, as set forth in the Monroe doctrine, but to protect her citizens from the influence of cheap labor and over-work. For cheap labor means a cheap people, and dear labor a dear people. The foundation of the Republic is equality.

Questions

1. How does McNeill define freedom for working men and women?

2. Why does he consider the "wage-system" of labor incompatible with republican government?

━━━━━━━

102. Henry George, *Progress and Poverty* (1879)

Source: Henry George, **Progress and Poverty** *[1879] (New York, 1884), pp. 489–96.*

Dissatisfaction with social conditions in the Gilded Age extended well beyond aggrieved workers. Alarmed by fear of class warfare and the growing power of concentrated wealth, social thinkers offered numerous plans for change. Among the most influential was Henry George, whose *Progress and Poverty* became one of the era's great best-sellers. Its extraordinary success testified to what George called "a wide-spread consciousness . . . that there is something *radically* wrong in the present social organization."

George's book began with a famous statement of "the problem" suggested by its title—the expansion of poverty alongside material progress. His solution was the "single tax," which would replace other taxes with a levy on increases in the value of real estate. The single tax would be so high that it would prevent speculation in both urban and rural land, and land would then become available to aspiring businessmen and urban working men seeking to become farmers. Whether or not they believed in George's solution, millions of readers responded to his clear explanation of economic relationships and his stirring account of how the "unjust and unequal distribution of wealth" long thought to be confined to the Old World had made its appearance in the New.

━━━━━━━

THE EVILS ARISING from the unjust and unequal distribution of wealth, which are becoming more and more apparent as modern civilization goes on, are not incidents of progress, but tendencies which must bring progress to a halt; that they will not cure themselves, but, on the contrary, must, unless their cause is removed, grow greater and greater, until they sweep us back into barbarism by the road every previous civilization has trod. But it also shows that these evils are not imposed by natural laws; that they spring solely from social mal-adjustments which ignore natural laws, and that in removing their cause we shall be giving an enormous impetus to progress.

The poverty which in the midst of abundance, pinches and embrutes men, and all the manifold evils which flow from it, spring from a denial of justice. In permitting the monopolization of the natural opportunities which nature freely offers to all, we have ignored the fundamental law of justice—for so far as we can see, when we view things upon a large scale, justice seems to be the supreme law of the universe. But by sweeping away this injustice and asserting the rights of all men to natural opportunities, we shall conform ourselves to the law—we shall remove the great cause of unnatural inequality in the distribution of wealth and power; we shall abolish poverty; tame the ruthless passions of greed; dry up the springs of vice and misery; light in dark places the lamp of knowledge; give new vigor to invention and a fresh impulse to discovery; substitute political strength for political weakness; and make tyranny and anarchy impossible.

The reform I have proposed accords with all that is politically, socially, or morally desirable. It has the qualities of a true reform, for it will make all other reforms easier. What is it but the carrying out in letter and spirit of the truth enunciated in the Declaration of Independence—the "self-evident" truth that is the heart and soul of the Declaration—*"That all men are created equal; that they are endowed by their Creator with certain inalienable rights; that among them are life, liberty, and the pursuit of happiness!"*

These rights are denied when the equal right to land—on which and by which men alone can live—is denied. Equality of political rights will not compensate for the denial of the equal right to the bounty of nature. Political liberty, when the equal right to land is denied, becomes, as population increases and invention goes on, merely the liberty to compete for employment at starvation wages. This is the truth that we have ignored. And so there come beggars in our streets and tramps on our roads; and poverty enslaves men whom we boast are political sovereigns; and want breeds ignorance that our schools cannot enlighten; and citizens vote as their masters dictate; and the demagogue usurps the part of the statesman; and gold weighs in the scales of justice; and in high places sit those who do not pay to civic virtue even the compliment of hypocrisy; and the pillars of the republic that we thought so strong already bend under an increasing strain.

We honor Liberty in name and in form. We set up her statues and sound her praises. But we have not fully trusted her. And with our growth so grow her demands. She will have no half service!

Liberty! it is a word to conjure with, not to vex the ear in empty boastings. For Liberty means Justice, and Justice is the natural law—the law of health and symmetry and strength, of fraternity and co-operation.

They who look upon Liberty as having accomplished her mission when she has abolished hereditary privileges and given men the ballot, who think of her as having no further relations to the every-day affairs of life, have not seen her real grandeur—to them the poets who have sung of her must seem rhapsodists, and her martyrs fools! As the sun is the lord of life, as well as of light; as his beams not merely pierce the clouds, but support all growth, supply all motion, and call forth from what would otherwise be a cold and inert mass, all the infinite diversities of being and beauty, so is liberty to mankind. It is not for an abstraction that men have toiled and died; that in every age the witnesses of Liberty have stood forth, and the martyrs of Liberty have suffered.

We speak of Liberty as one thing, and virtue, wealth, knowledge, invention, national strength and national independence as other things. But, of all these, Liberty is the source, the mother, the necessary condition. She is to virtue what light is to color; to wealth what sunshine is to grain; to knowledge what eyes are to sight. She is the genius of invention, the brawn of national strength, the spirit of national independence. Where Liberty rises, there virtue grows, wealth increases, knowledge expands, invention multiplies human powers, and in strength and spirit the freer nation rises among her neighbors as Saul amid his brethren—taller and fairer. Where Liberty sinks, there virtue fades, wealth diminishes, knowledge is forgotten, invention ceases, and empires once mighty in arms and arts become a helpless prey to freer barbarians!

• • •

The fiat has gone forth! With steam and electricity, and the new powers born of progress, forces have entered the world that will either compel us to a higher plane or overwhelm us, as nation after nation, as civilization after civilization, have been overwhelmed before. It is the delusion which precedes destruction that sees in the popular unrest with which the civilized world is feverishly pulsing, only the passing effect of ephemeral causes. Between democratic ideas and the aristocratic adjustments of society there is an irreconcilable conflict. Here in the United States, as there in Europe, it may be seen arising. We cannot go on permitting men to vote and forcing them to tramp. We cannot go on educating boys and girls in our public schools and then refusing them the right to earn an honest living. We cannot go on prating of the inalienable rights of man and then denying the inalienable right to the bounty of the Creator.

Questions

1. Why does George write that Americans have not "fully trusted" Liberty?

2. What does he see as the major threats to American freedom?

103. Edward Bellamy, *Looking Backward* (1888)

Source: Edward Bellamy, **Looking Backward** *2000–1887 (Boston, 1888), pp. 42–55, 262–63.*

Even more influential than *Progress and Poverty* was *Looking Backward*, a novel by Edward Bellamy published in 1888. The book recounts the experiences of Julian West, who falls asleep in the late nineteenth century only to awaken in the year 2000, in a world where cooperation has replaced class strife and cutthroat competition. Inequality has been banished and with it the idea of liberty as a condition to be achieved through individual striving free of governmental restraint. Freedom, Bellamy insisted, was a social condition, resting on interdependence, not autonomy.

From today's vantage point, Bellamy's utopia—with citizens required to labor for years in an Industrial Army controlled by a single Great Trust—seems a chilling social blueprint. Yet the book not only inspired the creation of hundreds of Nationalist clubs devoted to bringing into existence the world of 2000 but left a profound mark on a generation of reformers and intellectuals. For Bellamy held out the hope of retaining the material abundance made possible by industrial capitalism while eliminating inequality. In proposing that the state guarantee economic security to all, Bellamy proposed a far-reaching expansion of the idea of freedom.

"IN GENERAL," I said, "what impresses me most about the city is the material prosperity on the part of the people which its magnificence implies."

"I would give a great deal for just one glimpse of the Boston of your day," replied Dr. Leete. "No doubt, as you imply, the cities of that period were rather shabby affairs. If you had the taste to make them splendid, which I would not be so rude as to question, the general poverty resulting from your extraordinary industrial system would not have given you the means. Moreover, the excessive individualism which then prevailed was inconsistent with much public spirit.

What little wealth you had seems almost wholly to have been lavished in private luxury. Nowadays, on the contrary, there is no destination of the surplus wealth so popular as the adornment of the city, which all enjoy in equal degree."

• • •

"What solution, if any, have you found for the labor question? It was the Sphinx's riddle of the nineteenth century, and when I dropped out the Sphinx was threatening to devour society, because the answer was not forthcoming. It is well worth sleeping a hundred years to learn what the right answer was, if, indeed, you have found it yet."

"As no such thing as the labor question is known nowadays," replied Dr. Leete, "and there is no way in which it could arise, I suppose we may claim to have solved it. Society would indeed have fully deserved being devoured if it had failed to answer a riddle so entirely simple. In fact, to speak by the book, it was not necessary for society to solve the riddle at all. It may be said to have solved itself. The solution came as the result of a process of industrial evolution which could not have terminated otherwise. All that society had to do was to recognize and coöperate with that evolution, when its tendency had become unmistakable."

• • •

"The fact that the desperate popular opposition to the consolidation of business in a few powerful hands had no effect to check it proves that there must have been a strong economical reason for it. The small capitalists, with their innumerable petty concerns, had in fact yielded the field to the great aggregations of capital, because they belonged to a day of small things and were totally incompetent to the demands of an age of steam and telegraphs and the gigantic scale of its enterprises. To restore the former order of things, even if possible, would have involved returning to the day of stage-coaches. Oppressive and intolerable as was the régime of the great consolidations of capital, even its victims, while they cursed it, were forced to admit the prodigious increase of efficiency which had been imparted to the national industries, the vast economies effected by

concentration of management and unity of organization, and to confess that since the new system had taken the place of the old the
wealth of the world had increased at a rate before undreamed of. To
be sure this vast increase had gone chiefly to make the rich richer, increasing the gap between them and the poor; but the fact remained
that, as a means merely of producing wealth, capital had been proved
efficient in proportion to its consolidation. The restoration of the
old system with the subdivision of capital, if it were possible, might
indeed bring back a greater equality of conditions, with more individual dignity and freedom, but it would be at the price of general
poverty and the arrest of material progress."

• • •

"It would seem to follow, from what you have said, that wives are
in no way dependent on their husbands for maintenance."

"Of course they are not," replied Dr. Leete, "nor children on their
parents either, that is, for means of support, though of course they
are for the offices of affection. The child's labor, when he grows up,
will go to increase the common stock, not his parents', who will be
dead, and therefore he is properly nurtured out of the common stock.
The account of every person, man, woman, and child, you must understand, is always with the nation directly, and never through any
intermediary, except, of course, that parents, to a certain extent, act
for children as their guardians. You see that it is by virtue of the relation of individuals to the nation, of their membership in it, that they
are entitled to support; and this title is in no way connected with or
affected by their relations to other individuals who are fellow members of the nation with them. That any person should be dependent
for the means of support upon another would be shocking to the
moral sense as well as indefensible on any rational social theory.
What would become of personal liberty and dignity under such an
arrangement? I am aware that you called yourselves free in the nineteenth century. The meaning of the word could not then, however,
have been at all what it is at present, or you certainly would not have
applied it to a society of which nearly every member was in a position

of galling personal dependence upon others as to the very means of life, the poor upon the rich, or employed upon employer, women upon men, children upon parents.

Questions

1. Why does Bellamy's character Dr. Leete state that the meaning of the word "free" could not have meant the same thing in the nineteenth century as it does in 2000?

2. How does Bellamy suggest that the transition to a society of harmony and equality will take place?

104. Walter Rauschenbusch and the Social Gospel (1912)

Source: Walter Rauschenbusch, **Christianizing the Social Order** *(New York, 1912), pp. 41–44.*

The Baptist clergyman Walter Rauschenbusch, who began preaching in New York City in 1886, was a bridge between the Gilded Age and the Progressive era of the early twentieth century. Appalled by the low wages and dire living conditions of his poor parishioners, Rauschenbusch rejected the idea, common among the era's Protestant preachers, that poverty arose from individual sins like drinking and sabbath breaking. In sermons and, in the early twentieth century, in widely read books, he developed what came to be called the Social Gospel. Rauschenbush insisted that devout Christians rediscover the "social wealth of the Bible," and especially Jesus' concern for the poor. Freedom and spiritual self-development, he argued, required an equalization of wealth and power and unbridled competition mocked the Christian ideal of brotherhood.

The Social Gospel movement originated as an effort to reform Protestant churches by expanding their appeal in poor urban neighborhoods and making them more attentive to the era's social ills. Its adherents established missions and relief programs in urban areas that attempted to alleviate poverty, combat child labor, and encourage the construction of better working-class housing.

THE CHIEF PURPOSE of the Christian Church in the past has been the salvation of individuals. But the most pressing task of the present is not individualistic. Our business is to make over an antiquated and immoral economic system; to get rid of laws, customs, maxims, and philosophies inherited from an evil and despotic past; to create just and brotherly relations between great groups and classes of society; and thus to lay a social foundation on which modern men individually can live and work in a fashion that will not outrage all the better elements in them. Our inherited Christian faith dealt with individuals; our present task deals with society.

The Christian Church in the past has taught us to do our work with our eyes fixed on another world and a life to come. But the business before us is concerned with refashioning this present world, making this earth clean and sweet and habitable. . . .

Twenty-five years ago the social wealth of the Bible was almost undiscovered to most of us. We used to plow it six inches deep for crops and never dreamed that mines of anthracite were hidden down below. Even Jesus talked like an individualist in those days and seemed to repudiate the social interest when we interrogated him. He said his kingdom was not of this world; the things of God had nothing to do with the things of Caesar; the poor we would always have with us; and his ministers must not be judges and dividers when Labor argued with Capital about the division of the inheritance. To-day he has resumed the spiritual leadership of social Christianity, of which he was the founder. It is a new tribute to his mastership that the social message of Jesus was the first great possession which social Christianity rediscovered. . . .

With true Christian instinct men have turned to the Christian law of love as the key to the situation. If we all loved our neighbor, we should "treat him right," pay him a living wage, give sixteen ounces to the pound, and not charge so much for beef. But this appeal assumes that we are still living in the simple personal relations of the good old times, and that every man can do the right thing when he wants to do it. But suppose a business man would be glad indeed to pay his young women the $12 a week which they need for a decent living, but all his competitors are paying from $7 down to $5. Shall he love himself into bankruptcy? In a time of industrial depression shall he employ men whom he does not need? And if he does, will his five loaves feed the five thousand unemployed that break his heart with their hungry eyes? If a man owns a hundred shares of stock in a great corporation, how can his love influence its wage scale with that puny stick? The old advice of love breaks down before the hugeness of modern relations. We might as well try to start a stranded ocean liner with the oar which poled our old dory from the mud banks many a time. It is indeed love that we want, but it is socialized love. Blessed be the love that holds the cup of water to thirsty lips. We can never do without the plain affection of man to man. But what we most need today is not the love that will break its back drawing water for a growing factory town from a well that was meant to supply a village, but a love so large and intelligent that it will persuade an ignorant people to build a system of waterworks up in the hills, and that will get after the thoughtless farmers who contaminate the brooks with typhoid bacilli, and after the lumber concern that is denuding the watershed of its forests. We want a new avatar of love.

Questions

1. Why does Rauschenbusch argue that "the salvation of individuals" is not sufficient to address social problems?

2. What does he urge Christians to do to alleviate poverty?

CHAPTER 17

Freedom's Boundaries, at Home and Abroad, 1890–1900

105. The Populist Platform (1892)

Source: The World Almanac, 1893 *(New York, 1893), pp. 83–85.*

Like industrial workers, small farmers in the late nineteenth century faced increasing economic difficulties. Through the Farmers Alliance and the People's (or Populist) Party, farmers sought to remedy their condition. The era's greatest political insurgency, the party's major base lay in the cotton and wheat belts of the South and West, but it also sought to appeal to industrial workers.

The Populist platform of 1892, adopted at the party's Omaha convention, remains a classic document of American reform. It spoke of a nation "brought to the verge of moral, political, and material ruin" by political corruption and economic inequality. The platform put forth a long list of proposals to restore democracy and economic opportunity, many of which would be adopted during the next half century, including government control of the currency and a graduated income tax, and asserted that rural and urban workers shared an identity of interest. In addition, Populists called for public ownership of the railroads to guarantee farmers inexpensive access to markets for their crops.

Preamble

The conditions which surround us best justify our co-operation; we meet in the midst of a nation brought to the verge of moral, political, and material ruin. Corruption dominates the ballot-box, the Legislatures, the Congress, and touches even the ermine of the bench. The people are demoralized; most of the States have been compelled to isolate the voters at the polling places to prevent universal intimidation and bribery. The newspapers are largely subsidized or muzzled, public opinion silenced, business prostrated, homes covered with mortgages, labor impoverished, and the land concentrating in the hands of capitalists. The urban workmen are denied the right to organize for self-protection, imported pauperized labor beats down their wages, a hireling standing army, unrecognized by our laws, is established to shoot them down, and they are rapidly degenerating into European conditions. The fruits of the toil of millions are boldly stolen to build up colossal fortunes for a few, unprecedented in the history of mankind; and the possessors of those, in turn, despise the Republic and endanger liberty. From the same prolific womb of governmental injustice we breed the two great classes—tramps and millionaires.

The national power to create money is appropriated to enrich bondholders; a vast public debt payable in legal tender currency has been funded into gold-bearing bonds, thereby adding millions to the burdens of the people.

Silver, which has been accepted as coin since the dawn of history, has been demonetized to add to the purchasing power of gold by decreasing the value of all forms of property as well as human labor, and the supply of currency is purposely abridged to fatten usurers, bankrupt enterprise, and enslave industry. A vast conspiracy against mankind has been organized on two continents, and it is rapidly taking possession of the world. If not met and overthrown at once it forebodes terrible social convulsions, the destruction of civilization, or the establishment of an absolute despotism.

We have witnessed for more than a quarter of a century the struggles of the two great political parties for power and plunder, while grievous wrongs have been inflicted upon the suffering people. We charge that the controlling influences dominating both these parties have permitted the existing dreadful conditions to develop without serious effort to prevent or restrain them. Neither do they now promise us any substantial reform. They have agreed together to ignore, in the coming campaign, every issue but one. They propose to drown the outcries of a plundered people with the uproar of a sham battle over the tariff, so that capitalists, corporations, national banks, rings, trusts, watered stock, the demonetization of silver and the oppressions of the usurers may all be lost sight of. They propose to sacrifice our homes, lives, and children on the altar of mammon; to destroy the multitude in order to secure corruption funds from the millionaires.

Assembled on the anniversary of the birthday of the nation, and filled with the spirit of the grand general and chief who established our independence, we seek to restore the government of the Republic to the hands of "the plain people," with which class it originated. We assert our purposes to be identical with the purposes of the National Constitution; to form a more perfect union and establish justice, insure domestic tranquillity, provide for the common defence, promote the general welfare, and secure the blessings of liberty for ourselves and our posterity.

We declare that this Republic can only endure as a free government while built upon the love of the whole people for each other and for the nation; that it cannot be pinned together by bayonets; that the civil war is over, and that every passion and resentment which grew out of it must die with it, and that we must be in fact, as we are in name, one united brotherhood of free men.

Our country finds itself confronted by conditions for which there is no precedent in the history of the world; our annual agricultural productions amount to billions of dollars in value, which must, within a few weeks or months, be exchanged for billions of dollars' worth of commodities consumed in their production; the existing currency supply is wholly inadequate to make this exchange; the results are falling prices, the formation of combines and rings, the impoverishment of the producing class. We pledge ourselves that if given power we will labor to correct these evils by wise and reasonable legislation, in accordance with the terms of our platform.

We believe that the power of government—in other words, of the people—should be expanded (as in the case of the postal service) as rapidly and as far as the good sense of an intelligent people and the teachings of experience shall justify, to the end that oppression, injustice, and poverty shall eventually cease in the land.

While our sympathies as a party of reform are naturally upon the side of every proposition which will tend to make men intelligent, virtuous, and temperate, we nevertheless regard these questions, important as they are, as secondary to the great issues now pressing for solution, and upon which not only our individual prosperity but the very existence of free institutions depend; and we ask all men to first help us to determine whether we are to have a republic to administer before we differ as to the conditions upon which it is to be administered, believing that the forces of reform this day organized will never cease to move forward until every wrong is remedied and equal rights and equal privileges securely established for all the men and women of this country.

PLATFORM

We declare, therefore—

First.—That the union of the labor forces of the United States this day consummated shall be permanent and perpetual; may its spirit enter into all hearts for the salvation of the Republic and the uplifting of mankind.

Second.—Wealth belongs to him who creates it, and every dollar taken from industry without an equivalent is robbery. "If any will not work, neither shall he eat." The interests of rural and civic labor are the same; their enemies are identical.

Third.—We believe that the time has come when the railroad corporations will either own the people or the people must own the railroads, and should the government enter upon the work of owning and managing all railroads, we should favor an amendment to the Constitution by which all persons engaged in the government service shall be placed under a civil-service regulation of the most rigid character, so as to prevent the increase of the power of the national administration by the use of such additional government employees.

Finance.—We demand a national currency, safe, sound, and flexible, issued by the general government only, a full legal tender for all debts, public and private, and that without the use of banking corporations, a just, equitable, and efficient means of distribution direct to the people, at a tax not to exceed 2 per cent per annum, to be provided as set forth in the sub-treasury plan of the Farmers' Alliance, or a better system; also by payments in discharge of its obligations for public improvements.

1. We demand free and unlimited coinage of silver and gold at the present legal ratio of 16 to 1.

2. We demand that the amount of circulating medium be speedily increased to not less than $50 per capita.

3. We demand a graduated income tax.

4. We believe that the money of the country should be kept as much as possible in the hands of the people, and hence we demand that all State and national revenues shall be limited to the necessary expenses of the government, economically and honestly administered.

5. We demand that postal savings banks be established by the government for the safe deposit of the earnings of the people and to facilitate exchange.

Transportation.—Transportation being a means of exchange and a public necessity, the government should own and operate the railroads in the interest of the people. The telegraph, telephone, like the post-office system, being a necessity for the transmission of news, should be owned and operated by the government in the interest of the people.

Land.—The land, including all the natural sources of wealth, is the heritage of the people, and should not be monopolized for speculative purposes, and alien ownership of land should be prohibited. All land now held by railroads and other corporations in excess of their actual needs, and all lands now owned by aliens should be reclaimed by the government and held for actual settlers only.

Questions

1. How does the Omaha platform identify the main threats to American liberty?

2. How did the Populists seek to rethink the relationship between government power and freedom?

---

106. John Marshall Harlan, Dissent in *Plessy v. Ferguson* (1896)

Source: **Plessy v. Ferguson, *163 U. S. 537 (1896).***

The Supreme Court's decision in 1896 in *Plessy v. Ferguson* was a key step in the nation's long retreat from the ideal of equal rights for American citizens regardless of race, embodied in the laws and constitutional amendments of Reconstruction. In *Plessy*, the Court gave its approval to state laws requiring separate facilities for blacks and whites. The case arose from Louisiana, where the legislature had required railroad companies to maintain a separate car or section for black passengers. In its 8–1 decision, the court upheld the Louisiana law, arguing that separate facilities did not discriminate so long as they were "separate but equal."

The lone dissenter, John Marshall Harlan, reprimanded the majority with an oft-quoted comment: "our Constitution is color-blind." Stigmatizing a group because of its race, he continued, was a "badge of slavery," which should be held unconstitutional under the Thirteenth Amendment, which had abolished the institution. As Harlan predicted, states reacted to the *Plessy* decision by passing laws mandating racial segregation in every aspect of southern life.

WHILE THERE MAY be in Louisiana persons of different races who are not citizens of the United States, the words in the act, "white and colored races," necessarily include all citizens of the United States of both races residing in that State. So that we have before us a state enactment that compels, under penalties, the separation of the two races in railroad passenger coaches, and makes it a crime for a citizen of either race to enter a coach that has been assigned to citizens of the other race.

Thus the State regulates the use of a public highway by citizens of the United States solely upon the basis of race.

However apparent the injustice of such legislation may be, we have only to consider whether it is consistent with the Constitution of the United States.

That a railroad is a public highway, and that the corporation which owns or operates it is in the exercise of public functions, is not, at this day, to be disputed.

• • •

In respect of civil rights, common to all citizens, the Constitution of the United States does not, I think, permit any public authority to know the race of those entitled to be protected in the enjoyment of such rights. Every true man has pride of race, and under appropriate circumstances when the rights of others, his equals before the law, are not to be affected, it is his privilege to express such pride and to take such action based upon it as to him seems proper. But I deny that any legislative body or judicial tribunal may have regard to the race of citizens when the civil rights of those citizens are involved. Indeed, such legislation, as that here in question, is inconsistent not only with that equality of rights which pertains to citizenship, National and State, but with the personal liberty enjoyed by every one within the United States.

The Thirteenth Amendment does not permit the withholding or the deprivation of any right necessarily inhering in freedom. It not only struck down the institution of slavery as previously existing in the United States, but it prevents the imposition of any burdens or disabilities that constitute badges of slavery or servitude. It decreed universal civil freedom in this country. This court has so adjudged. But that amendment having been found inadequate to the protection of the rights of those who had been in slavery, it was followed by the Fourteenth Amendment, which added greatly to the dignity and glory of American citizenship, and to the security of personal liberty, by declaring that "all persons born or naturalized in the United States and subject to the jurisdiction thereof, are citizens of the United States and of the State wherein they reside," and that "no State shall make or enforce any law which shall abridge the privileges or immunities of citizens of the United States; nor shall any State deprive any person of life, liberty or property without due process of law, nor deny to any person within its jurisdiction the equal protection of the laws." These two amendments, if enforced according to their true intent and meaning, will protect all the civil rights that pertain to freedom and citizenship. Finally, and to the end that no citizen should be denied, on account of his race, the privilege of participating in the political control of his country, it was declared by the Fifteenth Amendment that "the right of citizens of the United States to vote shall not be denied or abridged by the United States or by any State on account of race, color or previous condition of servitude."

• • •

It was said in argument that the statute of Louisiana does not discriminate against either race, but prescribes a rule applicable alike to white and colored citizens. But this argument does not meet the difficulty. Every one knows that the statute in question had its origin in the purpose, not so much to exclude white persons from railroad cars occupied by blacks, as to exclude colored people from coaches occupied by or assigned to white persons. Railroad corporations of Louisiana did not make discrimination among whites in the matter of accommodation for travellers. The thing to accomplish was, under the guise of giving equal accommodation for white and blacks, to compel the latter to keep to themselves while travelling in railroad passenger coaches. No one would be so wanting in candor as to assert the contrary. The fundamental objection, therefore, to the statute is that it interferes with the personal freedom of citizens. "Personal liberty," it has been well said, "consists in the power of locomotion, of changing situations, or removing one's person to whatsoever places one's own inclination may direct, without imprisonment or restraint, unless by due course of law." If a white man and a black man choose to occupy the same public conveyance on a public highway, it is their right to do so, and no government, proceeding alone on grounds of race, can prevent it without infringing the personal liberty of each.

• • •

The white race deems itself to be the dominant race in this country. And so it is, in prestige, in achievements, in education, in wealth and in power. So, I doubt not, it will continue to be for all time, if it remains true to its great heritage and holds fast to the principles of constitutional liberty. But in view of the Constitution, in the eye of the law, there is in this country no superior, dominant, ruling class of citizens. There is no caste here. Our Constitution is color-blind, and neither knows nor tolerates classes among citizens. In respect of civil rights, all citizens are equal before the law. The humblest is the peer of the most powerful. The law regards man as man, and takes no account of his surroundings or of his color when his civil rights as guaranteed by the supreme law of the land are involved. It is, therefore, to be regretted that this high tribunal, the final expositor of the fundamental law of the land, has reached the conclusion that it is competent for a State to regulate the enjoyment by citizens of their civil rights solely upon the basis of race.

In my opinion, the judgement this day rendered will, in time, prove to be quite as pernicious as the decision made by this tribunal in the *Dred Scott case.* It was adjudged in that case that the descendants of Africans who were imported into this country and sold as slaves were not included nor intended to be included under the word "citizens" in the Constitution, and could not claim any of the rights and privileges which that instrument provided for and secured to citizens of the United States; that at the time of the adoption of the Constitution they were "considered as a subordinate and inferior class of beings, who had been subjugated by the dominant race and, whether emancipated or not, yet remained subject to their authority, and had no rights or privileges but such as those who held the power and the government might choose to grant them."

• • •

I am of opinion that the statute of Louisiana is inconsistent with the personal liberty of citizens, white and black, in that State, and hostile to both the spirit and letter of the Constitution of the United States. If laws of like characters should be enacted in the several States of the Union, the effect would be in the highest degree mischievous. Slavery, as an institution tolerated by law would, it is true, have disappeared from our country, but there would remain a power in the States, by sinister legislation, to interfere with the full enjoyment of the blessings of freedom; to regulate civil rights, common to all citizens, upon the basis of race; and to place in a condition of legal inferiority a large body of American citizens, now constituting a part of the political community called the people of the United States, for whom, and by whom through representatives, our government is administered. Such a system is inconsistent with the guarantee given by the Constitution to each State of a republican form of government, and may be stricken down by Congressional action, or by the courts in the discharge of their solemn duty to maintain the supreme law of the land, anything in the constitution or laws of any State to the contrary notwithstanding.

Questions

1. Why does Harlan consider laws requiring racial segregation to be violations of the freedom blacks had won during the Civil War?

2. What does Harlan mean by the phrase, "our Constitution is color-blind"?

107. Ida B. Wells, *Crusade for Justice* (ca. 1892)

Source: From The Crusade for Justice: The Autobiography of Ida. B Wells, *ed. Alfreda M. Duster, pp. 47–52, 64–71, 78–81. Copyright © The University of Chicago Press. Reprinted with permission.*

Racial segregation was only one part of a comprehensive system of racial inequality that was firmly put into place during the 1890s. Those blacks who sought to challenge the system or who refused to accept the demeaning behavior that was a daily feature of southern life faced not only overwhelming political and legal power but also the threat of violent reprisal. In every year between 1883 and 1905, more than fifty persons, the vast majority of them black men, were lynched in the South—that is, murdered by a mob. Lynching continued well into the twentieth century.

Many victims of lynchings were accused after their deaths of having raped a white woman. Many white southerners considered preserving the purity of white womanhood a justification for extralegal vengeance. Yet, in nearly all cases, as Ida B. Wells argued in a newspaper editorial after a Memphis lynching in 1892, the charge of rape was a "bare lie." Born a slave in Mississippi in 1862, Wells had become a schoolteacher and editor. Her essay condemning the lynching of three black men in Memphis led a mob to destroy her newspaper, the *Memphis Free Press*, while she was out of the city. Wells remained in the North, where she became the nation's leading antilynching crusader. In her autobiography, which remained unpublished until 1970, Wells described the Memphis lynching and the beginnings of the antilynching movement.

———

WHILE I WAS thus carrying on the work of my newspaper, . . . there came the lynching in Memphis which changed the whole course of my life. . . .

Thomas Moss, Calvin McDowell, and Henry Stewart owned and operated a grocery store in a thickly populated suburb. . . . There was already a grocery owned and operated by a white man who hitherto had had a monopoly on the trade of this thickly populated colored suburb. Thomas's grocery changed all that, and he and his associates were made to feel that they were not welcome by the white grocer. . . .

One day some colored and white boys quarreled over a game of marbles and the colored boys got the better of the fight which followed. . . . Then the challenge was issued that the vanquished whites were coming on Saturday night to clean out [Thomas's] Colored People's Grocery Company. . . . Accordingly the grocery company armed several men and stationed them in the rear of the store on that fatal Saturday night, not to attack but repel a threatened attack. . . . The men stationed there had seen several white men stealing through the rear door and fired on them without a moment's pause. Three of these men were wounded, and others fled and gave the alarm. . . . Over a hundred colored men were dragged from their homes and put in jail on suspicion.

All day long on that fateful Sunday white men were permitted in the jail to look over the imprisoned black men. . . . The mob took out of their cells Thomas Moss, Calvin McDowell, and Henry Stewart, the three officials of the People's Grocery Company. They were loaded on a switch engine of the railroad which ran back of the jail, carried a mile north of the city limits, and horribly shot to death. One of the morning papers held back its edition in order to supply its

readers with the details of that lynching.... The mob took possession of the People's Grocery Company, helping themselves to food
and drink, and destroyed what they could not eat or steal. The credi-
tors had the place closed and a few days later what remained of the
stock was sold at auction. Thus, with the aid of city and county authorities and the daily papers, that white grocer had indeed put an
end to his rival Negro grocer as well as to his business....

Like many another person who had read of lynchings in the
South, I had accepted the idea meant to be conveyed—that although
lynching was irregular and contrary to law and order, unreasoning
anger over the terrible crime of rape led to the lynching; that perhaps
the brute deserved death anyhow and the mob was justified in taking his life.

But Thomas Moss, Calvin McDowell and Henry Stewart had been
lynched in Memphis, one of the leading cities of the South, in which
no lynching had taken place before, with just as much brutality as
other victims of the mob; and they had committed no crime against
white women. This is what opened my eyes to what lynching really
was. An excuse to get rid of Negroes who were acquiring wealth and
property and thus keep the race terrorized and "keep the nigger
down." I then began an investigation of every lynching I read about.
I stumbled on the amazing record that every case of rape reported ...
became such only when it became public.

Many cases were like that of the lynching which happened in Tu-
nica County, Mississippi. The Associated Press reporter said, "The big
burly brute was lynched because he had raped the seven-year-old
daughter of the sheriff." I visited the place afterward and saw the girl,
who was a grown woman more than seventeen years old. She had
been found in the lynched Negro's cabin by her father, who had led
the mob against him in order to save his daughter's reputation. That
Negro was a helper on the farm....

It was with these and other stories in mind in that last week in
May 1892 that I wrote the following editorial:

Eight Negroes lynched since last issue of the *Free Speech*. They were charged with killing white men and five with raping white women. Nobody in this section believes the old thread-bare lie that Negro men assault white women. If Southern white men are not careful they will overreach themselves and a conclusion will be drawn which will be very damaging to the moral reputation of their women.

This editorial furnished at last the excuse for doing what the white leaders of Memphis had long been wanting to do: put an end to the *Free Speech*. . . .

Having lost my paper, had a price put on my life, and been made an exile from home for hinting at the truth, I felt that I owed it to myself and to my race to tell the whole truth now that I was where I could do so freely. Accordingly, the fourth week in June, the *New York Age* had a seven-column article on the front page giving names, dates and places of many lynchings for alleged rape. This article showed conclusively that my editorial in the *Free Speech* was based on facts of illicit association between black men and white women.

Such relationships between white men and colored women were notorious, and had been as long as the two races had lived together in the South. . . .

• • •

The more I studied the situation, the more I was convinced that the Southerner had never gotten over his resentment that the Negro was no longer his plaything, his servant, and his source of income. The federal laws for Negro protection passed during Reconstruction had been made a mockery by the white South where it had not secured their repeal. This same white South had secured political control of its several states, and as soon as white southerners came into power they began to make playthings of Negro lives and property. This still seemed not enough "to keep the nigger down."

Here came lynch law to stifle Negro manhood which defended itself, and the burning alive of Negroes who were weak enough to accept favors from white women. The many unspeakable and unprintable tortures to which Negro rapists (?) of white women were subjected were for the purpose of striking terror into the hearts of other Negroes who might be thinking of consorting with willing white women.

I found that in order to justify these horrible atrocities to the world, the Negro was branded as a race of rapists, who were especially after white women. I found that white men who had created a race of mulattoes by raping and consorting with Negro women were still doing so wherever they could; these same white men lynched, burned and tortured Negro men for doing the same thing with white women; even when the white women were willing victims.

That the entire race should be branded as moral monsters and despoilers of white womanhood and childhood was bound to rob us of all the friends we had and silence any protests that they might make for us. For all these reasons it seemed a stern duty to give the facts I had collected to the world. . . .

About two months after my appearance in the columns in the *New York Age*, two colored women remarked on my revelations during a visit with each other and said they thought that the women of New York and Brooklyn should do something to show appreciation of my work and to protest the treatment which I had received. . . . A committee of two hundred and fifty women was appointed, and they stirred up sentiment throughout the two cities which culminated in a testimonial at Lyric Hall on 5 October 1892.

This testimonial was conceded by the oldest inhabitants to be the greatest demonstration ever attempted by race women for one of their number. . . . The leading colored women of Boston and Philadelphia had been invited to join in this demonstration, and they came, a brilliant array . . . behind a lonely, homesick girl who was an exile because she had tried to defend the manhood of her race. . . .

So many things came out of that wonderful testimonial.

First it was the beginning of the club movement among the colored women in this country. The women of New York and Brooklyn decided to continue that organization, which they called the Women's Loyal Union. These were the first strictly women's clubs organized in those cities. Mrs. Ruffin of Boston, who came over to that testimonial . . . called a meeting of the women at her home to meet me, and they organized themselves into the Woman's Era Club of that city. Mrs. Ruffin had been a member of the foremost clubs among white women in Boston for years, but this was her first effort to form one among colored women. . . .

Second, that testimonial was the beginning of public speaking for me. I have already said that I had not before made speeches, but invitations came from Philadelphia, Wilmington, Delaware, Chester, Pennsylvania, and Washington, D. C. . . .

In Philadelphia . . . Miss Catherine Impey of Street Somerset, England, was visiting Quaker relatives of hers in the city and at the same time was trying to learn what she could about the color question in this country. She was the editor of *Anti-Caste*, a magazine published in England in behalf of the natives of India, and she was therefore interested in the treatment of darker races everywhere . . . The third great result of that wonderful testimonial in New York the previous month [followed]. . . . The interview between Miss Impey and myself resulted in an invitation to England and the beginning of the worldwide campaign against lynching.

Questions

1. What social conditions seem to have given rise to the Memphis lynching?

2. What does Wells see as the contributions of the antilynching movement?

108. Saum Song Bo, Chinese-American Protest, from *American Missionary* (1885)

Source: **American Missionary,** *Vol. 39 (October 1885), p. 290.*

Blacks were not the only group to find their rights receding in the late nine-teenth century. Leaders of both political parties expressed vicious opinions regarding immigrants from China, and labor unions, including the Knights of Labor, which claimed to welcome all workers, barred them from mem-bership. Beginning in 1882, Congress temporarily excluded immigrants from China from entering the country altogether. Although nonwhites had long been prohibited from becoming naturalized citizens, this was the first time that race had been used to exclude an entire group of people from coming to the United States. Congress renewed the restriction ten years later and made it permanent in 1902.

During the mid-1880s, a national campaign sought to raise funds to build the pedestal on which the Statue of Liberty, a gift from France, would rest. Saum Song Bo, a Chinese-American writer, contrasted Americans' cele-bration of liberty with their actual treatment of the Chinese. (He also noted that in their colonies in Southeast Asia, the French themselves were guilty of depriving local residents, including the Chinese, of their liberty.)

Sir:

A paper was presented to me yesterday for inspection, and I found it to be specially drawn up for subscription among my countrymen to-ward the Pedestal Fund of the Bartholdi Statue of Liberty. Seeing that the heading is an appeal to American citizens, to their love of coun-try and liberty, I feel that my countrymen and myself are honored in being thus appealed to as citizens in the cause of liberty. But the word liberty makes me think of the fact that this country is the land of liberty for men of all nations except the Chinese. I consider it as an insult to us Chinese to call on us to contribute toward building in this land a pedestal for a statue of Liberty. That statue represents

Liberty holding a torch which lights the passage of those of all nations who come into this country. But are the Chinese allowed to come? As for the Chinese who are here, are they allowed to enjoy liberty as men of all other nationalities enjoy it? Are they allowed to go about everywhere free from the insults, abuses, assaults, wrongs, and injuries from which men of other nationalities are free?

If there be a Chinaman who came to this country when a lad, who has passed through an American institution of learning of the highest grade, who has so fallen in love with American manners and ideas that he desires to make his home in this land, and who, seeing that his countrymen demand one of their own number to be their legal adviser, representative, advocate, and protector, desires to study law, can he be a lawyer? By the law of this nation, he, being a Chinaman, cannot become a citizen, and consequently cannot be a lawyer.

And this statue of Liberty is a gift to a people from another people who do not love or value liberty for the Chinese. Are not the Annamese and Tonquinese Chinese, to whom liberty is as dear as to the French? What right have the French to deprive them of their liberty?

Whether this statute against the Chinese or the statue to Liberty will be the more lasting monument to tell future ages of the liberty and greatness of this country, will be known only to future generations.

Liberty, we Chinese do love and adore thee; but let not those who deny thee to us, make of thee a graven image and invite us to bow down to it.

Saum Song Bo

Questions

1. Why does Bo feel that the Chinese do not "enjoy liberty" in the same way as other Americans do?

2. Why does he refer to France's treatment of its colonial subjects in making his argument?

109. Frances E. Willard, *Women and Temperance* (1883)

Source: Frances E. Willard, Women and Temperance *(Hartford, Conn., 1883), pp. 43–46.*

Founded in 1874, the Women's Christian Temperance Union (WCTU) grew to become the era's largest female organization, with a membership by 1890 of 150,000. Under the banner of Home Protection, it moved from demanding the prohibition of alcoholic beverages (blamed for leading men to squander their wages on drink and treat their wives abusively) to a comprehensive program of economic and political reform including the right to vote. Women, insisted Frances Willard, the group's president, must abandon the idea that "weakness" and dependence was their nature and join assertively in movements to change society.

To HELP FORWARD the coming of Christ into all departments of life, is, in its last analysis, the purpose and aim of the W. C. T. U. For we believe this correlation of New Testament religion with philanthropy, and of the church with civilization, is the perpetual miracle which furnishes the only sufficient antidote to current skepticism. Higher toward the zenith climbs the Sun of Righteousness, making circle after circle of human endeavor and achievement warm and radiant with the healing of its beams. First of all, in our gospel temperance work, this heavenly light penetrated the gloom of the individual, tempted heart (that smallest circle, in which all others are involved), illumined its darkness, melted its hardness, made it a sweet and sunny place—a temple filled with the Holy Ghost.

Having thus come to the heart of the drinking man in the plenitude of his redeeming power, Christ entered the next wider circle, in which two human hearts unite to form a home, and here, by the revelation of her place in His kingdom, He lifted to an equal level with her husband the gentle companion who had supposed herself happy in being the favorite vassal of her liege lord. "There is neither male nor female in Christ Jesus;" this was the "open sesame," a declaration utterly opposed to all custom and tradition, but so steadily the light has shone, and so kindly has it made the heart of man, that without strife of tongues, or edict of sovereigns, it is coming now to pass that in proportion as any home is really Christian, the husband and the wife are peers in dignity and power. There are no homes on earth where woman is "revered, beloved," and individualized in character and work, so thoroughly as the fifty thousand in America where "her children arise up and call her blessed, her husband also, and he praiseth her" because of her part in the work of our W. C. T. U.

• • •

But the modern temperance movement, born of Christ's gospel and cradled at His altars, is rapidly filling one more circle of influence, wide as the widest zone of earthly weal or woe, and that is government. "The government shall be upon His shoulder." "Unto us a King is given." "He shall reign whose right it is." "He shall not fail, nor be discouraged until he hath set judgment in the earth." "For at the name of Jesus every knee shall bow, and every tongue confess that Christ is Lord to the glory of God the Father." "Thy kingdon come, thy will be done *on earth.*" Christ shall reign—not visibly, but invisibly; not in form, but in fact; not in substance, but in essence, and the day draws nigh! Then surely the traffic in intoxicating liquors as a drink will no longer be protected by the statute book, the lawyer's plea, the affirmation of the witness, and decision of the judge. And since the government is, after all, a circle that include all hearts, all homes, all churches, all societies, does it not seem as if intelligent loyalty to Christ the King would cause each heart that loves Him to feel in duty bound to use all the power it could gather to itself in helping choose the framers of these more righteous laws? But let it be remembered that for every Christian man who has a voice in making and enforcing laws there are at least two Christian women who have no voice at all. Hence, under such circumstances as now exist, His militant army must ever be powerless to win those legislative battles which, more than any others, affect the happiness of aggregate humanity. But the light gleams already along the sunny hilltops of the nineteenth century of grace. Upon those who in largest numbers love Him who has filled their hearts with peace and their homes with blessing, slowly dawns the consciousness that they may—nay, better still, *they ought* to—ask for power to help forward the coming of their Lord in government—to throw the safeguard of their prohibition ballots around those who have left the shelter of their arms only to be entrapped by the saloons that bad men legalize and set along the streets.

Questions

1. What religious convictions seem to inspire Willard's crusade against liquor?

2. Why does Willard believe that women should enjoy the right to vote?

110. Rev. Charles G. Ames on the Anti-Imperialist Movement (1898)

Source: "Address of the Rev. Charles G. Ames," Anti-Imperialism. Speeches at the Meeting in Faneuil Hall, Boston, June 15, 1898 *(Boston, 1898), pp. 9–16.*

As a result of the Spanish-American War of 1898, the United States acquired an overseas empire. America's entry into the ranks of imperial powers sparked an intense debate over the relationship between political democracy, race, and American citizenship. The right of every people to self-government was one of the main principles of the Declaration of Independence. In the aftermath of the Spanish-American War, however, nationalism, democracy, and American freedom emerged more closely identified than ever with notions of Anglo-Saxon superiority. Unlike previously acquired areas, new territories like the Philippines and Puerto Rico were denied both independence and a future path to statehood.

Opponents of imperialism formed the Anti-Imperialist League, a coalition of writers and social reformers who believed American energies should be directed at home, businessmen fearful of the cost of maintaining overseas outposts, and racists who did not wish to bring nonwhite populations into the United States. In a speech at an anti-imperialist meeting in Boston, the Rev. Charles G. Ames illustrated the complex combination of motives that went into anti-imperialism.

WE ARE TOLD that it is "our duty" to extend to the struggling people of the Philippines the same help and protection we have pledged to Cuba. Did we take a pledge to conquer and annex Cuba? We laid much stress on the fact that the suffering was "at our very doors;" then, almost before we have lifted a finger to deliver Cuba, we set up a claim to Spanish possessions on the other side of the globe! American interests were deeply involved in the Cuban disorders; can we give any similar reason for laying hand on the Asiatic Archipelago?

I trust that we shall everywhere leave better order than we found; but to swallow these islands whole may prove a more indigestible meal than all the imported material we are trying to incorporate into our body politic at home.

Let us face the facts and the underlying problem. We speak with contempt of the Spanish title to the islands. What other title can we acquire by conquest? Next we must govern either with or without the consent of the people. If with their consent, it must be expressed through republican forms; that is, by suffrage. Is there a man in America who wishes those seven millions of Malays, Negritos and Chinamen for fellow-citizens and joint rulers of this Republic? But if we govern them without their consent, it must be by military occupation,—by force; that is, by the Spanish method, though we shall not copy the Spanish cruelty. There is no third possibility; we must set up our home form of government,—state or territorial,—or we must have a governor-general, backed by soldiers, and supported by a navy much more powerful than would be required for a mere protectorate, which does not require annexation or control.

But the scheme of conquest does not end with the acquisition of the Philippines: it only begins there. The imperial programme includes a chain of island possessions. The European powers are dividing the Asiatic, African and Polynesian world among themselves; we are to go in for a share of the booty. We are to take foreign lands as Spain took Mexico and Peru; as England originally took her part of North America; as France acquired Canada and Louisiana. And we are to do it by war; by the right of might. Can we not show the world a more excellent way?

What will be the effect on our domestic policy? How can we undertake to rule subject provinces in distant parts of the globe without trampling on the principles of free government? Once accepting this way of dealing with other people, how long will it be before some occasion will arise for applying it at home? In committing ourselves to permanent military methods of government anywhere, we give up the republic, for we abandon its fundamental principle, even while boasting of the name.

Great standing armies are consistent with monarchy: they are even necessary. But they are the menace and terror of popular government: they compel centralization of power; more than that, they tend to sidetrack republican equality by creating a caste. Even in Massachusetts, ex-soldiers enjoy more rights than other men; they are a preferred and privileged class. What begins in gratitude for honorable service may easily create a precedent and a policy. Ever since the civil war, our presidents, with a single exception, have all been men of the army. As a rule returning soldiers, whatever their fitness or want of fitness, can play the game of politics with loaded dice whenever they choose.

The imperial scheme requires us to go very deeply into military and naval expenditure, that we may be ever on fighting footing. We must girdle the earth with strategic possession, every one of which must be fortified and garrisoned. They will be of little value in peace, since nearly all the world is open to commerce. In war they would be remote and exposed, inviting attack and requiring defence. Points of weakness every one of them! Further, we create the necessity of spending billions on fortifications for our extended coast line, by assuming an attitude of defiance and aggression—toward all the world. Let American mothers take notice: They are to raise boys to kill and be killed. Why do we mince such little matters? We are to be a great military nation! Our industry is to foot the bills. If you object, you are no patriot! But where will be the republic?

Our present system of government, resting on the intelligent choice of the people and their loving covenant, is probably the strongest in existence. It will bear any amount of strain so long as it is sound at the centre. All that a wise and virtuous king can do for his dependent subjects, that and better can a wise and virtuous people do for their independent selves; for, by the heavenly help, we who are neither very wise nor very virtuous have carried our ship of state through a storm that would have foundered the staunchest monarchy on earth. We need never despair of the republic till the people are seduced from its principles; as they surely will be if we are ever drawn into the Old World's military maelstrom. For militarism lives everywhere, as it must live, by sucking and poisoning the blood of liberty.

The policy of imperialism threatens to change the temper of our people, and to put us into a permanent attitude of arrogance, testiness and defiance toward other nations. The conditions which compel us to seek alliances are sure to breed antagonisms. If we form alliances for security, we lose our independence; if for plunder, we lose our character.

If once we enter the field of international conflict as a great military and naval power, we shall be one more bully among bullies: we shall only add one more to the list of oppressors of mankind by compelling other nations to increase their armaments on our account; and none will suffer for the folly so much as our own toiling millions.

Some of us who have shared the fortunes of our country through two wars are not happy witnesses of the levity with which many of our journalists and some of our statesmen treat of war, as if it were in itself more desirable and more honorable than peace.

In the present state of public feeling, you can hardly fasten on any man a worse brand of odium than to say he is in favor of "peace at any price." I should like to see a part of that odium transferred to those who appear to be in favor of *war at any price*. I am still of the opinion that peace is the more valuable article, and that we can steadily work towards it without becoming a nation of milk-sops.

The programme of imperialism reads to me like a declaration of war for the new century as well as for the remaining years of the old. I read in it also a contemptuous mockery of all our highest lessons— a setting at naught of the great Prophet of Brotherhood and a demand for Barabbas. Poor Christian as I am, it grieves and shames me to see a generation instructed by the Prince of Peace proposing to set him on a dunce's stool and to crown him with a fool's cap, while shouting hosannas to the great god Jingo, who seems, on both sides of the water, to be the modern representative of both Mars and Moloch.

In the light of our American doctrine of democracy, as well as in the light of what we still call the gospel, every war is a family quarrel and a family misfortune. There must be some rational limit to our right to injure, disable and despoil an enemy. We have duties of humanity even toward wretched Spain; and not less because the republicans of that country are our natural allies. Of course we shall conquer, for what can a poor cripple do in the grasp of a giant? Yet magnanimity and moderation toward a beaten foe may win our noblest victory and save future generations in both countries from bitter and burning hatred.

Questions

1. Why does Ames believe that empire is incompatible with American democracy?

2. Why does he feel that "Malays, Negritos and Chinamen" ought not to become "fellow citizens"?

111. Albert Beveridge, a Defense of Imperialism (1900)

Source: Congressional Record, *56th Congress, 1st Session, pp. 704–12.*

Albert Beveridge, elected to the Senate from Indiana in 1899, became one of the most outspoken proponents of the new imperialism. The United States, he insisted, ventured abroad not for material gain or national power, but to bring "a new day of freedom" to the peoples of the world. He echoed the claim of President William McKinley that America's was a "benevolent" imperialism, rooted in a national mission to uplift backward cultures and spread liberty across the globe. Nonwhite peoples, he believed were not capable of self-government. But in a speech in the Senate in 1900 he also pointed to the practical benefits the country would enjoy by maintaining possession of the Philippines.

MR. PRESIDENT, THE times call for candor. The Philippines are ours forever, "territory belonging to the United States," as the Constitution calls them. And just beyond the Philippines are China's illimitable markets. We will not retreat from either. We will not repudiate our duty in the archipelago. We will not abandon our opportunity in the Orient. We will not renounce our part in the mission of our race, trustee, under God, of the civilization of the world. And we will move forward to our work, not howling out regrets like slaves whipped to their burdens, but with gratitude for a task worthy of our strength, and thanksgiving to Almighty God that He has marked us as His chosen people, henceforth to lead in the regeneration of the world.

This island empire is the last land left in all the oceans. If it should prove a mistake to abandon it, the blunder once made would be irretrievable. If it proves a mistake to hold it, the error can be corrected when we will. Every other progressive nation stands ready to relieve us.

But to hold it will be no mistake. Our largest trade henceforth must be with Asia. The Pacific is our ocean. More and more Europe will manufacture the most it needs, secure from its colonies the most it consumes. Where shall we turn for consumers of our surplus? Geography answers the question. China is our natural customer. She is nearer to us than to England, Germany, or Russia, the commercial powers of the present and the future. They have moved nearer to China by securing permanent bases on her borders. The Philippines give us a base at the door of all the East.

Lines of navigation from our ports to the Orient and Australia; from the Isthmian Canal to Asia; from the Oriental ports to Australia, converge at and separate from the Philippines. They are a self-supporting, dividend-paying fleet, permanently anchored at a spot selected by the strategy of Providence, commanding the Pacific. And the Pacific is the ocean of the commerce of the future. Most future wars will be conflicts for commerce. The power that rules the Pacific, therefore, is the power that rules the world. And, with the Philippines, that power is and will forever be the American Republic....

Nothing is so natural as trade with one's neighbors. The Philippines make us the nearest neighbors of all the East. Nothing is more natural than to trade with those you know. This is the philosophy of all advertising. The Philippines bring us permanently face to face with the most sought-for customers of the world. National prestige, national propinquity, these and commercial activity are the elements of commercial success. The Philippines give the first; the character of the American people supply the last. It is a providential conjunction of all the elements of trade, of duty, and of power. If we are willing to go to war rather than let England have a few feet of frozen Alaska, which affords no market and commands none, what should we not do rather than let England, Germany, Russia, or Japan have all the Philippines? And no man on the spot can fail to see that this would be their fate if we retired. . . .

Here, then, Senators, is the situation. Two years ago there was no land in all the world which we could occupy for any purpose. Our commerce was daily turning toward the Orient, and geography and trade developments made necessary our commercial empire over the Pacific. And in that ocean we had no commercial, naval, or military base. To-day we have one of the three great ocean possessions of the globe, located at the most commanding commercial, naval, and military points in the eastern seas, within hail of India, shoulder to shoulder with China, richer in its own resources than any equal body of land on the entire globe, and peopled by a race which civilization demands shall be improved. Shall we abandon it? That man little knows the common people of the Republic, little understands the instincts of our race, who thinks we will not hold it fast and hold it forever, administering just government by simplest methods. . . .

But, Senators, it would be better to abandon this combined garden and Gibraltar of the Pacific, and count our blood and treasure already spent a profitable loss, than to apply any academic arrangement of self-government to these children. They are not capable of self-government. How could they be? They are not of a self-governing race. They are Orientals, Malays, instructed by Spaniards in the latter's worst estate.

They know nothing of practical government except as they have witnessed the weak, corrupt, cruel, and capricious rule of Spain. What magic will anyone employ to dissolve in their minds and characters those impressions of governors and governed which three centuries of misrule has created? What alchemy will change the oriental quality of their blood and set the self-governing currents of the

American pouring through their Malay veins? How shall they, in the twinkling of an eye, be exalted to the heights of self-governing peoples which required a thousand years for us to reach, Anglo-Saxon though we are? . . .

The three best educators on the island at different times made to me the same comparison, that the common people in their stupidity are like their caribou bulls. They are not even good agriculturists. Their waste of cane is inexcusable. Their destruction of hemp fiber is childish. They are incurably indolent. They have no continuity or thoroughness of industry. They will quit work without notice and amuse themselves until the money they have earned is spent. They are like children playing at men's work.

No one need fear their competition with our labor. No reward could beguile, no force compel, these children of indolence to leave their trifling lives for the fierce and fervid industry of high-wrought America. The very reverse is the fact. One great problem is the necessary labor to develop these islands—to build the roads, open the mines, clear the wilderness, drain the swamps, dredge the harbors. The natives will not supply it. A lingering prejudice against the Chinese may prevent us from letting them supply it. Ultimately, when the real truth of the climate and human conditions is known, it is barely possible that our labor will go there. Even now young men with the right moral fiber and a little capital can make fortunes there as planters. . . .

The Declaration of Independence does not forbid us to do our part in the regeneration of the world. If it did, the Declaration would be wrong, just as the Articles of Confederation, drafted by the very same men who signed the Declaration, was found to be wrong. The Declaration has no application to the present situation. It was written by self-governing men for self-governing men. . . .

Senators in opposition are estopped from denying our constitutional power to govern the Philippines as circumstances may demand, for such power is admitted in the case of Florida, Louisiana, Alaska. How, then, is it denied in the Philippines? Is there a geographical interpretation to the Constitution? Do degrees of longitude fix constitutional limitations? Does a thousand miles of ocean diminish constitutional power more than a thousand miles of land? . . .

Mr. President, this question is deeper than any question of party politics; deeper than any question of the isolated policy of our country even; deeper even than any question of constitutional power. It is elemental. It is racial. God has not been preparing the English-speaking and Teutonic peoples for a thousand years for nothing but vain and idle self-contemplation and self-admiration. No! He has made us the master organizers of the world to establish system where chaos reigns. He has given us the spirit of progress to overwhelm the forces of reaction throughout the earth. He has made us adept in government that we may administer government among savage and senile peoples. Were it not for such a force as this the world would relapse into barbarism and night. And of all our race He has marked the American people as His chosen nation to finally lead in the regeneration of the world. This is the divine mission of America, and it holds for us all the profit, all the glory, all the happiness possible to man. We are trustees of the world's progress, guardians of its righteous peace. The judgment of the Master is upon us: "Ye have been faithful over a few things; I will make you ruler over many things."

Questions

1. What economic benefits does Beveridge foresee from the acquisition of the Philippines?

2. What does Beveridge see as the "divine mission" of the United States?

CHAPTER 18

The Progressive Era, 1900–1916

112. Manuel Gamio on a Mexican-American Family and American Freedom (ca. 1926)

Source: "The Santella Family," Mexican Immigration to the United States, 1926–1928, Gamio Collection, Bancroft Library, University of California at Berkeley. Reprinted with permission of The Bancroft Library.

The early twentieth century was a period of massive immigration to the United States. Most of the newcomers arrived from southern and eastern Europe, but between 1900 and 1930, some 1 million Mexicans also entered the country. Like their predecessors, the new immigrants arrived imagining the United States as a land of freedom, where all persons could worship as they pleased, enjoyed economic opportunity, and had been emancipated from the oppressive social hierarchies of their homelands.

During the 1920s, the sociologist Manuel Gamio conducted interviews of Mexican-American immigrants in Los Angeles. This excerpt from his report on the Santella family, one better off and "whiter" than most Mexican immigrants, reveals the intergenerational tensions that American freedom inspired within immigrant families.

———

THE FOLLOWING INFORMATION concerning the Santella family was obtained by conversation with them and by observing them for it has been a long time that we have known them.

In 1915, on account of the Mexican revolution, which was at its height, Mr. Santella, his wife and his children, who are seven, five girls and two boys, came to the United States, going to live in San Antonio, Texas. As they are a well-to-do family they lived with every comfort possible in a house which was rented to them on San Pedro Street. I understand that they own a number of pieces of property in Mexico City, among them the private residence of the family, which according to the picture which I have before me is a beautiful colonial style building. On San Pedro Street live the wealthiest class of the Mexican colony, or rather, a number of the wealthier members who make up a sort of "high society" in the midst of the great majority of the Mexican colony, which is made up of persons of the working classes.

• • •

After five years of residence in San Antonio all the members of the family talked English and had conformed to the American customs with the exception of the father and the mother. The eldest of the young women married a young American who was manager of a jewelry shop. Two years later the youngest married a brother of this American. This other man was an employee of the same jewelry shop. It seems that these marriages didn't please the father for he constantly declared at the time that these young men didn't "belong to society." The brother who went to Europe returned to San Antonio, Texas, and later moved to Los Angeles, California, where he married a young American girl.

The other male member of the family is much given to the radio and occupies himself with the selling and buying of them, their installation, etc., but he doesn't help the family in any way and he is supported by his father.

The musician has met with good success during his stay in Los Angeles for he is director of the symphonic orchestra of the "Figueroa" theatre located in one of the colonies in Los Angeles. He also has made several adaptations of music for the theatre and movies and has composed several pieces, all of which has given him a certain amount of name and a good place among the artistic elements of Los Angeles.

Before going on we ought to say that this family is white for the grandparents of the father were French and those of the mother were Spaniards. Two of the sisters are blondes and the others are brunettes; the brothers are dark.

Tired of living in San Antonio and of seeing himself obliged to continuously travel between Mexico and the United States, the father decided to permanently return to Mexico in order to be able to watch over his interests there, letting his wife choose the place where she would rather live. The mother with her unmarried daughter and her son decided to come to live in Los Angeles, where they are now living. They live in an apartment in a residence on South Bronson Street, which leads to Hollywood. Their relations are largely with Americans. The family owns a Buick automobile, which the young ladies run.

The father, therefore, lives in Mexico City, where the members of the family only go for visits. The mother lives with her three unmarried daughters and her son. The married son lives in a house that faces the family and the two married daughters live in San Antonio, Texas.

The daughters have worked at different times in Los Angeles against the will of their parents, they say, in the movies as extras representing Spanish types.

The mother says that she likes life in the United States, for the comfort that there is, the quietness and because she finds less danger for her daughters. Here she goes with freedom to the grocery store, clothing store or wherever it may be and buys whatever she wishes without anyone paying attention to her. She lives as she wants and without as many social obligations as in Mexico, where she had to follow such and such a custom, have a great number of servants, and always having to meet a great number of social requirements which bothered her a great deal. She says, nevertheless, that she doesn't like the American customs in the matter of the liberty and way of behaving of the young women of this country, [the] customs and ways of being by which her daughters have been influenced and which greatly concerns her. On the other hand, she likes this country for the progress which it has made and she says that she only likes to go back to Mexico for visits. And since her daughters have married she considers herself obligated to live here in order to help them in everything possible and above all else it happens that the climate of Los Angeles is very good for her.

The youngest of the girls was studying in a high school in San Antonio and later continued her studies in Los Angeles but a little after arriving in this city she entered into relations with a young Englishman who is now her fiancé and she will be married to him within a few months. She quit school on account of this and also wishing to be independent and earn herself the money needed for her clothes and other wants she decided to go to work in spite of the opposition of her father and mother. She is now the secretary of a doctor. She receives the patients who come to his clinic, answers the telephone calls and takes charge of answering the correspondence of her chief for she knows shorthand and typewriting. She receives $20.00 a week for this work with which she buys her dresses, shoes, etc. This young lady who is seventeen years old is the most Americanized of all according to what her mothers and sisters say.

Questions

1. What evidence does the report provide about the spread of consumer culture in early twentieth-century America?

2. What differences in attitudes toward Americanization and gender relations within the Santella family are revealed in Gamio's report?

113. Charlotte Perkins Gilman, *Women and Economics* (1898)

Source: Charlotte Perkins Gilman, Women and Economics *(Boston, 1898), pp. 20–21, 152–57, 210–11.*

During the Progressive Era, the working woman—immigrant and native, working class and professional—became a symbol of female emancipation. The growing number of younger women who desired a life-long career, wrote Charlotte Perkins Gilman in her influential book *Women and Economics* (1898), offered evidence of a "spirit of personal independence" that pointed to a coming transformation of both economic and family life. In the home, Gilman argued, women experienced not fulfillment but oppression, and the housewife was an unproductive parasite, little more than a servant to her husband and children. By condemning women to a life of domestic drudgery, prevailing gender norms made them incapable of contributing to society or enjoying freedom in any meaningful sense of the word. Gilman devised plans for communal nurseries, cafeterias, and laundries, to help free married women from "house service." Her writings had a strong impact on the first generation of twentieth-century feminists.

————————————

IT IS NOT motherhood that keeps the housewife on her feet from dawn till dark; it is house service, not child service. Women work longer and harder than most men, and not solely in maternal duties. The savage mother carries the burdens, and does all menial service for the tribe. The peasant mother toils in the fields, and the workingman's wife in the home. Many mothers, even now, are wage-earners for the family, as well as bearers and rearers of it. And the women who are not so occupied, the women who belong to rich men,—here perhaps is the exhaustive devotion to maternity which is supposed to justify an admitted economic dependence. But we do not find it even among these. Women of ease and wealth provide for their children better care than the poor woman can; but they do not spend more time upon it themselves, nor more care and effort. They have other occupation.

• • •

The working power of the mother has always been a prominent factor in human life. She is the worker *par excellence*, but her work is not such as to affect her economic status. Her living, all that she gets,—food, clothing, ornaments, amusements, luxuries,—these bear no relation to her power to produce wealth, to her services in the house, or to her motherhood. These things bear relation only to the man she marries, the man she depends on,—to how much he has and how much he is willing to give her.

• • •

A truer spirit is the increasing desire of young girls to be independent, to have a career of their own, at least for a while, and the growing objection of countless wives to the pitiful asking for money, to the beggary of their position. More and more do fathers give their daughters, and husbands their wives, a definite allowance,—a separate bank account,—something which they can play is all their own. The spirit of personal independence in the women of to-day is sure proof that a change has come.

For a while the introduction of machinery which took away from the home so many industries deprived woman of any importance as an economic factor; but presently she arose, and followed her lost wheel and loom to their new place, the mill. To-day there is hardly an industry in the land in which some women are not found. Everywhere throughout America are women workers outside the unpaid labor of the home, the last census giving three million of them. This is so patent a fact, and makes itself felt in so many ways by so many persons, that it is frequently and widely discussed. Without here going into its immediate advantages or disadvantages from an industrial point of view, it is merely instanced as an undeniable proof of the radical change in the economic position of women that is advancing upon us. She is assuming new relations from year to year before our eyes; but we, seeing all social facts from a personal point of view, have failed to appreciate the nature of the change.

• • •

The growing individualization of democratic life brings inevitable change to our daughters as well as to our sons. Girls do not all like to sew, many do not know how. Now to sit sewing together, instead of being a harmonizing process, would generate different degrees of restlessness, of distaste, and of nervous irritation. And, as to the reading aloud, it is not so easy now to choose a book that a well-educated family of modern girls and their mother would all enjoy together. As the race become more specialized, more differentiated, the simple lines of relation in family life draw with less force, and the more complex lines of relation in social life draw with more force; and this is a perfectly natural and desirable process for women as well as for men.

• • •

Economic independence for women necessarily involves a change in the home and family relation. But, if that change is for the advantage of individual and race, we need not fear it. It does not involve a change in the marriage relation except in withdrawing the element of economic dependence, nor in the relation of mother to child save to improve it. But it does involve the exercise of human faculty in women, in social service and exchange rather than in domestic service solely. This will of course require the introduction of some other form of living than that which now obtains. It will render impossible the present method of feeding the world by means of millions of private servants, and bringing up children by the same hand.

It is a melancholy fact that the vast majority of our children are reared and trained by domestic servants,—generally their mothers, to be sure, but domestic servants by trade. To become a producer, a factor in the economic activities of the world, must perforce interfere with woman's present status as a private servant. House mistress she may still be, in the sense of owning and ordering her home, but housekeeper or house-servant she may not be—and be anything else. Her position as mother will alter, too. Mother in the sense of bearer and rearer of noble children she will be, as the closest and dearest, the one most honored and best loved; but mother in the sense of exclusive individual nursery-maid and nursery-governess she may not be—and be anything else.

Questions

1. Why does Gilman foresee a "radical change in the economic position of women"?

2. What changes in family life does she envision as a result of the growing economic independence of women?

---

114. John Mitchell, "The Workingman's Conception of Industrial Liberty" (1910)

Source: John Mitchell, "The Workingman's Conception of Industrial Liberty," American Federationist *(May 1910), pp. 405–410.*

During the Progressive Era, the ideas of "industrial freedom" and "industrial democracy," which had entered the political vocabulary in the Gilded Age, moved to the center of political discussion. Many Progressives believed that the key to increasing industrial freedom lay in empowering workers to participate in economic decision making via strong unions. In the article that follows, John Mitchell, head of the United Mine Workers' Union, pointedly contrasts workers' understanding of "industrial liberty" with prevailing laissez-faire definitions of freedom inherited from the Gilded Age and enforced by the courts during the Progressive Era. When legislatures tried to regulate working conditions to improve the status of labor, courts overturned the laws as violations of freedom—freedom not only of the employers but of workers themselves. Workers, he observed, "feel that they are being guaranteed the liberties they do not want and denied the liberty that is of real value to them."

WHILE THE DECLARATION of Independence established civil and political liberty, it did not, as you all know, establish industrial liberty. For nearly one hundred years following the Declaration of Independence, chattel slavery was a recognized and legal institution in our civilization. And real industrial liberty was not even established with the abolition of chattel slavery; because liberty means more than the right to choose the field of one's employment. He is not a free man whose family must buy food today with the money that is earned tomorrow. He is not really free who is forced to work unduly long hours and for wages so low that he can not provide the necessaries of life for himself and his family; who must live in a crowded tenement and see his children go to work in the mills, the mines, and the factories before their bodies are developed and their minds trained. To have freedom a man must be free from the harrowing fear of hunger and want; he must be in such a position that by the exercise of reasonable frugality he can provide his family with all of the necessities and the reasonable comforts of life. He must be able to educate his children and to provide against sickness, accident, and old age.

• • •

In carrying on this contest for new liberties and new laws and broader concepts of old laws, we may seem at times to be running counter to established authority, but closer investigation will demonstrate that we are defending and not violating the organic laws upon which the Government is founded. It is not my wish to introduce matters controversial in character, but events in the recent past upon which there is much misinformation and no small public sentiment, may, I hope, justify brief allusion to these concrete problems, because they illustrate most forcefully the workingman's conception of industrial liberty.

Some time ago the legislature of the State of Illinois enacted a law prohibiting the employment of women in factories for more than sixty hours in any one week or more than ten hours in any one day. It was the judgment of the members of this legislature that society was directly interested in the health and happiness of its women wage-earners. Physicians and scientific men of the highest possible standing had testified that more than ten hours' work in a mill or a factory was detrimental to the health of the woman and dangerous to the generations that were to follow. Shortly thereafter, at the instigation of her employer, a woman working in a Chicago box factory brought suit in the courts to have the law declared unconstitutional, setting up the claim that she was unable in ten hours' work to earn sufficient wages to maintain herself, and that therefore this act limiting her hours of labor in effect deprived her of her liberty and property without due process of law. The court agreed with her and declared the law to be unconstitutional; and the consequence is that thousands upon thousands of wage-earning women in the State of Illinois who demanded the passage of this act are now required to work from eleven to fourteen hours per day in order that this one woman acting for her employer—her lawsuit financed by him—might have the liberty of working more than ten hours per day. The very ground upon which this woman made her complaint—namely, that she could not earn enough money in ten hours to maintain herself—renders ridiculous and absurd her plea that her liberty had been abridged.

• • •

A number of years ago the legislatures of several coal producing States enacted laws requiring employers to pay the wages of their workmen in lawful money of the United States and to cease the practice of paying wages in merchandise. From time immemorial it had been the custom of coal companies to conduct general supply stores, and the workingmen were required, as a condition of employment, to accept products in lieu of money in return for services rendered. This system was a great hardship to the workmen, as by it competition was eliminated entirely and the prices charged for supplies sold from these company stores were much higher than goods could be purchased for in the open market. The question of the constitutionality of this legislation was carried into the courts and by the highest tribunal it was declared to be an invasion of the workman's liberty to deny him the right to accept merchandise in lieu of money as payment of his wages.

These cases are selected because they illustrate the general policy of the organized labor movement. We are trying constantly to secure laws that will protect those in our social life who are least able to protect themselves. There is scarcely a law on the statute books of any State or of the Nation, throwing the protecting arm of the Government about the weak and the defenseless, that has not had its inspiration in the minds of the organized workmen. True, they have had the assistance of good men and good women from other walks of life, but the burden of these efforts has fallen upon the much-maligned organizations of labor. Surely it will not be denied that in seeking laws for the protection of women and children, the workingmen are rendering a real service to the Nation and to society and that they are promoting in the best sense the liberty and the happiness of the people.

The cases I have cited, however, are typical of hundreds of instances in which laws that have been enacted for the protection of the workingmen have been declared by the courts to be unconstitutional, on the grounds that they invaded the liberty of the workingpeople. To understand the attitude of the workingmen in matters of this kind, it is necessary to bear in mind that all this legislation was championed by them and was enacted at their solicitation, and when the courts declare such laws unconstitutional—basing their decisions upon the hypothesis that the liberty of the workman is invaded—is it not natural that the workingmen should feel that they are being guaranteed the liberties they do not want and denied the liberty that is of real value to them? May they not exclaim, with Madame Roland, "O Liberty! Liberty! How many crimes are committed in thy name!"

• • •

I have tried in this brief address to present at least one phase of the workingman's conception of industrial liberty, but my chief purpose has been to convey to you the spirit of patriotism which underlies the whole movement for better conditions of life and labor. The labor movement is primarily and fundamentally a moral movement. While attention is attracted to it by its strikes and its struggles yet the battles it fights in defense of the poor and the helpless are but phases of the great movement which is making for the physical, the mental, and the moral uplift of the people. Behind and above the demand for higher wages and shorter hours stands the greater movement for better men, for happier women, and for joyous children; for homes, for books, for pictures and music, for the things that make for culture and refinement. The labor movement stands for the essential principles of religion and morality; for temperance; for decency, and for dignity.

Questions

1. What does Mitchell see as the purposes of the labor movement?

2. What would be necessary to establish "real industrial liberty" as understood by Mitchell?

---

115. The Industrial Workers of the World and the Free Speech Fights (1909)

Source: Elizabeth Gurley Flynn, "The Free-Speech Fight at Spokane," **International Socialist Review, Vol. 16 (December 1909), pp. 483–89.**

The most prominent union of the Progressive Era, the American Federation of Labor, mainly represented the most privileged American workers— skilled industrial and craft laborers, nearly all of them white, male, and native born. In 1905, a group of unionists who rejected the AFL's exclusionary policies formed the Industrial Workers of the World (IWW), which sought to mobilize the immigrant factory labor force, migrant timber and agricultural workers, women, blacks, even the despised Chinese.

But what really attracted attention to the IWW was its battle for freedom of speech. Lacking union halls, its organizers relied on songs, street theater, impromptu organizing meetings, and street corner gatherings to spread their message and attract support. In response to IWW activities, officials in Los Angeles, Spokane, Denver, and more than a dozen other cities limited or prohibited outdoor meetings. To arouse popular support, the IWW filled the jails with members who defied local law by speaking in public. In nearly all the free-speech fights, the IWW eventually forced local officials to give way. "Whether they agree or disagree with its methods or aims," wrote one journalist, "all lovers of liberty everywhere owe a debt to this organization for . . . [keeping] alight the fires of freedom."

THE WORKING CLASS of Spokane are engaged in a terrific conflict, one of the most vital of the local class struggles. It is a fight for more than free speech. It is to prevent the free press and labor's right to organize from being throttled. The writers of the associated press newspapers have lied about us systematically and unscrupulously. It is only through the medium of the Socialist and labor press that we can hope to reach the ear of the public.

The struggle was precipitated by the I.W.W. and it is still doing the active fighting, namely, going to jail. But the principles for which we are fighting have been endorsed by the Socialist Party and the Central Labor Council of the A.F. of L. [American Federation of Labor].

The I.W.W. in Spokane is composed of "floaters," men who drift from harvest fields to lumber camps from east to west. They are men without families and are fearless in defense of their rights but as they are not the "home guard" with permanent jobs, they are the type upon whom the employment agents prey. With alluring signs detailing what short hours and high wages men can get in various sections, usually far away, these leeches induce the floater to buy a job, paying exorbitant rates, after which they are shipped out a thousand miles from nowhere. The working man finds no such job as he expected but one of a few days' duration until he is fired to make way for the next "easy mark."

The I.W.W. since its inception in the northwest has carried on a determined, relentless fight on the employment sharks and as a result the business of the latter has been seriously impaired. Judge Mann in the court a few days ago remarked: "I believe all this trouble is due to the employment agencies," and he certainly struck the nail on the head. "The I.W.W. must go," the sharks decreed last winter and a willing city council passed an ordinance forbidding all street meetings within the fire limits. This was practically a suppression of free speech because it stopped the I.W.W. from holding street meetings in the only districts where working men congregate. In August the Council modified their decision to allow religious bodies to speak on the streets, thus frankly admitting their discrimination against the I.W.W.

The I.W.W. decided that fall was the most advantageous time for the final conflict because the members of the organization drift back into town with their "stake" to tide them over the winter.

A test case was made about three weeks ago when Fellow Worker Thompson spoke on the street. At his trial on November 2nd the ordinance of August was declared unconstitutional by Judge Mann. He made a flowery speech in which he said that the right of free speech was "God given" and "inalienable," but with the consistency common to legal lights ruled that the *first ordinance* was now in vogue. Members of the Industrial Workers of the World thereupon went out on the street and spoke. They were all arrested and to our surprise the next morning were charged with disorderly conduct, which came under another ordinance. It looked as if the authorities hardly dared to fight it out on the ordinance forbidding free speech. From that time on, every day has witnessed the arrests of many members of the Industrial Workers of the World, Socialists and W.F. of M. [Western Federation of Miners] men.

On the third of November the headquarters of the I.W.W. was raided by Chief of Police Sullivan and his gang. They arrested James Wilson, editor of the *Industrial Worker*, James P. Thompson, local organizer, C. L. Filigno, local secretary, and A. E. Cousins, associate editor, on a charge of criminal conspiracy. E. J. Foote, acting editor of the *Industrial Worker*, was arrested out of the lawyer's office on the next day. The idea of the police was presumably to get "the leaders," as they are ignorant enough to suppose that by taking a few men they can cripple a great organization. The arrest of these men is serious, however, as they are charged with a state offense and are liable to be railroaded to the penitentiary for five years.

The condition of the city jail is such that it cannot be described in decent language. Sufficient to say, that the boys have been herded twenty-eight to thirty at a time in a 6×8 cell known as the sweat box. The steam has been turned on full blast until the men were ready to drop from exhaustion. Several have been known to faint before being removed. Then they were placed in an ice-cold cell and as a result of this inhuman treatment several are now in so precarious a condition that we fear they will die. After this preliminary punishment they were ordered to work on the rock pile and when they refused were placed on a diet of bread and water. Many of the boys, with a courage that is remarkable, refused even that. This is what the capitalist press sneeringly alluded to as a "hunger strike." The majority has been sentenced to thirty days. Those who repeated the terrible crime of saying "Fellow Workers" on the street corner were given thirty days, one hundred dollars' fine and costs. The trials have given additional proof to our much-disputed charge that justice in the United States is a farce. Fellow Worker Little was asked by the Judge what he was doing when arrested. He answered "reading the Declaration of Independence." "Thirty days," said the Judge. The next fellow worker had been reading extracts from the *Industrial Worker* and it was thirty days for him. We are a "classy" paper ranked with the Declaration of Independence as too incendiary for Spokane.

A case in point illustrates how "impartial" the court is. A woman from a notorious resort in this city which is across the street from the city hall and presumably operated under police protection appeared and complained against a colored soldier charged with disorderly conduct. The case was continued. The next case was an I.W.W.

speaker. The Judge without any preliminaries asked "were you speaking on the street?" When the defendant replied "Yes" the Judge sternly ordered thirty days, one hundred dollars' fine and costs.

Fellow Worker Knust, one of our best speakers, was brutally beaten by an officer and he is at present in the hospital. Mrs. Frenette, one of our women members, was also struck by an officer. Some of the men inside the jail have black eyes and bruised faces. One man has a broken jaw, yet these men were not in such a condition when they were arrested.

Those serving sentence have been divided into three groups, one in the city jail, another in an old abandoned and partly wrecked schoolhouse and the third at Fort Wright, guarded by negro soldiers. These outrages are never featured in the local leading papers. It might be detrimental to the Washington Water Power-owned government. The usual lies about the agitators being ignorant foreigners, hoboes and vags [vagrants] are current. Assuming that most of those arrested were foreigners, which is not the case, there are 115 foreigners and 136 Americans, it would certainly reflect little credit on American citizens that outsiders have to do the fighting for what is guaranteed in the American constitution. Most of the boys have money. They are not what could be called "vags," although that would not be to their discredit, but they do not take their money to jail with them. They believe in leading a policeman not into temptation. They are intelligent, level-headed working men fighting for the rights of their class.

The situation assumed such serious proportions that a committee of the A.F. of L., the Socialist Party and the I.W.W. went before the City Council requesting the repeal of the present ordinance and the passage of one providing for orderly meetings at reasonable hours. All of these committees, without qualification, endorsed free speech and made splendid talks before the Council. Two gentlemen appeared against us. One was an old soldier over 70 years of age with strong prejudices against the I.W.W. and the other president of the Fidelity National Bank of Spokane; yet these two presumably carried more

weight than the twelve thousand five hundred citizens the three committees collectively represented. We were turned down absolutely and
a motion was passed that no further action would be taken upon the
present ordinance until requests came from the Mayor and Chief of Police. The Mayor, on the strength of this endorsement by a body of old fo-
gies who made up all the mind they possess years ago, called upon the
acting governor for the militia. His request was refused, however, and
the acting governor is quoted as saying that he saw no disturbance.

The "Industrial Worker" appeared on time yesterday much to the
chagrin and amazement of the authorities. Perhaps they now understand that every member in turn will take their place in the editorial
chair before our paper will be suppressed.

The organization is growing by leaps and bounds. Men are coming
in from all directions daily to go to jail that their organization may live.

Questions

1. Why was freedom of speech so important to labor organizations like the
IWW?

2. What does the IWW's experience reveal about the status of civil liberties
in early twentieth-century America?

---

116. Margaret Sanger on "Free Motherhood," from *Woman and the New Race* (1920)

Source: Margaret Sanger, **Woman and the New Race** *(New York, 1929), pp.
1, 47–48, 94–95, 226–32. Reprinted with permission of Alexander Sanger,
Executor of the Estate of Margaret Sanger.*

The word "feminism" entered the political vocabulary for the first time in
the years before World War I. It expressed not only traditional demands
such as the right to vote and greater economic opportunities for women

but a quest for free sexual expression and reproductive choice as essential to women's emancipation. The law banned not only the sale of birth control devices but distributing information about them.

More than any other individual, Margaret Sanger, one of eleven children of an Irish-American working-class family, placed the issue of birth control at the heart of the new feminism. She began openly advertising birth control devices in her own journal, *The Woman Rebel*. In 1916, Sanger opened a clinic in a working-class neighborhood of Brooklyn and began distributing contraceptive devices to poor Jewish and Italian women, an action for which she was sentenced to a month in prison. Like the IWW free-speech fights, Sanger's experience revealed how laws set rigid limits to Americans' freedom of expression.

⸻

THE MOST FAR-REACHING social development of modern times is the revolt of woman against sex servitude. The most important force in the remaking of the world is a free motherhood. Beside this force, the elaborate international programmes of modern statesmen are weak and superficial. Diplomats may formulate leagues of nations and nations may pledge their utmost strength to maintain them, statesmen may dream of reconstructing the world out of alliances, hegemonies and spheres of influence, but woman, continuing to produce explosive populations, will convert these pledges into the proverbial scraps of paper; or she may, by controlling birth, lift motherhood to the plane of a voluntary, intelligent function, and re-make the world. When the world is thus remade, it will exceed the dream of statesman, reformer and revolutionist.

• • •

Most women who belong to the workers' families have no accurate or reliable knowledge of contraceptives, and are, therefore, bringing children into the world so rapidly that they, their families and their class are overwhelmed with numbers. Out of these numbers … have grown many of the burdens with which society in general is weighted; out of them have come, also, the want, disease, hard living conditions and general misery of the workers.

The women of this class are the greatest sufferers of all. Not only do they bear the material hardships and deprivations in common with the rest of the family, but in the case of the mother, these are intensified. It is the man and the child who have first call upon the insufficient amount of food. It is the man and the child who get the recreation, if there is any to be had, for the man's hours of labor are usually limited by law or by his labor union.

It is the woman who suffers first from hunger, the woman whose clothing is least adequate, the woman who must work all hours, even though she is not compelled, as in the case of millions, to go into a factory to add to her husband's scanty income. It is she, too, whose health breaks first and most hopelessly, under the long hours of work, the drain of frequent childbearing, and often almost constant nursing of babies. There are no eight-hour laws to protect the mother against overwork and toil in the home; no laws to protect her against ill health and the diseases of pregnancy and reproduction. In fact there has been almost no thought or consideration given for the protection of the mother in the home of the workingman.

• • •

The basic freedom of the world is woman's freedom. A free race cannot be born of slave mothers. A woman enchained cannot choose but give a measure of that bondage to her sons and daughters. No woman can call herself free who does not own and control her body. No woman can call herself free until she can choose consciously whether she will or will not be a mother.

It does not greatly alter the case that some women call themselves free because they earn their own livings, while others profess freedom because they defy the conventions of sex relationship. She who earns her own living gains a sort of freedom that is not to be undervalued, but in quality and in quantity it is of little account beside the untrammeled choice of mating or not mating, of being a mother or not being a mother. She gains food and clothing and shelter, at least, without submitting to the charity of her companion, but the earning of her own living does not give her the development of her inner sex urge, far deeper and more powerful in its outworkings than any of these externals. In order to have that development, she must still meet and solve the problem of motherhood.

With the so-called "free" woman, who chooses a mate in defiance of convention, freedom is largely a question of character and audacity. If she does attain to an unrestricted choice of a mate, she is still in a position to be enslaved through her reproductive powers. Indeed, the pressure of law and custom upon the woman not legally married is likely to make her more of a slave than the woman fortunate enough to marry the man of her choice.

• • •

Voluntary motherhood implies a new morality—a vigorous, constructive, liberated morality. That morality will, first of all, prevent the submergence of womanhood into motherhood. It will set its face against the conversion of women into mechanical maternity and toward the creation of a new race.

Woman's role has been that of an incubator and little more. She has given birth to an incubated race. She has given to her children what little she was permitted to give, but of herself, of her personality, almost nothing. In the mass, she has brought forth quantity, not quality. The requirement of a male dominated civilization has been numbers. She has met that requirement.

It is the essential function of voluntary motherhood to choose its own mate, to determine the time of childbearing and to regulate strictly the number of offspring. Natural affection upon her part, instead of selection dictated by social or economic advantage, will give her a better fatherhood for her children. The exercise of her right to decide how many children she will have and when she shall have them will procure for her the time necessary to the development of other faculties than that of reproduction. She will give play to her tastes, her talents and her ambitions. She will become a full-rounded human being.

• • •

A free womanhood turns of its own desire to a free and happy motherhood, a motherhood which does not submerge the woman, but, which is enriched because she is unsubmerged. When we voice, then, the necessity of setting the feminine spirit utterly and absolutely free, thought turns naturally not to rights of the woman, nor indeed of the mother, but to the rights of the child—of all children in the world. For this is the miracle of free womanhood, that in its freedom it becomes the race mother and opens its heart in fruitful affection for humanity.

Questions

1. How does Sanger define "free womanhood"?

2. How does she believe access to birth control will change women's lives?

---

117. Carlos Montezuma, "What Indians Must Do" (1914)

Source: Carlos Montezuma, "What Indians Must Do," Quarterly Journal, *Vol. 2 (1914), pp. 294–99.*

Many Indian intellectuals during the Progressive era were not unsympathetic to the basic goals of federal Indian policy, including the transformation of communal landholdings on reservations into family farms. But Carlos Montezuma became an outspoken critic. Born in Arizona, he had been captured as a child by members of a neighboring tribe and sold to a traveling photographer, who brought him to Chicago, where Montezuma attended school and eventually obtained a medical degree. In the article that follows, published in the journal of the Society of American Indians, Montezuma condemned federal paternalism toward the Indians and called for the abolition of the Bureau of Indian Affairs. Convinced that outsiders exerted too much power over life on the reservations, he insisted that self-determination was the only way for Indians to escape poverty and marginalization. Montezuma's writings had little influence at the time on government policy, but Indian activists would later rediscover him as a forerunner of Indian radicalism.

━━━━━━━━━

WE MUST FREE ourselves. Our peoples' heritage is freedom. Freedom reigned in their whole make-up. They harmonized with nature and lived accordingly. Preaching freedom to our people on reservations does not make them free any more than you can, by preaching, free those prisoners who are in the penitentiary. Reservations are prisons where our people are kept to live and die, where equal possibilities, equal education and equal responsibilities are unknown. . . .

We must do away with the Indian Bureau. The reservation system has debarred us as a race from acquiring that knowledge to appreciate our property. The government after teaching us how to live without work has come to the conclusion "that the Indians are not commercialists" and, therefore, "we (his guardian) will remove them as we think best and use them as long as our administration lasts and make friends." The Indian Department has drifted into commercialism at the expense of our poor benighted people. So they go on and say, "Let us not allot those Indians on that sweet flowing water because there are others who will profit by damming it up and selling it out to the newcomers; that the Indians do not use or develop their lands; five acres of irrigated land is all that one Indian can manage, but in order to be generous, we will give him ten acres and close up the books and call it square; that their vast forest does them no good, before the Indian can open his eyes let us transfer it to the Forestry Reserve Department. Never mind, let the Indian scratch for his wood to cook with and to warm himself in the years to come; that the Indians have no use for rivers, therefore, we will go into damming business and build them on their lands without their consent. Pay? No! Why should we?" They give us "C" class water instead of "A" class. They have got us! Why? Because we do not know the difference.

"In this valley the Indians have too much land. We will move them from where they have lived for centuries" (by Executive order in behalf of the coming settlers). Even if he had cultivated and claims more than that, we will allot that Indian only ten acres. If he rebels and makes trouble, we will put him in jail until he is ready to behave himself." This poor Indian may try to get an Indian friend to help him out of his predicament. But right there the Indian helper is balked by the Indian Department and is told he is not wanted on the reservation. When an Indian collects money from among his tribe to defray expenses to Washington and back in order to carry their complaints, and to be heard and considered in their rights, the superintendent with the aid of the Indian policeman takes this Indian, takes the money away from him and gives back the money to those who contributed, put[s] him in jail and brands him as a grafter. . . .

The sooner the Government abolishes the Indian Bureau, the better it will be for we Indians in every way. The system that has kept alive the Indian Bureau has been instrumental in dominating over our race for fifty years. In that time the Indian's welfare has grown to the secondary and the Indian Bureau the whole thing, and therefore a necessary political appendage of the government. It sends out exaggerated and wonderful reports to the public in order to suck the blood of our race, so that it may have perpetual life to sap your life, my life and our children's future prospects. There are many good things to say about the Indian Department. It started out right with our people. It fed them, clothed them and protected them from going outside of the reservations. It was truly a place of refuge. Then they were dominated by agents; now they are called superintendents. On the reservation our people did not act without the consent of the Superintendent; they did not express themselves without the approval of the Superintendent, and *they did not dare to think*, for that would be to rival, to the Superintendent. Yesterday, today, our people are in the same benighted condition. As Indians they are considered nonentities. They are not anything to themselves and not anything to the world. . . .

We must be independent. When with my people for a vacation in Arizona I must live outdoors; I must sleep on the ground; I must cook in the fire on the ground; I must sit on the ground, I must eat nature's food and I must be satisfied with inconveniences that I do not enjoy at my Chicago home. Yet those blood relations of mine are independent, happy, because they were born and brought up in that environment, while as a greenhorn I find myself dependent and helpless in such simple life. In order for we Indians to be independent in the whirl of this other life, we must get into it and used to it and live up to its requirements and take our chances with the rest of our fellow creatures. Being caged up and not permitted to develop our facilities has made us a dependent race. We are looked upon as hopeless to save and hopeless to do anything for ourselves. The only Christian way, then, is to leave us alone and let us die in that condition. The conclusion is true that we will die that way if we do not hurry and get out of it and hustle for our salvation. Did you ever notice how other races hustle and bustle in order to achieve independence? Reservations Indians must do the same as the rest of the wide world.

Questions

1. How does Montezuma believe Indians can "free ourselves"?

2. Why does Montezuma call for the abolition of the Indian Bureau?

---

118. Woodrow Wilson and the New Freedom (1912)

Source: "Address to the New York Press Club, September 9, 1912," Arthur S. Link, ed., The Papers of Woodrow Wilson *(Princeton, N.J., 1966–1994), Vol. 25, pp. 122–25. © 1978 Princeton University Press.*

The four-way presidential contest of 1912 between President William Howard Taft, former president Theodore Roosevelt, Woodrow Wilson, and Socialist Eugene V. Debs became a national debate on the relationship between political and economic freedom in the age of big business. Public attention focused particularly on the battle between Wilson, the Democratic candidate, and Roosevelt, running as the standard-bearer of the new Progressive Party, over the role of the federal government in securing economic freedom. Both believed increased government action necessary to preserve individual freedom, but they differed about the dangers of increasing the government's power and the inevitability of economic concentration. Wilson called his approach the New Freedom. He envisioned the federal government strengthening antitrust laws, protecting the right of workers to unionize, and actively encouraging small businesses. Wilson feared big government as much as the power of the corporations. He warned that corporations were as likely to corrupt government as to be managed by it, a forecast that proved remarkably accurate.

―――――――――

YOU HAVE IN this new party [the Progressive Party] two things—a political party and a body of social reformers. Will the political party contained in it be serviceable to the social reformers? I do not think that I am mistaken in picking out as the political part of that platform the part which determines how the government is going to stand related to the central problems upon which its freedom depends. The freedom of the Government of the United States depends upon getting separated from, disentangled from, those interests which have enjoyed, chiefly enjoyed, the patronage of that government. Because the trouble with the tariff is not that it has been protective, for in recent years it has been much more than protective. It has been one of the most colossal systems of deliberate patronage that has ever been conceived. And the main trouble with it is that the protection stops where the patronage begins, and that if you could lop off the patronage, you would have taken away most of the objectionable features of the so-called protection.

This patronage, this special privilege, these favors doled out to some persons and not to all, have been the basis of the control which has been set up over the industries and over the enterprises of this country by great combinations. Because we forgot, in permitting a regime of free competition to last so long, that the competitors had ceased to be individuals or small groups of individuals, and it had come to be a competition between individuals or small groups on the one hand and enormous aggregations of individuals and capital on the other; and that, after that contrast in strength had been created in fact, competition, free competition, was out of the question, that it was then possible for the powerful to crush the weak.

That isn't competition; that is warfare. And because we did not check the free competition soon enough, because we did not check it at the point where pigmies entered the field against giants, we have created a condition of affairs in which the control of industry, and to a large extent the control of credit in this country, upon which industry feeds and in which all new enterprises must be rooted, is in the hands of a comparatively small and very compact body of men. These are the gentlemen who have in some instances, perhaps in more than have been exhibited by legal proof, engaged in what we are now expected to call "unreasonable combinations in restraint of trade." They have indulged themselves beyond reason in the exercise of that power which makes competition practically impossible.

Very well then, the test of our freedom for the next generation lies here. Are we going to take that power away from them, or are we going to leave it with them? You can take it away from them if you regulate competition and make it impossible for them to do some of the things which they have been doing. You leave it with them if you legitimatize and regulate monopoly. And what the platform of the new party proposes to do is exactly that.

It proposes to start where we are, and, without altering the established conditions of competition, which are conditions which affect it. We shall say what these giants shall do and to what the pigmies shall submit, and we shall do that not by law, for if you will read the plank in its candid statement—for it is perfectly candid—you will find that it rejects regulation by law and proposes a commission which shall have the discretion itself to undertake what the plank calls "constructive regulation." It shall make its rules as it goes along.

As it handles these giants, so shall it shape its course. That, gentlemen, is nothing more than a legitimatized continuation of the present order of things, with the alliance between the great interests and the government open instead of covert.

• • •

Liberty has never come from the government. Liberty has always come from the subjects of the government. The history of liberty is a history of resistance. The history of liberty is a history of the limitation of governmental power, not the increase of it. Do these gentlemen dream that in the year 1912 we have discovered a unique exception to the movement of human history? Do they dream that the whole character of those who exercise power has changed, that it is no longer a temptation? Above all things else, do they dream that men are bred great enough now to be a Providence over the people over whom they preside?

• • •

[Theodore Roosevelt believes that] big business and the government could live on amicable terms with one another. . . .

Now, I say that in that way lies no thoroughfare for social reform, and that those who are hopeful of social reform through the instrumentality of that party ought to realize that in the very platform itself is supplied the demonstration that it is not a serviceable instrument. They do propose to serve civilization and humanity, but they can't serve civilization and humanity with that kind of government.

Questions

1. Why does Wilson say, "the history of liberty is a history of the limitation of governmental power"?

2. How does he propose to protect "our freedom for the next generation"?

119. The Progressive Party Platform (1912)

Source: Donald B. Johnson, comp., National Party Platforms *(Urbana, Ill., 1978), Vol. 1, pp. 175–79.*

Drafted by a group of female activists, labor reformers, and social scientists, the Progressive Party platform of 1912 laid out a blueprint for a modern, democratic welfare state, complete with women's suffrage, federal supervision of corporate enterprise, national labor and health legislation for women and children, an eight-hour work day and "living wage" for all workers, and a national system of social insurance covering unemployment, medical care, and old age. Described by the party's presidential candidate, Theodore Roosevelt, as the "most important document" since the end of the Civil War, the platform brought together many of the streams of thought and political experiences that flowed into Progressivism and anticipated many policies adopted two decades later during the New Deal. In economic matters it reflected Roosevelt's New Nationalism, which envisioned heavy taxes on personal and corporate fortunes, and federal regulation of industries including railroads, mining, and oil. Unlike Wilson, Roosevelt insisted that big business was here to stay and that federal government must protect the public interest by regulating its activities.

***

THE CONSCIENCE OF the people, in a time of grave national problems, has called into being a new party, born of the nation's sense of justice. We of the Progressive party here dedicate ourselves to the fulfillment of the duty laid upon us by our fathers to maintain the government of the people, by the people and for the people whose foundations they laid.

We hold with Thomas Jefferson and Abraham Lincoln that the people are the masters of their Constitution, to fulfill its purposes and to safeguard it from those who, by perversion of its intent, would convert it into an instrument of injustice. In accordance with the needs of each generation the people must use their sovereign powers to establish and maintain equal opportunity and industrial justice, to secure which this Government was founded and without which no republic can endure.

This country belongs to the people who inhabit it. Its resources, its business, its institutions and its laws should be utilized, maintained or altered in whatever manner will best promote the general interest.

It is time to set the public welfare in the first place.

The Old Parties

Political parties exist to secure responsible government and to execute the will of the people.

From these great tasks both of the old parties have turned aside. Instead of instruments to promote the general welfare, they have become the tools of corrupt interests which use them impartially to serve their selfish purposes. Behind the ostensible government sits enthroned an invisible government owing no allegiance and acknowledging no responsibility to the people.

To destroy this invisible government, to dissolve the unholy alliance between corrupt business and corrupt politics is the first task of the statesmanship of the day.

The deliberate betrayal of its trust by the Republican party, the fatal incapacity of the Democratic party to deal with the new issues of the new time, have compelled the people to forge a new instrument of government through which to give effect to their will in laws and institutions.

Unhampered by tradition, uncorrupted by power, undismayed by the magnitude of the task, the new party offers itself as the instrument of the people to sweep away old abuses, to build a new and nobler commonwealth.

A Covenant with the People

This declaration is our covenant with the people, and we hereby bind the party and its candidates in State and Nation to the pledges made herein.

The Rule of the People

The National Progressive party, committed to the principles of government by a self-controlled democracy expressing its will through representatives of the people, pledges itself to secure such alterations in the fundamental law of the several States and of the United States as shall insure the representative character of the government.

In particular, the party declares for direct primaries for the nomination of State and National officers, for nation-wide preferential primaries for candidates for the presidency; for the direct election of United States Senators by the people; and we urge on the States the policy of the short ballot, with responsibility to the people secured by the initiative, referendum and recall.

• • •

Nation and State

Up to the limit of the Consititution, and later by amendment of the Constitution, it found necessary, we advocate bringing under effective national jurisdiction those problems which have expanded beyond reach of the individual States.

It is as grotesque as it is intolerable that the several States should by unequal laws in matter of common concern become competing commercial agencies, barter the lives of their children, the health of their women and the safety and well being of their working people for the benefit of their financial interests.

The extreme insistence on States' rights by the Democratic party in the Baltimore platform demonstrates anew its inability to understand the world into which it has survived or to administer the affairs of a union of States which have in all essential respects become one people.

EQUAL SUFFRAGE

The Progressive party, believing that no people can justly claim to be a true democracy which denies political rights on account of sex, pledges itself to the task of securing equal suffrage to men and women alike.

CORRUPT PRACTICES

We pledge our party to legislation that will compel strict limitation of all campaign contributions and expenditures, and detailed publicity of both before as well as after primaries and elections.

PUBLICITY AND PUBLIC SERVICE

We pledge our party to legislation compelling the registration of lobbyists; publicity of committee hearings except on foreign affairs, and recording of all votes in committee; and forbidding federal appointees from holding office in State or National political organizations, or taking part as officers or delegates in political conventions for the nomination of elective State or National officials.

THE COURTS

The Progressive party demands such restriction of the power of the courts as shall leave to the people the ultimate authority to determine fundamental questions of social welfare and public policy. To secure this end, it pledges itself to provide:

1. That when an Act, passed under the police power of the State, is held unconstitutional under the State Constitution, by the courts, the people, after an ample interval for deliberation, shall have an

opportunity to vote on the question whether they desire the Act to become law, notwithstanding such decision.

2. That every decision of the highest appellate court of a State declaring an Act of the Legislature unconstitutional on the ground of its violation of the Federal Constitution shall be subject to the same review by the Supreme Court of the United States as is now accorded to decisions sustaining such legislation.

• • •

SOCIAL AND INDUSTRIAL JUSTICE

The supreme duty of the Nation is the conservation of human resources through an enlightened measure of social and industrial justice. We pledge ourselves to work unceasingly in State and Nation for:

Effective legislation looking to the prevention of industrial accidents, occupational diseases, overwork, involuntary unemployment, and other injurous effects incident to modern industry;

The fixing of minimum safety and health standards for the various occupations, and the exercise of the public authority of State and Nation, including the Federal Control over interstate commerce, and the taxing power, to maintain such standards;

The prohibition of child labor;

Minimum wage standards for working women, to provide a "living wage" in all industrial occupations;

The general prohibition of night work for women and the establishment of an eight hour day for women and young persons;

One day's rest in seven for all wage workers;

The eight hour day in continuous twenty-four-hour industries;

The abolition of the convict contract labor system; substituting a system of prison production for governmental consumption only; and the application of prisoners' earnings to the support of their dependent families;

Publicity as to wages, hours and conditions of labor; full reports upon industrial accidents and diseases, and the opening to public inspection of all tallies, weights, measures and check systems on labor products:

Standards of compensation for death by industrial accident and injury and trade disease which will transfer the burden of lost earnings from the families of working people to the industry, and thus to the community;

The protection of home life against the hazards of sickness, irregular employment and old age through the adoption of a system of social insurance adapted to American use;

The development of the creative labor power of America by lifting the last load of illiteracy from American youth and establishing continuation schools for industrial education under public control and encouraging agricultural education and demonstration in rural schools;

The establishment of industrial research laboratories to put the methods and discoveries of science at the service of American producers;

We favor the organization of the workers, men and women, as a means of protecting their interests and of promoting their progress.

• • •

Health

We favor the union of all the existing agencies of the Federal Government dealing with the public health into a single national health service without discrimination against or for any one set of therapeutic methods, school of medicine, or school of healing with such additional powers as may be necessary to enable it to perform efficiently such duties in the protection of the public from preventable diseases as may be properly undertaken by the Federal authorities, including the executing of existing laws regarding pure food, quarantine and cognate subjects, the promotion of vital statistics and the extension of the registration area of such statistics, and co-operation with the health activities of the various States and cities of the Nation.

BUSINESS

We believe that true popular government, justice and prosperity go hand in hand, and, so believing, it is our purpose to secure that large measure of general prosperity which is the fruit of legitimate and honest business, fostered by equal justice and by sound progressive laws.

We demand that the test of true prosperity shall be the benefits conferred thereby on all the citizens, not confined to individuals or classes, and that the test of corporate efficiency shall be the ability better to serve the public; that those who profit by control of business affairs shall justify that profit and that control by sharing with the public the fruits thereof.

We therefore demand a strong National regulation of inter-State corporations. The corporation is an essential part of modern business. The concentration of modern business, in some degree, is both inevitable and necessary for national and international business efficiency. But the existing concentration of vast wealth under a corporate system, unguarded and uncontrolled by the Nation, has placed in the hands of a few men enormous, secret, irresponsible power over the daily life of the citizen—a power insufferable in a free Government and certain of abuse.

This power has been abused, in monopoly of National resources, in stock watering, in unfair competition and unfair privileges, and finally in sinister influences on the public agencies of State and Nation. We do not fear commercial power, but we insist that it shall be exercised openly, under publicity, supervision and regulation of the most efficient sort, which will preserve its good while eradicating and preventing its ill.

To that end we urge the establishment of a strong Federal administrative commission of high standing, which shall maintain permanent active supervision over industrial corporations engaged in inter-State commerce, or such of them as are of public importance, doing for them what the Government now does for the National banks, and what is now done for the railroads by the Inter-State Commerce Commission.

Such a commission must enforce the complete publicity of those corporation transactions which are of public interest; must attack unfair competition, false capitalization and special privilege, and by continuous trained watchfulness guard and keep open equally all the highways of American commerce.

Thus the business man will have certain knowledge of the law, and will be able to conduct his business easily in conformity therewith; the investor will find security for his capital; dividends will be rendered more certain, and the savings of the people will be drawn naturally and safely into the channels of trade.

Under such a system of constructive regulation, legitimate business, freed from confusion, uncertainty and fruitless litigation, will develop normally in response to the energy and enterprise of the American business man.

We favor strengthening the Sherman Law by prohibiting agreement to divide territory or limit output; refusing to sell to customers who buy from business rivals; to sell below cost in certain areas while maintaining higher prices in other places: using the power of transportation to aid or injure special business concerns; and other unfair trade practices.

• • •

Questions

1. What reforms does the platform propose to improve the functioning of American democracy?

2. How does the platform seem to define economic freedom?

CHAPTER 19

Safe for Democracy: The United States and World War I, 1916–1920

120. Woodrow Wilson on America and the World (1916)

Source: "An Address in Detroit to Businessmen, July 10, 1916," Arthur S. Link, ed., The Papers of Woodrow Wilson *(Princeton, N.J., 1966–1994), Vol. 37, pp. 383–86.*

More than any other individual, Woodrow Wilson articulated a new vision of America's relationship to the rest of the world. His foreign policy, called by historians "liberal internationalism," rested on the conviction that economic and political progress went hand in hand. Thus, greater worldwide freedom would follow inevitably from increased American investment and trade abroad. Wilson believed that the United States had a responsibility to teach other peoples the lessons of democracy. Moreover, he was convinced that the export of American manufactured goods and investments would encourage the spread of democratic ideals. To Wilson, expanding American economic influence served a higher purpose than mere profit. Wilson feared that American businessmen had yet to learn how to market their goods overseas. In 1916, with Europe embroiled in World War I but the United States still neutral, he urged businessmen to abandon their "provincial views" and think in global terms.

━━━━━━

THESE ARE DAYS of incalculable change, my fellow citizens. It is impossible for anybody to predict anything that is certain, in detail, with regard to the future, either of this country or of the world, in the large movements of business. But one thing is perfectly clear, and that is that the United States will play a new part, and that it will be a part of unprecedented opportunity and of greatly increased responsibility.

The United States has had a very singular history in respect of its business relationships with the rest of the world. I have always believed, and I think you have always believed, that there is more business genius in the United States than anywhere else in the world. And yet America has apparently, been afraid of touching too intimately the great processes of international exchange. America, of all countries in the world, has been timid and has not, until recently, has not, until within the last two or three years, provided itself with the fundamental instrumentalities for playing a large part in the trade of the world. America, which ought to have had the broadest vision of any nation, has raised up an extraordinary number of provincial thinkers—men who thought provincially about business, men who thought that the United States was not ready to take her competitive part in the struggle for the peaceful conquest of the world. For anybody who reflects philosophically upon the history of this country, that is the most amazing fact about it.

But the time for provincial thinkers has gone by. We must play a great part in the world, whether we choose it or not. Do you know the significance of this single fact—that, within the last year or two we have, speaking in large terms, ceased to be a debtor nation and become a creditor nation, that we have more of the surplus gold of the world than we ever had before, and that our business hereafter is to be to lend and to help and to promote the great peaceful enterprises of the world. We have got to finance the world in some important degree, and those who finance the world must understand it and rule it with their spirits and with their minds. We cannot cabin and confine ourselves any longer. So that, as I said, I came here to congratulate you upon the great role that lies ahead of you to play. This is a salesmanship congress, and hereafter salesmanship will have to be closely related in its outlook and scope to statesmanship, to international statesmanship. It will have to be touched with an intimate comprehension of the conditions of business and enterprise throughout the round globe, because America will have to place her goods by running her intelligence ahead of her goods. No amount of mere push, no amount of mere hustling, or, to speak in the western language, no amount of mere rustling, no amount of mere active enterprise, will suffice.

• • •

What do we all most desire when the present tragical confusion of the world's affairs is over? We desire permanent peace, do we not? Permanent peace can grow in only one soil. That is the soil of actual good will, and good will cannot exist without mutual comprehension. Charles Lamb, the English writer, made a very delightful remark that I have long treasured in my memory. He stuttered a little bit, and he said of someone who was not present. "I h-h-hate that m-man." And someone said, "Why, Charles, I didn't know you knew him." "Oh," he said, "I-I-I don't; I-I can't h-hate a m-man I know." That is a profound human remark. You can't hate a man you know. I know some rascals whom I have tried to hate. I have tried to head them off as rascals, but I have been unable to hate them. I have liked them. And so, not to compare like with unlike, in the relationship of nations with each other, many of our antagonisms are based upon misunderstandings, and, as long as you do not understand a country you cannot trade with it. As long as you cannot take its point of view, you cannot commend your goods to its purchase. As long as you go to it with a supercilious air, for example, and patronize it, and, then, as we have tried to do in some less developed countries, tell them that that is what they ought to want, whether they want it or not, you can't do business with them. You have got to approach them just as you really ought to approach all matters of human relationship.

These people who give their money to philanthropy, for example, but cannot for the life of them see from the point of view of those for whose benefit they are giving the money, are not philanthropists. They endow and promote philanthropy, but you cannot be a philanthropist unless you love all sorts and conditions of men. The great barrier in this world, I have sometimes thought, is not the barrier of principle, but the barrier of taste. Certain classes of society find certain other classes of society distasteful to them. They don't like the way they dress. They don't like the infrequency with which they bathe. They don't like to consort with them under the conditions in which they live, and, therefore, they stand at a distance from them. And it is impossible for them to serve them, because they do not understand them and do not feel that common pulse of humanity and that common school of experience which is the only thing which binds us together and educates us in the same fashion.

This, then, my friends, is the simple message that I bring to you. Lift your eyes to the horizon of business. Do not look too close at the little processes with which you are concerned, but let your thoughts and your imaginations run abroad throughout the whole world. And, with the inspiration of the thought that you are Americans and are meant to carry liberty and justice and the principles of humanity wherever you go, go out and sell goods that will make the world more comfortable and more happy, and convert them to the principles of America.

Questions

1. Why does Wilson believe that increased American trade with other countries will promote liberty throughout the world?

2. What changes in business practices does Wilson feel are necessary for businessmen to compete in the world economy?

121. Carrie Chapman Catt, Address to Congress on Women's Suffrage (1917)

Source: *Carrie Chapman Catt,* An Address to the Congress of the United States *(New York, 1917).*

Carrie Chapman Catt, a long-time campaigner for votes for women, served as president of the National American Women Suffrage Association from 1900 to 1904 and again from 1915 to 1920. Many women activists had been associated with the pacifist movement and opposed American entry into World War I. In 1917, Catt shocked them by announcing the association's support for the Wilson administration and American participation in World War I. Catt reasoned that by taking part in the war effort, women would finally win the right to vote.

In the winter of 1917, Catt addressed the Congress urging support for a constitutional amendment to enfranchise women. In support of her argument, she invoked the nation's founding principles, and Wilson's claim that the United States was the leader in the worldwide struggle for democracy. Catt's strategy bore fruit when Congress in 1918 approved the Nineteenth Amendment, which became part of the constitution two years later.

WOMAN SUFFRAGE IS INEVITABLE....

First, the history of our country. Ours is a nation born of revolution, of rebellion against a system of government so securely entrenched in the customs and traditions of human society that in 1776 it seemed impregnable. From the beginning of things, nations had been ruled by kings and for kings, while the people served and paid the cost. The American Revolutionists boldly proclaimed the heresies: "Taxation without representation is tyranny." "Governments derive their just powers from the consent of the governed." The colonists won, and the nation which was established as a result of their victory has held unfailingly that these two fundamental principles of democratic government are not only the spiritual source of our national existence but have been our chief historic pride and at all times the sheet anchor of our liberties.

Eighty years after the Revolution, Abraham Lincoln welded those two maxims into a new one: "Ours is a government of the people, by the people, and for the people." Fifty years more passed and the president of the United States, Woodrow Wilson, in a mighty crisis of the nation, proclaimed to the world: "We are fighting for the things which we have always carried nearest to our hearts: for democracy, for the right of those who submit to authority to have a voice in their own government."

All the way between these immortal aphorisms political leaders have declared unabated faith in their truth. Not one American has arisen to question their logic in the 141 years of our national existence. However stupidly our country may have evaded the logical application at times, it has never swerved from its devotion to the theory of democracy as expressed by those two axioms....

With such a history behind it, how can our nation escape the logic it has never failed to follow, when its last unenfranchised class calls for the vote? Behold our Uncle Sam floating the banner with one hand, "Taxation without representation is tyranny," and with the other seizing the billions of dollars paid in taxes by women to whom he refuses "representation." Behold him again, welcoming the boys of twenty-one and the newly made immigrant citizen to "a voice in their own government" while he denies that fundamental right of democracy to thousands of women public school teachers from whom many of these men learn all they know of citizenship and patriotism, to women college presidents, to women who preach in our pulpits, interpret law in our courts, preside over our hospitals, write books and magazines, and serve in every uplifting moral and social enterprise. Is there a single man who can justify such inequality of treatment, such outrageous discrimination? Not one....

Second, the suffrage for women already established in the United States makes women suffrage for the nation inevitable. When Elihu Root, as president of the American Society of International Law, at the eleventh annual meeting in Washington, April 26, 1917, said, "The world cannot be half democratic and half autocratic. It must be all democratic or all Prussian. There can be no compromise," he voiced a general truth. Precisely the same intuition has already taught the blindest and most hostile foe of woman suffrage that our nation cannot long continue a condition under which government in half its territory rests upon the consent of half of the people and in the other half upon the consent of all the people; a condition which grants representation to the taxed in half of its territory and denies it in the other half; a condition which permits women in some states to share in the election of the president, senators, and representatives and denies them that privilege in others. It is too obvious to require demonstration that woman suffrage, now covering half our territory, will eventually be ordained in all the nation. No one will deny it. The only question left is when and how will it be completely established.

Third, the leadership of the United States in world democracy compels the enfranchisement of its own women. The maxims of the Declaration were once called "fundamental principles of government." They are now called "American principles" or even "Americanisms." They have become the slogans of every movement toward political liberty the world around, of every effort to widen the suffrage for men or women in any land. Not a people, race, or class striving for freedom is there anywhere in the world that has not made our axioms the chief weapon of the struggle. More, all men and women the world around, with farsighted vision into the verities of things, know that the world tragedy of our day is not now being waged over the assassination of an archduke, nor commercial competition, nor national ambitions, nor the freedom of the seas. It is a death grapple between the forces which deny and those which uphold the truths of the Declaration of Independence....

Do you realize that in no other country in the world with democratic tendencies is suffrage so completely denied as in a considerable number of our own states? There are thirteen black states where no suffrage for women exists, and fourteen others where suffrage for women is more limited than in many foreign countries.

Do you realize that when you ask women to take their cause to state referendum you compel them to do this: that you drive women of education, refinement, achievement, to beg men who cannot read for their political freedom?

Do you realize that such anomalies as a college president asking her janitor to give her a vote are overstraining the patience and driving women to desperation?

Do you realize that women in increasing numbers indignantly resent the long delay in their enfranchisement?

Your party platforms have pledged women suffrage. Then why not be honest, frank friends of our cause, adopt it in reality as your own, make it a party program, and "fight with us"? As a party measure—a measure of all parties—why not put the amendment through Congress and the legislatures? We shall all be better friends, we shall have a happier nation, we women will be free to support loyally the party of our choice, and we shall be far prouder of our history.

"There is one thing mightier than kings and armies"—aye, than Congresses and political parties—"the power of an idea when its time has come to move." The time for woman suffrage has come. The woman's hour has struck. If parties prefer to postpone action longer and thus do battle with this idea, they challenge the inevitable. The idea will not perish; the party which opposes it may. Every delay, every trick, every political dishonesty from now on will antagonize the women of the land more and more, and when the party or parties which have so delayed women suffrage finally let it come, their sincerity will be doubted and their appeal to the new voters will be met with suspicion. This is the psychology of the situation. Can you afford the risk? Think it over.

We know you will meet opposition. There are a few "women haters" left, a few "old males of the tribe," . . . who know better than women what is good for them. There are women, too, with "slave souls" and "clinging vines" for backbones. There are female dolls and male dandies. But the world does not wait for such as these, nor does liberty pause to heed the plaint of men and women with a grouch. She does not wait for those who have a special interest to serve, nor a selfish reason for depriving other people of freedom. Holding her torch aloft, liberty is pointing the way onward and upward and saying to America, "Come."

To you and the supporters of our cause in Senate and House, and the number is large, the suffragists of the nation express their grateful thanks. This address is not meant for you. We are more truly appreciative of all you have done than any words can express. We ask you to make a last, hard fight for the amendment during the present session. Since last we asked a vote on this amendment, your position has been fortified by the addition to suffrage territory of Great Britain, Canada, and New York.

Some of you have been too indifferent to give more than casual attention to this question. It is worthy of your immediate consideration. A question big enough to engage the attention of our allies in wartime is too big a question for you to neglect.

Some of you have grown old in party service. Are you willing that those who take your places by and by shall blame you for having failed to keep pace with the world and thus having lost for them a party advantage? Is there any real gain for you, for your party, for your nation by delay? Do you want to drive the progressive men and women out of your party?

Some of you hold to the doctrine of states' rights as applying to woman suffrage. Adherence to that theory will keep the United States far behind all other democratic nations upon this question. A theory which prevents a nation from keeping up with the trend of world progress cannot be justified.

Gentlemen, we hereby petition you, our only designated representatives, to redress our grievances by the immediate passage of the Federal Suffrage Amendment and to use your influence to secure its ratification in your own state, in order that the women of our nation may be endowed with political freedom before the next presidential election, and that our nation may resume its world leadership in democracy.

Woman suffrage is coming—you know it. Will you, Honorable

Senators and Members of the House of Representatives, help or hinder it?

Questions

1. Why does Catt claim that denying women the right to vote violates the principle of democracy?

2. How does Catt characterize women who do not support the campaign for suffrage?

---

122. Eugene V. Debs, Speech to the Jury (1918)

Source: **The Debs White Book** *(Girard, Kans., 1920), pp. 37–57.*

Despite President Wilson's claim that the United States entered World War I in 1917 to "make the world safe for democracy," American intervention was followed at home by the most massive suppression of freedom of expression in the country's history. The Espionage Act of 1917 prohibited not only spying and interfering with the draft but also "false statements" that might impede military success. In 1918, the Sedition Act made it a crime to make spoken or printed statements intended to cast "contempt, scorn, or disrepute" on the "form of government" or that advocated interference with the war effort.

The government charged over 2,000 persons with violating these laws. The most prominent victim was Eugene V. Debs, the leader of the Socialist Party, convicted in 1918 under the Espionage Act for delivering an antiwar speech. Before his sentencing, Debs gave the court a lesson in the history of American freedom, tracing the tradition of dissent from Tom Paine to the abolitionists and pointing out that the nation had never engaged in a war without internal opposition. Sentenced to ten years in prison, Debs was released in 1921 by Woodrow Wilson's successor, Warren G. Harding.

MAY IT PLEASE the court, and gentlemen of the jury:

For the first time in my life I appear before a jury in a court of law to answer to an indictment for crime. I am not a lawyer. I know little about court procedure, about the rules of evidence or legal practice. I know only that you gentlemen are to hear the evidence brought against me, that the court is to instruct you in the law, and that you are then to determine by your verdict whether I shall be branded with criminal guilt and be consigned, perhaps to the end of my life, in a felon's cell.

• • •

I wish to admit the truth of all that has been testified to in this proceeding. I have no disposition to deny anything that is true. I would not, if I could, escape the results of an adverse verdict. I would not retract a word that I have uttered that I believe to be true to save myself from going to the penitentiary for the rest of my days.

Gentlemen, you have heard the report of my speech at Canton on June 16, and I submit that there is not a word in that speech to warrant the charges set out in the indictment. I admit having delivered the speech. I admit the accuracy of the speech in all of its main features as reported in this proceeding.

In what I had to say there my purpose was to have the people understand something about the social system in which we live and to prepare them to change this system by perfectly peaceable and orderly means into what I, as a Socialist, conceive to be a real democracy.

From what you heard in the address of the counsel for the prosecution, you might naturally infer that I am an advocate of force and violence. It is not true. I have never advocated violence in any form. I have always believed in education, in intelligence, in enlightenment; and I have always made my appeal to the reason and to the conscience of the people.

I admit being opposed to the present social system. I am doing what little I can, and have been for many years, to bring about a change that shall do away with the rule of the great body of the people by a relatively small class and establish in this country an industrial and social democracy.

• • •

Washington, Jefferson, Franklin, Paine and their compeers were the rebels of their day. When they began to chafe under the rule of a foreign king and to sow the seed of resistance among the colonists they were opposed by the people and denounced by the press.... But they had the moral courage to be true to their convictions, to stand erect and defy all the forces of reaction and detraction; and that is why their names shine in history, and why the great respectable majority of their day sleep in forgotten graves.

• • •

William Lloyd Garrison, Wendell Phillips, Elizabeth Cady Stanton, Susan B. Anthony, Gerrit Smith, Thaddeus Stevens and other leaders of the abolition movement who were regarded as public enemies and treated accordingly, were true to their faith and stood their ground. They are all in history. You are now teaching your children to revere their memories, while all of their detractors are in oblivion.

• • •

From the beginning of the war to this day I have never by word or act been guilty of the charges embraced in this indictment. If I have criticized, if I have condemned, it is because I believed it to be my duty, and that it was my right to do so under the laws of the land. I have had ample precedents for my attitude. This country has been engaged in a number of wars and every one of them has been condemned by some of the people, among them some of the most eminent men of their time. The war of the American Revolution was violently opposed. The Tory press representing the "upper classes" denounced its leaders as criminals and outlaws.

The war of 1812 was opposed and condemned by some of the most influential citizens; the Mexican war was vehemently opposed and bitterly denounced, even after the war had been declared and was in progress, by Abraham Lincoln, Charles Sumner, Daniel Webster, Henry Clay and many other well-known and influential citizens.

These men denounced the President, they condemned his administration while the war was being waged, and they charged in substance that the war was a crime against humanity. They were not indicted; they were not charged with treason nor tried for crime. They are honored today by all of their countrymen.

The Civil War between the states met with violent resistance and passionate condemnation. In the year 1864 the Democratic Party met in national convention at Chicago and passed a resolution condemning the war as a failure. What would you say if the Socialist Party were to meet in convention today and condemn the present war as a failure? You charge us with being disloyalists and traitors. Were the Democrats of 1864 disloyalists and traitors because they condemned the war as a failure?

And if so, why were they not indicted and prosecuted accordingly? I believe in the Constitution. Isn't it strange that we Socialists stand almost alone today in upholding and defending the Constitution of the United States? The revolutionary fathers who had been oppressed under king rule understood that free speech, a free press and the right of free assemblage by the people were fundamental principles in democratic government.

• • •

That is the right I exercised at Canton on the sixteenth day of last June; and for the exercise of that right, I now have to answer to this indictment. I believe in the right of free speech, in war as well as in peace. I would not, under any circumstances suppress free speech. It is far more dangerous to attempt to gag the people than to allow them to speak freely what is in their hearts.

I have told you that I am no lawyer, but it seems to me that I know enough to know that if Congress enacts any law that conflicts with this provision in the Constitution, that law is void. If the Espionage Law finally stands, then the Constitution of the United States is dead. If that law is not the negation of every fundamental principle established by the Constitution, then certainly I am unable to read or to understand the English language.

• • •

I am not on trial here. There is an infinitely greater issue that is being tried today in this court, though you may not be conscious of it. American institutions are on trial here before a court of American citizens. The future will render the final verdict.

Questions

1. Why does Debs insist that the Espionage Act represents "the negation of every fundamental principle established by the Constitution"?

2. Why does Debs recount the history of political dissent and opposition to previous American wars?

123. Randolph Bourne, "Trans-National America" (1916)

Source: Randolph Bourne, "Trans-National America," Atlantic Monthly, Vol. 118 (July 1916), pp. 86–97.

The increased immigration of the early twentieth century heightened awareness of ethnic and racial difference and spurred among many native-born Americans demands for "Americanization"—the creation of a more homogenous national culture. A minority of Progressives questioned Americanization efforts and insisted on respect for immigrant subcultures. Randolph Bourne's 1916 essay, "Trans-National America," exposed the fundamental flaw in the Americanization model. No single model of American culture existed, Bourne pointed out. Interaction between individuals and groups had produced the nation's music, poetry, and other cultural expressions. Bourne envisioned a democratic, cosmopolitan society in which immigrants and natives alike submerged their group identities in a new "trans-national" culture. Once the United States entered World War I, however, the Americanization campaign intensified. But Bourne's arguments would be rediscovered later in the twentieth century, when a more pluralistic vision of American society took hold.

———

No REVERBERATORY EFFECT of the great war has caused American public opinion more solicitude than the failure of the "melting-pot." The discovery of diverse nationalistic feelings among our great alien population has come to most people as an intense shock. It has brought out the unpleasant inconsistencies of our traditional beliefs. We have had to watch hard-hearted old Brahmins virtuously indignant at the spectacle of the immigrant refusing to be melted, while they jeer at patriots like Mary Antin who write about "our forefathers." We have had to listen to publicists who express themselves as stunned by the evidence of vigorous nationalistic and cultural movements in this country among Germans, Scandinavians, Bohemians, and Poles, while in the same breath they insist that the alien shall be forcibly assimilated to that Anglo-Saxon tradition which they unquestioningly label "American."

As the unpleasant truth has come upon us that assimilation in this country was proceeding on lines very different from those we had marked out for it, we found ourselves inclined to blame those who were thwarting our prophecies. The truth became culpable. We blamed the war, we blamed the Germans. And then we discovered with a moral shock that these movements had been making great headway before the war even began. We found that the tendency, reprehensible and paradoxical as it might be, has been for the national clusters of immigrants, as they became more and more firmly established and more and more prosperous, to cultivate more and more assiduously the literatures and cultural traditions of their homelands. Assimilation, in other words, instead of washing out the memories of Europe, made them more and more intensely real. Just as these clusters became more and more objectively American, did they become more and more German or Scandinavian or Bohemian or Polish.

To face the fact that our aliens are already strong enough to take a share in the direction of their own destiny, and that the strong cultural movements represented by the foreign press, schools, and colonies are a challenge to our facile attempts, is not, however, to admit the failure of Americanization. It is not to fear the failure of democracy. It is rather to urge us to an investigation of what Americanism may rightly mean. It is to ask ourselves whether our ideal has been broad or narrow—whether perhaps the time has not come to assert a higher ideal than the "melting-pot." Surely we cannot be certain of our spiritual democracy when, claiming to melt the nations within us to a comprehension of our free and democratic institutions, we fly into panic at the first sign of their own will and tendency. We act as if we wanted Americanization to take place only on our own terms, and not by the consent of the governed. All our elaborate machinery of settlement and school and union, of social and political naturalization, however, will move with friction just in so far as it neglects to take into account this strong and virile insistence that America shall be what the immigrant will have a hand in making it, and not what a ruling class, descendant of those British stocks which were the first permanent immigrants, decide that America shall be made. This is the condition which confronts us, and which demands a clear and general readjustment of our attitude and our ideal.

· · ·

The non-English American can scarcely be blamed if he sometimes thinks of the Anglo-Saxon predominance in America as little more than a predominance of priority. The Anglo-Saxon was merely the first immigrant, the first to found a colony. He has never really ceased to be the descendant of immigrants, nor has he ever succeeded in transforming that colony into a real nation, with a tenacious, richly woven fabric of native culture. Colonials from the other nations have come and settled down beside him. They found no definite native culture which should startle them out of their colonialism, and consequently they looked back to their mother-country, as the earlier Anglo-Saxon immigrant was looking back to his. What has been offered the newcomer has been the chance to learn English, to become a citizen, to salute the flag. And those elements of our ruling classes who are responsible for the public schools, the settlements, all the organizations for amelioration in the cities, have every reason to be proud of the care and labor which they have devoted to absorbing the immigrant. His opportunities the immigrant has taken to gladly, with almost a pathetic eagerness to make his way in the new land without friction or disturbance. The common language has made not only for the necessary communication, but for all the amenities of life.

If freedom means the right to do pretty much as one pleases, so long as one does not interfere with others, the immigrant has found freedom, and the ruling element has been singularly liberal in its treatment of the invading hordes. But if freedom means a democratic cooperation in determining the ideals and purposes and industrial and social institutions of a country, then the immigrant has not been free, and the Anglo-Saxon element is guilty of just what every dominant race is guilty of in every European country: the imposition of its own culture upon the minority peoples. The fact that this imposition has been so mild and, indeed, semiconscious does not alter its quality. And the war has brought out just the degree to which that purpose of "Americanizing," that is, "Anglo-Saxonizing," the immigrant has failed.

• • •

There is no distinctively American culture. It is apparently our lot rather to be a federation of cultures. This we have been for half a century, and the war has made it ever more evident that this is what we are destined to remain.

• • •

What we have achieved has been rather a cosmopolitan federation of national colonies, of foreign cultures, from whom the sting of devastating competition has been removed. America is already the world-federation in miniature, the continent where for the first time in history has been achieved that miracle of hope, the peaceful living side by side, with character substantially preserved, of the most heterogenous peoples under the sun. Nowhere else has such contiguity been anything but the breeder of misery. Here, notwithstanding our tragic failures of adjustment, the outlines are already too clear not to give us a new vision and a new orientation of the American mind in the world.

We cannot Americanize America worthily by sentimentalizing and moralizing history. When the best schools are expressly renouncing the questionable duty of teaching patriotism by means of history, it is not the time to force shibboleth upon the immigrant. This form of Americanization has been heard because it appealed to the vestiges of our old sentimentalized and moralized patriotism. This has so far held the field as the expression of the new American's new devotion. The inflections of other voices have been drowned. They must be heard. We must see if the lesson of the war has not been for hundreds of these later Americans a vivid realization of their trans-nationality; a new consciousness of what America meant to them as a citizenship in the world. It is the vague historic idealisms which have provided the fuel for the European flame. Our American ideal can make no progress until we do away with this romantic gilding of the past.

Questions

1. Why does Bourne write that the "melting-pot" had failed?

2. Why does he argue that immigrants "have not been free"?

124. W. E. B. Du Bois, "Returning Soldiers" (1919)

Source: *"Returning Soldiers,"* The Crisis *(May 19, 1919, pp. 13–14). W. W. Norton & Company wishes to thank the Crisis Publishing Company, Inc., the publisher of the magazine of the National Association for the Advancement of Colored People, for the use of this material first published in the May 1919 issue of* Crisis Magazine. *Reprinted with permission.*

Scholar, poet, agitator, father of pan-Africanism, founder of the National Association for the Advancement of Colored People (NAACP), W. E. B. Du Bois was one of the towering figures of twentieth-century America. As editor of *The Crisis*, the NAACP's magazine, Du Bois brought the plight and achievements of black Americans to hundreds of thousands of readers.

When the United States entered World War I, Du Bois called on blacks to "close ranks" and enlist in the army, even though the military subjected them to pervasive discrimination. As in the Civil War, he argued, military service would stake a claim to equal citizenship. But as race riots erupted in many American cities, Du Bois's hopes disintegrated. In 1919, he issued a searing indictment of American race relations, and called on returning black soldiers to take up the struggle for racial justice.

WE ARE RETURNING from war! The Crisis and tens of thousands of black men were drafted into a great struggle. For bleeding France and what she means and has meant and will mean to us and humanity and against the threat of German race arrogance, we fought gladly and to the last drop of blood; for America and her highest ideals, we fought in far-off hope; for the dominant southern oligarchy entrenched in Washington, we fought in bitter resignation. For the America that represents and gloats in lynching, disfranchisement, caste, brutality and devilish insult—for this, in the hateful up-turning and mixing of things, we were forced by vindictive fate to fight, also.

But today we return! We return from the slavery of uniform which the world's madness demanded us to don to the freedom of civil garb. We stand again to look America squarely in the face and call a spade a spade. We sing: This country of ours, despite all its better souls have done and dreamed, is yet a shameful land.

It *lynches.*

And lynching is barbarism of a degree of contemptible nastiness unparalleled in human history. Yet for fifty years we have lynched two Negroes a week, and we have kept this up right through the war.

It *disfranchises* its own citizens.

Disfranchisement is the deliberate theft and robbery of the only protection of poor against rich and black against white. The land that disfranchises its citizens and calls itself a democracy lies and knows it lies.

It encourages *ignorance.*

It has never really tried to educate the Negro. A dominant minority does not want Negroes educated. It wants servants, dogs, whores and monkeys. And when this land allows a reactionary group by its stolen political power to force as many black folk into these categories as it possibly can, it cries in contemptible hypocrisy: "They threaten us with degeneracy; they cannot be educated."

It *steals* from us.

It organizes industry to cheat us. It cheats us out of our land; it cheats us out of our labor. It confiscates our savings. It reduces our wages. It raises our rent. It steals our profit. It taxes us without representation. It keeps us consistently and universally poor, and then feeds us on charity and derides our poverty.

It *insults* us.

It has organized a nation-wide and latterly a world-wide propaganda of deliberate and continuous insult and defamation of black blood wherever found. It decrees that it shall not be possible in travel nor residence, work nor play, education nor instruction for a black man to exist without tacit or open acknowledgment of his inferiority to the dirtiest white dog. And it looks upon any attempt to question or even discuss this dogma as arrogance, unwarranted assumption and treason.

This is the country to which we Soldiers of Democracy return. This is the fatherland for which we fought! But it is *our* fatherland. It was right for us to fight. The faults of *our* country are *our* faults. Under similar circumstances, we would fight again. But by the God of Heaven, we are cowards and jackasses if now that that war is over, we do not marshal every ounce of our brain and brawn to fight a sterner, longer, more unbending battle against the forces of hell in our own land.

We *return*.

We *return from fighting*.

We *return fighting*.

Make way for Democracy! We saved it in France, and by the Great Jehovah, we will save it in the United States of America or know the reason why.

Questions

1. Which aspects of the condition of black Americans in 1919 does Du Bois consider most "shameful"?

2. Why does he refer to black soldiers as "Soldiers of Democracy"?

125. Marcus Garvey on Africa for the Africans (1921)

Source: "Speech Delivered at Liberty Hall, New York City, August 21, 1921," *in Amy Jacques-Garvey, ed.,* **Philosophy and Opinions of Marcus Garvey** *(New York, 1923–1925), Vol. 2, pp. 93–97.*

World War I redrew the racial map of the United States. With immigration from Europe suspended, northern employers for the first time offered industrial jobs to southern blacks. The result was the Great Migration, in which tens of thousands of African-Americans left the rural South for cities like New York and Chicago. In the new, densely populated black ghettoes, disappointment with conditions in the North inspired widespread support for a separatist movement launched by Marcus Garvey, a recent immigrant from Jamaica. Throughout the world, Garvey pointed out, the war had inspired movements for national self-determination—in Ireland, eastern Europe, and

Europe's Asian and African colonies. Blacks, he insisted, should enjoy the same internationally recognized identity enjoyed by other peoples. The government soon deported Garvey after convicting him of mail fraud. But the massive following his movement achieved testified to the sense of both racial pride and betrayal kindled in black communities during and after the war.

———

FOUR YEARS AGO, realizing the oppression and the hardships from which we suffered, we organized ourselves into an organization for the purpose of bettering our condition, and founding a government of our own. The four years of organization have brought good results, in that from an obscure, despised race we have grown into a mighty power, a mighty force whose influence is being felt throughout the length and breadth of the world. The Universal Negro Improvement Association existed but in name four years ago, today it is known as the greatest moving force among Negroes. We have accomplished this through unity of effort and unity of purpose, it is a fair demonstration of what we will be able to accomplish in the very near future, when the millions who are outside the pale of the Universal Negro Improvement Association will have linked themselves up with us.

By our success of the last four years we will be able to estimate the grander success of a free and redeemed Africa. In climbing the heights to where we are today, we have had to surmount difficulties, we have had to climb over obstacles, but the obstacles were stepping stones to the future greatness of this Cause we represent. Day by day we are writing a new history, recording new deeds of valor performed by this race of ours. It is true that the world has not yet valued us at our true worth but we are climbing up so fast and with such force that every day the world is changing its attitude towards us. Wheresoever you turn your eyes today you will find the moving influence of the Universal Negro Improvement Association among Negroes from all corners of the globe. We hear among Negroes the cry of "Africa for the Africans." This cry has become a positive, determined one. It is a cry that is raised simultaneously the world over because of the universal oppression that affects the Negro. You who are congregated here tonight as Delegates representing the hundreds of branches of the Universal Negro Improvement Association in different parts of the world will realize that we in New York are positive in this great desire of a free and redeemed Africa. We have established this Liberty Hall as the centre from which we send out the sparks of liberty to the four corners of the globe, and if you have caught the spark in your section, we want you to keep it a-burning for the great Cause we represent.

There is a mad rush among races everywhere towards national independence. Everywhere we hear the cry of liberty, of freedom, and a demand for democracy. In our corner of the world we are raising the cry for liberty, freedom and democracy. Men who have raised the cry for freedom and liberty in ages past have always made up their minds to die for the realization of the dream. We who are assembled in this Convention as Delegates representing the Negroes of the world give out the same spirit that the fathers of liberty in this country gave out over one hundred years ago. We give out a spirit that knows no compromise, a spirit that refuses to turn back, a spirit that says "Liberty or Death", and in prosecution of this great ideal—the ideal of a free and redeemed Africa, men may scorn, men may spurn us, and may say that we are on the wrong side of life, but let me tell you that way in which you are travelling is just the way all peoples who are free have travelled in the past. If you want liberty you yourselves must strike the blow. If you must be free you must become so through your own effort, through your own initiative. Those who have discouraged you in the past are those who have enslaved you for centuries and it is not expected that they will admit that you have a right to strike out at this late hour for freedom, liberty and democracy.

• • •

It falls to our lot to tear off the shackles that bind Mother Africa. Can you do it? You did it in the Revolutionary War. You did it in the

Civil War; You did it at the Battles of the Marne and Verdun; You did it in Mesopotamia. You can do it marching up the battle heights of Africa. Let the world know that 400,000,000 Negroes are prepared to die or live as free men. Despise us as much as you care. Ignore us as much as you care. We are coming 400,000,000 strong. We are coming with our woes behind us, with the memory of suffering behind us— woes and suffering of three hundred years—they shall be our inspiration. My bulwark of strength in the conflict for freedom in Africa, will be the three hundred years of persecution and hardship left behind in this Western Hemisphere. The more I remember the suffering of my fore-fathers, the more I remember the lynchings and burnings in the Southern States of America, the more I will fight on even though the battle seems doubtful. Tell me that I must turn back, and I laugh you to scorn. Go on! Go on! Climb ye the heights of liberty and cease not in well doing until you have planted the banner of the Red, the Black and the Green on the hilltops of Africa.

Questions

1. How does Garvey define black freedom?

2. How do you think Garvey felt that African independence would benefit black Americans?

126. John A. Fitch on the Great Steel Strike (1919)

Source: John A. Fitch, "The Closed Shop," The Survey (November 8, 1919), pp. 53–56, 86, 91.

Among American workers, wartime language linking patriotism with democracy and freedom inspired hopes that an era of social justice was at hand. In 1919, over 4 million workers engaged in strikes—the greatest wave of labor unrest in American history. The strike wave reached its peak in the era's greatest labor uprising, the steel strike. Centered in Pittsburgh and Chicago, this united some 365,000 mostly immigrant workers in demands for union recognition, higher wages, and an eight-hour workday. Before 1917, the steel mills were little autocracies, where managers arbitrarily established wages and working conditions and suppressed all efforts at union organizing. "For why this war?" asked a Polish immigrant steel worker at a union meeting attended by the writer John Fitch, who visited Pittsburgh to report on the strike. "For why we buy Liberty bonds? For the mills? No, for freedom and America—for everybody. No more [work like a] horse and wagon. For eight-hour day." By 1920, with middle-class opinion having turned against the labor movement and native-born workers abandoning their immigrant counterparts, the strike collapsed.

———

WHAT ARE THE chief issues in the steel strike? Is the strike revolution in disguise or is it a bona fide trade union struggle? Is the issue the closed union shop or the closed anti-union shop? Is the strike an effort of a minority to dominate, led by rank outsiders who came into the steel district as professional agitators? Or is it the expression of long pent-up desires held by large numbers of genuine steel workers, under a welcomed leadership? Is it a fight of Americans against foreigners? Or is it an old-fashioned dispute of anti-union employers against organized labor in any form, such as has long since been threshed out and settled in other major American industries in favor of collective bargaining?

It was to obtain the latest evidence bearing on these questions at the point of greatest interest and of greatest friction that I went to Pittsburgh in mid-October at the time that the Senate committee under the chairmanship of Senator Kenyon went there for a similar reason. I attended the committee hearings and then went out to the mill towns to meet the strikers, the citizens, the police and everyone else whom I could reach. I got some evidence and herewith I pass it on just as it came to me:

• • •

It has been alleged that the strike is one of foreigners alone and that there is some sort of issue between them and the Americans. That is certainly not the case in Johnstown, Pa., where the Cambria Steel Company plant is completely tied up—Americans and foreigners standing firm together. It is not true in Cleveland where thousands of skilled Americans have joined the unions nor is it true in Youngstown and Steubenville, O., or in Gary or South Chicago. At all of those points Americans in large numbers are in the unions and are out on strike.

In the Pittsburgh mill towns, however, it is apparent that the strikers are largely foreign-born and that the Americans are at work. Everywhere you encounter irritation. "These organizers didn't appeal to the Americans," you are told; "they just went among the foreigners." This is what you are told everywhere by business and professional men.

The cleavage between native American stock and foreigners, long a marked feature of life in Pittsburgh mill towns, has been accentuated during this strike. Among the strikers I found naturalized citizens and native-born citizens, but they were all Hunkies because they or their fathers were born in Europe. One young fellow was of the third generation in this country. His grandfather came from Hungary in 1848, about the time America was going wild over Louis Kossuth, the Hungarian patriot. But he is a Hunky. I was especially interested when I learned that his father also is a steel worker and on strike. "Your father must have been working in '92," I remarked, wondering if he were in the famous Homestead strike of that year. "Working in '92?" he demanded, growing red in the face. "The hell he was! He was on strike. Let me tell you scabbing doesn't run in our family." I hastened to explain that I had no intention of accusing his father of being a strike breaker.

In the Pittsburgh district the Americans are mostly at work. Whether this is due to their superior economic condition—the best jobs all belong to the Americans—or whether it is their distrust of the Hunky or their fear of discharge and blacklist, it is difficult to say. It is certain that they have had experience with the reprisals that follow organizing campaigns. It is plain also that forces opposed to the strike are making the most of the traditional antagonism between Americans and Hunkies. But the foreigners represent two-thirds of the employes in most steel mills. In any strike, therefore, a majority of the strikers would probably be foreigners.

• • •

Since 1909 unionism has not been permitted at any steel corporation mill and in most of them there is no collective bargaining of any sort. There has even been refusal to receive petitions—as in the case of groups of workmen in McKeesport and Braddock, who wanted the eight-hour day.

And these policies of ten years are still the policies of the United States Steel Corporation. During my recent trip to Pittsburgh, L. H. Burnett, assistant to the president of the Carnegie Steel Company, told me that committees of men might confer over grievances, but that if a committee wanted to negotiate with the officials over wages and hours, it would not be met. He stated that it was the policy of the company to discharge union men who were active or who were organizing within the plant.

Out in the mill towns the strikers told me of being discharged for joining the union. In half an hour at Homestead I talked with a half dozen men who claimed to have been disciplined in that way. I talked with three or four at Braddock and with two at Clairton, all of whom happened to be in strike headquarters when I called. Strikers are not permitted to gather in McKeesport, and I talked with no discharged men there, but business and professional men of that city who are opposed to the strike told me it had always been the policy of the National Tube Company to discharge men who were trying to organize a union. It was a McKeesport paper that remarked, in connection with Judge Gary's testimony at Washington that the United States Steel Corporation does not discharge men for joining unions, that Judge Gary "ought to know better than to make such a statement."

• • •

These open-hearth men work six days in the week in normal times, but during the war they worked seven days a week, working a long shift of twenty-four hours every second week. Blast furnace men spoke up and said they worked twelve hours a day and on a seven-day basis, all the time—twenty-four hours on at one week-end and twenty-four hours off at the next. Men on the rolls were twelve-hour, six-day men. Shop men, machinists, blacksmiths, mill wrights and repair men have a ten-hour day and a six-day week in theory, but when needed they must jump in and work until a breakdown is repaired. Twenty-four hours' continuous work is common, and thirty-six and forty-eight hours' by no means unknown.

• • •

I came away from Pittsburgh more than ever convinced that the issues of the strike are hours and the right of collective bargaining. Until there is such a reduction in hours of labor in the steel industry as will permit men to recuperate after a day's work, to mingle with their fellows and to play, there can be no opportunity for the development of good citizenship in the mill towns. So long as 50 per cent of the men work twelve hours a day, thousands of them seven days a week with a long shift of eighteen or twenty-four hours every second week, no one can claim for the steel industry the maintenance of an "American" standard of living.

• • •

In this strike the foreigners of Pittsburgh are shaking off that old reproach that they are undermining American standards of living. They are standing up and fighting for American standards and are doing it lawfully and with amazing patience while the constituted authorities are harassing them on every side. They are fighting for the restoration of constitutional guarantees, torn down by public officials of western Pennsylvania who have sworn to uphold the Constitution. Revolutionists? I went into a strikers' meeting in Homestead, and Joseph Cannon, an organizer and one of the orators of the American labor movement, was speaking. "Men," he was saying.

we want you to have eight hours so you can learn English. And then you must study American history. Read the Declaration of Independence. Read the history of the American Revolution of George Washington at Valley Forge, his soldiers without shoes in the dead of winter. Read of the hardships they endured and how they fought for liberty. And read of what the foreigners have done to build America. Why, men, did you know that 75 per cent of Washington's soldiers were foreigners? That 50 per cent of the men who fought to end the slavery of the black man in 1861 were foreign born? In every war America has ever had, the foreigner has played his part and has kept Old Glory flying.

You should have heard the thunder of applause. I stood where I could see the men's faces. Foreign-born they were for the most part, Slavic in origin almost altogether, and as they heard this appeal to American tradition every man stood the straighter, and the expression on every face was that of men who felt a kinship with the soldiers of Valley Forge.

These are the men whom it is proposed to "Americanize" as a remedy for industrial unrest. The best way to do that, I think, will be to Americanize their working conditions and their local government, so that they may have time for thinking and time and opportunity to hold such meetings as those they are holding now. Not since 1892 had there been such meetings in Homestead.

While in Pittsburgh, I heard about a great speech made at a strikers' meeting by a Pole. Someone who was there wrote it down for me. It was probably this immigrant's first public speech in the English language and it was something of a struggle; but he had something which had to be said.

"Mr. Chairman," he said. "Mr. Chairman—just like horse and wagon. Put horse in wagon, work all day. Take horse out of wagon—put in stable. Take horse out of stable, put in wagon. Same way like mills. Work all day. Come home—go sleep. Get up—go work in mills—come home. Wife say, 'John, children sick. You help with children.' You say, 'Oh, go to hell'—go sleep. Wife say, 'John, you go town.' You say, 'No'—go sleep. No know what the hell you do. For why this war? For why we buy Liberty bonds? For mills? No, for freedom and America—for everybody. No more horse and wagon. For eight-hour day."

Questions

1. How do the striking workers understand economic freedom?

2. Why do you think that in some instances, native-born and immigrant workers adopted different attitudes toward the strike?

CHAPTER 20

From Business Culture to Great Depression: The Twenties, 1920–1932

127. André Siegfried on the "New Society," from the *Atlantic Monthly* (1928)

Source: André Siegfried, "The Gulf Between," Atlantic Monthly, Vol. 141 (March 1928), pp. 289–95.

André Siegfried, a Frenchman who had visited the United States five times since the beginning of the century, commented in 1928 that American life had changed radically during the previous thirty years. A "new society," he wrote, came into being, in which Americans considered their "standard of living" a "sacred acquisition, which they will defend at any price." In this new "mass civilization," widespread acceptance of going into debt to purchase consumer goods had replaced the values of thrift and self-denial, central to nineteenth-century notions of upstanding character. Work, once seen as a source of pride in craft skill or collective empowerment via trade unions, now came to be valued as a path to individual fulfilment through consumption and entertainment. Siegfried considered the economy "sound" (a judgment soon to be disproven by the advent of the Great Depression), but worried that Americans seemed willing to sacrifice certain "personal" and "political liberties" in the name of economic efficiency and mass production.

━━━━━━

NEVER HAS EUROPE more eagerly observed, studied, discussed America; and never has America followed more carefully, discussed more closely, the discussions of Europe about the United States. At the same time, it is hardly excessive to state that never have the two continents been wider apart in their inspirations and ideals.

It is a widespread belief that the war is mainly responsible for that estrangement, especially, the aftermath of the war. I should be tempted to think that the deep reason is another one: Europe, after all, is not very different from what it was a generation ago; but there has been born since then a new America.

Such is the point I should like to discuss in the following pages, not *ex professo* and by summoning figures and statistics, but by plainly giving the impressions of a European who first knew the United States in 1898, and has since visited them again every four or five years. An American, thus looking at Europe, would of course have witnessed extraordinary changes, especially on account of the catastrophe of the war, but he would have to admit that the basis of the European civilization remains essentially the same. On the contrary, when I recall my impressions of the United States thirty years ago, I cannot avoid the thought that the very basis of the American civilization is no longer the same: a new society, whose foundation rests upon entirely different principles and methods, has come to life; the geographical, the moral centre of gravity of the country is no longer situated at the same place. It is not enough to say that a new period has grown out of the old; something entirely new has been created. Such a change did not clearly appear to me in 1901 or 1904; it was noticeable in 1914, and patent in 1919 and 1925.

• • •

Two principal facts seem to have brought a change the importance of which cannot be exaggerated. First, the conquest of the continent has been completed, and—all recent American historians have noted the significance of the event—the western frontier has disappeared: the pioneer is no longer needed, and, with him, the mystic dream of the West (the French would say the *mystique* of the West) has faded away. Thus came the beginning of the era of organization: the new problem was not to conquer adventurously but to produce methodically. The great man of the new generation was no longer a pioneer like Lincoln, nor a railroad magnate of the Hill type, but that genial *primaire* Henry Ford. From this time on, America has been no more an unlimited prairie with pure and infinite horizons, in which free men may sport like wild horses, but a huge factory of prodigious efficiency.

Thus was born—and this thanks solely to the American genius—a new conception of production, and, with the success of it, that wonderful progress in the standard of living of the American people. In this creation the United States was indebted for nothing essential to Europe. The rope was cut that had so long made of the new continent a persistent colony of the old. There appears to lie the main cause of the immense change which has made of the United States, in the twentieth century, a really new civilization, in which the legendary types of nineteenth-century America are in vain looked for by the traveler of to-day. Where is the hectic and semiwild millionaire of Abel Hermant in his *Transatlantiques?* Where is the gentleman cowboy of Bourget? Where is the old *gentilhomme* of the South, so long preserved in ice for our pleasure and delight? Above all, where is the liberty of the past—swallowed in one gulp by the ogre of efficiency?

• • •

This brings me to one definite conclusion: in the last twenty-five or thirty years America has produced a new civilization, whose centre is mid-continental, and for this reason, as well as because it owes little to us, is further away from Europe than before—it is American and autonomous. This may perhaps explain the growing estrangement between the old and new world.

Just before leaving the United States in the last days of 1925, after a six months' visit, I tried to sum up for myself, in a very short note which was not destined to be printed, my leading impressions of the present American civilization. It may be interesting to reproduce that note, not as giving any original view, but as representing, on the contrary, the spontaneous reaction of an average Frenchman—that is, of an average Western European.

'From an *economic point of view*, the country is sound,' because its prosperity is based, first on a boundless supply of natural produce, and second on an elaborate organization of industrial production, the perfection of which is nowhere approached in Europe.

'From the *point of view of civilization*, it is perhaps to be feared that standardization may, in the long run, tend to lessen the intellectual and artistic value of the American society—the part of the workingman in the factories where mass production is realized is not likely to increase his own value, as an individual; and in order to secure material comfort for the bulk of the American population it seems necessary to produce a common level of manufactured articles, which perhaps does not mark progress in comparison with the civilization of Europe.

'From a *moral point of view*, it is obvious that Americans have come to consider their standard of living as a somewhat sacred acquisition, which they will defend at any price. This means that they would be ready to make many an intellectual or even moral concession in order to maintain that standard.

'From a *political point of view*, it seems that the notion of efficiency in production is on the way to taking precedency of the very notion of liberty. In the name of efficiency one can obtain, from the American, all sorts of sacrifices in relation to his personal and even to certain of his political liberties.'

• • •

Mass production and mass civilization, its natural consequence, are the true characteristics of the new American society.

• • •

Lincoln, with his Bible and classical tradition, was easier for Europe to understand than Ford, with his total absence of tradition and his proud creation of new methods and new standards, especially conceived for a world entirely different from our own.

Questions

1. What are the most important elements of the "new society," according to Siegfried?

2. What "liberties" does he believe Americans are willing to sacrifice?

---

128. The Fight for Civil Liberties (1921)

Source: American Civil Liberties Union, The Fight for Free Speech *(New York, 1921), pp. 15–18.*

The repression of dissent under the Espionage and Sedition Acts of World War I sparked a new appreciation among some reformers of the importance of civil liberties. In 1917, a group of pacifists, Progressives shocked by wartime attacks on freedom of speech, and lawyers outraged at what they considered violations of Americans' legal rights formed the Civil Liberties Bureau. In 1920, it became the American Civil Liberties Union (ACLU). For the rest of the century, the ACLU would take part in most of the landmark legal cases that helped to bring about a "rights revolution." Its efforts helped to give meaning to traditional civil liberties, like freedom of speech, and invented new ones, like the right to privacy. When it began, however, the ACLU was a small, beleaguered organization. Its own pamphlets defending free speech were barred from the mails by postal inspectors.

One of the first documents issued by the ACLU was a general statement defining civil liberties, especially in areas where they had been violated during World War I. The group also insisted that civil liberties should apply equally to all Americans, regardless of race. Full protection of the rights outlined by the ACLU lay years in the future.

A Statement Defining the Position of the American Civil Liberties Union on the issues in the United States Today
(Adopted by the National Committee)

We stand on the general principle that all thought on matters of public concern should be freely expressed without interference. Orderly social progress is promoted by unrestricted freedom of opinion. The punishment of mere opinion, without overt acts, is never in the interest of orderly progress. Suppression of opinion makes for violence and bloodshed.

The principle of freedom of speech, press and assemblage, embodied in our constitutional law, must be reasserted in its application to American conditions today. That application must deal with various methods now used to repress new ideas and democratic movements. The following paragraphs cover the most significant of the tactics of repression in the United States today.

1. Free Speech. There should be no control whatever in advance over what any person may say. The right to meet and to speak freely without permit should be unquestioned.

There should be no prosecutions for the mere expression of opinion on matters of public concern, however radical, however violent. The expression of all opinions, however radical, should be tolerated. The fullest freedom of speech should be encouraged by setting aside special places in streets or parks and in the use of public buildings, free of charge, for public meetings of any sort.

2. Free Press. There should be no censorship over the mails by the post-office or any other agency at any time or in any way. Privacy of communication should be inviolate. Printed matter should never be subject to a political censorship. The granting or revoking of second class mailing privileges should have nothing whatever to do with a paper's opinions and policies.

If libelous, fraudulent, or other illegal matter is being circulated, it should be seized by proper warrant through the prosecuting authorities, not by the post-office department. The business of the post-office department is to carry the mails, not to investigate crime or to act as censors.

There should be no control over the distribution of literature at meetings or hand to hand in public or in private places. No system of licenses for distribution should be tolerated.

3. Freedom of Assemblage. Meetings in public places, parades and processions should be freely permitted, the only reasonable regulation being the advance notification to the police of the time and place. No discretion should be given the police to prohibit parades or processions, but merely to alter routes in accordance with the imperative demands of traffic in crowded cities. There should be no laws or regulations prohibiting the display of red flags or other political emblems.

The right of assemblage is involved in the right to picket in time of strike. Peaceful picketing, therefore, should not be prohibited, regulated by injunction, by order of court or by police edict. It is the business of the police in places where picketing is conducted merely to keep traffic free and to handle specific violations of law against persons upon complaint.

4. The Right to Strike. The right of workers to organize in organizations of their own choosing, and to strike, should never be infringed by law.

Compulsory arbitration is to be condemned not only because it destroys the workers' right to strike, but because it lays emphasis on one set of obligations alone, those of workers to society.

5. Law Enforcement. The practice of deputizing privately paid police as general police officers should be opposed. So should the attempts of private company employees to police the streets or property other than that of the company.

The efforts of private associations to take into their own hands the enforcement of law should be opposed at every point. Public officials, employes of private corporations, and leaders of mobs, who interfere with the exercise of the constitutionally established rights of free speech and free assembly, should be vigorously proceeded against.

The sending of troops into areas of industrial conflict to maintain law and order almost inevitably results in the government taking sides in an industrial conflict in behalf of the employer. The presence of troops, whether or not martial law is declared, very rarely affects the employer adversely, but it usually results in the complete denial of civil rights to the workers.

6. Search and Seizure. It is the custom of certain federal, state and city officials, particularly in cases involving civil liberty, to make arrests without warrant, to enter upon private property, and to seize papers and literature without legal process. Such practices should be contested. Officials so violating constitutional guarantees should be proceeded against.

7. The Right to a Fair Trial. Every person charged with an offense should have the fullest opportunity for a fair trial, for securing counsel and bail in a reasonable sum. In the case of a poor person, special aid should be organized to secure a fair trial, and when necessary, an appeal. The legal profession should be alert to defend cases involving civil liberty. The resolutions of various associations of lawyers against taking cases of radicals are wholly against the traditions of American liberty.

8. Immigration, Deportation and Passports. No person should be refused admission to the United States on the ground of holding objectionable opinions. The present restrictions against radicals of various beliefs is wholly opposed to our tradition of political asylum.

No alien should be deported merely for the expression of opinion or for membership in a radical or revolutionary organization. This is as un-American a practice as the prosecution of citizens for expression of opinion.

The attempt to revoke naturalization papers in order to declare a citizen an alien subject to deportation is a perversion of a law which was intended to cover only cases of fraud.

Citizenship papers should not be refused to any alien because of the expression of radical views, or activities in the cause of labor.

The granting of passports to or from the United States should not be dependent merely upon the opinions of citizens or membership in radical or labor organizations.

9. Liberty in Education. The attempts to maintain a uniform orthodox opinion among teachers should be opposed. The attempts of educational authorities to inject into public school and college instruction propaganda in the interest of any particular theory of society to the exclusion of others should be opposed.

10. Race Equality. Every attempt to discriminate between races in the application of all principles of civil liberty here set forth should be opposed.

How to Get Civil Liberty

We realize that these standards of civil liberty cannot be attained as abstract principles or as constitutional guarantees. Economic or political power is necessary to assert and maintain all "rights". In the midst of any conflict they are not granted by the side holding the economic and political power, except as they may be forced by the strength of the opposition. However, the mere public assertion of the principle of freedom of opinion in the words or deeds of individuals, or weak minorities, helps win recognition, and in the long run makes for tolerance and against resort to violence.

Today the organized movements of labor and of the farmers are waging the chief fight for civil liberty throughout the United States as part of their effort for increased control of industry. Publicity, demonstrations, political activities and legal aid are organized nationally and locally. Only by such an aggressive policy of insistence can rights be secured and maintained. The union of organized labor, the farmers, radical and liberal movements is the most effective means to this.

It is these forces which the American Civil Liberties Union serves in their efforts for civil liberty. The practical work of free speech demonstrations, publicity and legal defense is done primarily in the struggles of the organized labor and farmers movements.

Questions

1. In what ways can the ACLU's statement be seen as a reaction against violations of civil liberties before and during World War I?

2. Why does the ACLU identify "organized movements of labor and of the farmers" as waging the "chief fight" for civil liberties in the United States?

---

129. Clarence Darrow at the Scopes Trial (1924)

Source: Arthur Weinberg, ed., Attorney for the Damned *(New York, 1957), pp. 176–88.*

In 1925, a trial in Tennessee threw into sharp relief the division between traditional values and modern, secular culture. John Scopes, a teacher in a Tennessee public school, was arrested for violating a state law that prohibited the teaching of Charles Darwin's theory of evolution. The renowned labor lawyer Clarence Darrow defended Scopes. In his final argument, Darrow condemned the Tennessee law as a violation of freedom of thought and a recipe for conflict between the numerous religious groups that made up American society. The jury found Scopes guilty, although the Tennessee Supreme Court later overturned the decision on a technicality. Shortly after the trial ended, the movement for anti-evolution laws disintegrated. The battle would be rejoined, however, toward the end of the twentieth century, when fundamentalism reemerged as an important force in politics.

THIS CASE WE have to argue is a case at law, and hard as it is for me to bring my mind to conceive it, almost impossible as it is to put my mind back into the sixteenth century, I am going to argue it as if it was serious, and as if it was a death struggle between two civilizations.

We have been informed that the legislature has the right to prescribe the course of study in the public schools. Within reason, they no doubt have. They could not prescribe a course of study, I am inclined to think, under your constitution, which omitted arithmetic and geography and writing. Neither, under the rest of the constitution, if it shall remain in force in the state, could they prescribe it if the course of study was only to teach religion; because several hundred years ago, when our people believed in freedom, and when no men felt so sure of their own sophistry that they were willing to send a man to jail who did not believe them, the people of Tennessee adopted a constitution, and they made it broad and plain, and said that the people of Tennessee should always enjoy religious freedom in its broadest terms. So I assume that no legislature could fix a course of study which violated that.

• • •

I remember, long ago, Mr. Bancroft wrote this sentence, which is true: "That it is all right to preserve freedom in constitutions, but when the spirit of freedom has fled from the hearts of the people, then its matter is easily sacrificed under law." And so it is, unless there is left enough of the spirit of freedom in the state of Tennessee, and in the United States, there is not a single line of any constitution that can withstand bigotry and ignorance when it seeks to destroy the rights of the individual; and bigotry and ignorance are ever active. Here, we find today, as brazen and as bold an attempt to destroy learning as was ever made in the Middle Ages, and the only difference is we have not provided that they shall be burned at the stake, but there is time for that, Your Honor. We have to approach these things gradually.

• • •

The Bible is not one book. The Bible is made up of sixty-six books written over a period of about 1,000 years, some of them very early and some of them comparatively late. It is a book primarily of religion and morals. It is not a book of science. Never was and was never meant to be. Under it there is nothing prescribed that would tell you how to build a railroad or a steamboat or to make anything that would advance civilization. It is not a textbook or a text on chemistry.

It is not big enough to be. It is not a book on geology; they knew nothing about geology. It is not a book on biology; they knew nothing about it. It is not a work on evolution; that is a mystery. It is not a work on astronomy. The man who looked out at the universe and studied the heavens had no thought but that the earth was the center of the universe. But we know better than that. We know that the sun is the center of the solar system. And that there are an infinity of other systems around about us. They thought the sun went around the earth and gave us light and gave us night. We know better. We know the earth turns on its axis to produce days and nights. They thought the earth was created 4,004 years before the Christian Era. We know better. I doubt if there is a person in Tennessee who does not know better. They told it the best they knew. And while suns may change all you may learn of chemistry, geometry and mathematics, there are no doubt certain primitive, elemental instincts in the organs of man that remain the same. He finds out what he can and yearns to know more and supplements his knowledge with hope and faith.

That is the province of religion and I haven't the slightest fault to find with it. . . . If Mr. Scopes is to be indicted and prosecuted because he taught a wrong theory of the origin of life, why not tell him what he must teach? Why not say that you must teach that man was made of the dust; and still stranger, not directly from the dust, without taking any chances on it, whatever, that Eve was made out of Adam's rib? You will know what I am talking about.

• • •

Let us look at this act, Your Honor. Here is a law which makes it a crime to teach any theory of the origin of man excepting that contained in the divine account, which we find in the Bible. All right. Now that act applies to what? Teachers in the public schools. Now I have seen somewhere a statement of Mr. Bryan's that the fellow that made the pay check had a right to regulate the teachers. All right, let us see. I do not question the right of the legislature to fix the courses of study, but the state of Tennessee has no right under the police power of the State to carve out a law which applies to schoolteachers, a law which is a criminal statute and nothing else; which makes no effort to prescribe the school law or course of study. It says that John Smith who teaches evolution is a criminal if he teaches it in the public schools. There is no question about this act; there is no question where it belongs; there is no question of its origin. Nobody would claim that the act could be passed for a minute excepting that teaching evolution was in the nature of a criminal act; that it smacked of policemen and criminals and jails and grand juries; that it was in the nature of something that was criminal and, therefore, the State should forbid it.

It cannot stand a minute in this court on any theory than that it is a criminal act, simply because they say it contravenes the teaching of Moses without telling us what those teachings are. Now, if this is the subject of a criminal act, then it cannot make a criminal out of a teacher in the public schools and leave a man free to teach it in a private school. It cannot make it criminal for a teacher in the public schools to teach evolution, and for the same man to stand among the hustings and teach it: It cannot make it a criminal act for this teacher to teach evolution and permit books upon evolution to be sold in every store in the state of Tennessee and to permit the newspapers from foreign cities to bring into your peaceful community the horrible utterances of evolution. Oh, no, nothing like that. If the state of Tennessee has any force in this day of fundamentalism, in this day when religious bigotry and hatred is being kindled all over our land, see what can be done?

• • •

I will tell you what is going to happen, and I do not pretend to be a prophet, but I do not need to be a prophet to know. Your Honor knows the fires that have been lighted in America to kindle religious bigotry and hate. You can take judicial notice of them if you cannot of anything else. You know that there is no suspicion which possesses the minds of men like bigotry and ignorance and hatred.

If today you can take a thing like evolution and make it a crime to teach it in the public school, tomorrow you can make it a crime to teach it in the private school, and the next year you can make it a crime to teach it from the hustings or in the church. At the next session you may ban books and the newspapers. Soon you may set Catholic against Protestant and Protestant against Protestant, and try to foist your own religion upon the minds of men. If you can do one you can do the other. Ignorance and fanaticism is ever busy and needs feeding. Always it is feeding and gloating for more. To-day it is the public-school teachers, tomorrow the private. The next day the preachers and the lecturers, the magazines, the books, the newspapers. After a while, Your Honor, it is the setting of man against man and creed against creed until, with flying banners and beating drums, we are marching backward to the glorious ages of the sixteenth century when bigots lighted fagots to burn the men who dared to bring any intelligence and enlightenment and culture to the human mind.

Questions

1. What does Darrow mean when he calls the Scopes trial a "death struggle between two civilizations"?

2. Why does Darrow claim that the Tennessee law will "destroy learning" and increase religious bigotry?

---

130. Congress Debates Immigration (1921)

Source: Congressional Record, *67th Congress, 1st Session, pp. 511–15.*

Fears of foreign radicalism sparked by the labor upheavals immediately following World War I and the increased concern with "Americanizing" immigrants greatly strengthened pressures for wholesale immigration restriction. In 1921, Congress debated a proposal to limit immigration from

Europe temporarily to 357,000 per year (one third the annual average before the war). The excerpt that follows, from April 20, 1921, pitted Congressman Lucien W. Parrish, a Democrat from Texas, an advocate of immigration restriction, against Meyer London, a Socialist from New York and himself an immigrant from Poland.

Parrish's views prevailed. And three years later, Congress permanently limited European immigration to 150,000 per year, distributed according to a series of national quotas that severely restricted the numbers from southern and eastern Europe. The law aimed to ensure that descendants of the old immigrants forever outnumbered the children of the new. The law also barred the entry of all those ineligible for naturalized citizenship—that is, the entire population of Asia, even though Japan had fought on the American side in World War I. The quota system remained in place until the immigration reform act of 1965.

———

MR. PARRISH: We should stop immigration entirely until such a time as we can amend our immigration laws and so write them that hereafter no one shall be admitted except he be in full sympathy with our Constitution and laws, willing to declare himself obedient to our flag, and willing to release himself from any obligations he may owe to the flag of the country from which he came.

It is time that we act now, because within a few short years the damage will have been done. The endless tide of immigration will have filled our country with a foreign and unsympathetic element. Those who are out of sympathy with our Constitution and the spirit of our Government will be here in large numbers, and the true spirit of Americanism left us by our fathers will gradually become poisoned by this uncertain element.

The time once was when we welcomed to our shores the oppressed and downtrodden people from all the world, but they came to us because of oppression at home and with the sincere purpose of making true and loyal American citizens, and in truth and in fact they did adapt themselves to our ways of thinking and contributed in a substantial sense to the progress and development that our civilization has made. But that time has passed now; new and strange conditions have arisen in the countries over there; new and strange doctrines are being taught. The Governments of the Orient are being overturned and destroyed, and anarchy and bolshevism are threatening the very foundation of many of them, and no one can foretell what the future will bring to many of those countries of the Old World now struggling with these problems.

Our country is a self-sustaining country. It has taught the principles of real democracy to all the nations of the earth; its flag has been the synonym of progress, prosperity, and the preservation of the rights of the individual, and there can be nothing so dangerous as for us to allow the undesirable foreign element to poison our civilization and thereby threaten the safety of the institutions that our forefathers have established for us.

Now is the time to throw about this country the most stringent immigration laws and keep from our shores forever those who are not in sympathy with the American ideas. It is the time now for us to act and act quickly, because every month's delay increases the difficulty in which we find ourselves and renders the problems of government more difficult of solution. We must protect ourselves from the poisonous influences that are threatening the very foundation of the Governments of Europe; we must see to it that those who come here are loyal and true to our Nation and impress upon them that it means something to have the privileges of American citizenship. We must hold this country true to the American thought and the American ideals....

Mr. London: ... This bill is a continuation of the war upon humanity. It is an assertion of that exaggerated nationalism which never appeals to reason and which has for its main source the self-conceit of accumulated prejudice.

At whom are you striking in this bill? Why, at the very people whom a short while ago you announced you were going to emancipate. We sent 2,000,000 men abroad to make the world "safe for democracy," to liberate these very people. Now you shut the door to them. Yes. So far, we have made the world safe for hypocrisy and the

United States incidentally unsafe for the Democratic Party, temporarily at least. [Laughter.] The supporters of the bill claim that the law will keep out radicals. The idea that by restricting immigration you will prevent the influx of radical thought is altogether untenable....

Ideas can neither be shut in nor shut out. There is only one way of contending with an idea, and that is the old and safe American rule of free and untrammeled discussion. Every attempt to use any other method has always proven disastrous.

While purporting to be a temporary measure, just for a year or so, this bill is really intended to pave the way to permanent exclusion.

To prevent immigration means to cripple the United States. Our most developed industrial States are those which have had the largest immigration. Our most backward States industrially and in the point of literacy are those which have had no immigration to speak of.

The extraordinary and unprecedented growth of the United States is as much a cause as the effect of immigration.

Defenders of this bill thoughtlessly repeat the exploded theory that there have been two periods of immigration, the good period, which the chairman of the committee fixes up to the year 1900, and the bad period since. The strange thing about it is that at no time in history has any country made such rapid progress in industry, in science, and in the sphere of social legislation as this country has shown since 1900.

The new immigration is neither different nor worse, and besides that, identically the same arguments were used against the old immigration.

By this bill we, who have escaped the horrors of the war, will refuse a place of refuge to the victims of the war.

I repeat, this is an attempt at civilization. Progress is by no means a continuous or uninterrupted process. Many a civilization has been destroyed in the tortuous course of history and has been followed by hundreds or thousands of years of darkness. It is just possible that

unless strong men who love liberty will everywhere assert themselves, the world will revert to a state of savagery. Just now we hear
nothing but hatred, nothing but the ravings of the exaggerated I—"I
am of the best stock, I do not want to be contaminated; I have produced the greatest literature; my intellect is the biggest; my heart is
the noblest"—and this is repeated in every parliament, in every
country, by every fool all over the world. [Applause.]

Questions

1. Why does Parrish consider continued immigration dangerous?

2. Why does London argue that immigration restriction is based on "prejudice" rather than "reason"?

131. *Meyer v. Nebraska* and the Meaning of Liberty (1923)

Source: Opinion of the Court, **Meyer v. Nebraska** *262 U.S. 390 (1923).*

One expression of the anti-immigrant sentiment sparked by World War I
was the passage of laws by a number of states restricting teaching in foreign
languages. Robert Meyer, a parochial school teacher in Nebraska, was found
guilty of violating a 1919 law that mandated that all instruction be in English. The state supreme court upheld his conviction and Meyer appealed to
the U. S. Supreme Court, arguing that the law violated the Fourteenth
Amendment's guarantee of liberty to all citizens.

By a 7–2 vote, the Court declared the Nebraska law unconstitutional. The
decision expanded the freedom of all immigrant groups, and helped to lay
the groundwork for the court's decisions of the 1960s affirming a constitutional right to privacy.

THE SUPREME COURT of [Nebraska] affirmed the judgment of conviction.... It declared the offense charged and established was "the direct and intentional teaching of the German language as a distinct subject to a child who had not passed the eighth grade," in the parochial school maintained by Zion Evangelical Lutheran Congregation, a collection of Biblical stories being used therefore. And it held that the statute forbidding this did not conflict with the Fourteenth Amendment, but was a valid exercise of the police power. The following excerpts from the opinion sufficiently indicate the reasons advanced to support the conclusion:

> The salutary purpose of the statute is clear. The Legislature had seen the baneful effects of permitting foreigners, who had taken residence in this country, to rear and educate their children in the language of their native land. The result of that condition was found to be inimical to our own safety. To allow the children of foreigners, who had emigrated here, to be taught from early childhood the language of the country of their parents was to ... educate them so that they must always think in that language, and, as a consequence, naturally inculcate in them the ideas and sentiments foreign to the best interests of this country....

The problem for our determination is whether the statute as construed and applied unreasonably infringes the liberty guaranteed to the plaintiff in error by the Fourteenth Amendment:

> No state ... shall deprive any person of life, liberty or property without due process of law.

While this court has not attempted to define with exactness the liberty thus guaranteed ... without doubt, it denotes not merely freedom from bodily restraint but also the right of the individual to contract, to engage in any of the common occupations of life, to acquire useful knowledge, to marry, establish a home and bring up children, to worship God according to the dictates of his own conscience, and generally to enjoy those privileges long recognized at common law as essential to the orderly pursuit of happiness by free men. The established doctrine is that this liberty may not be interfered with, under the guise of protecting the public interest, by legislative action which is arbitrary or without reasonable relation to some purpose within the competency of the state to effect....

The American people have always regarded education and acquisition of knowledge as matters of supreme importance which should be diligently promoted. The Ordinance of 1787 declares: "Religion, morality and knowledge being necessary to good government and the happiness of mankind, schools and the means of education shall forever be encouraged." Corresponding to the right of control, it is the natural duty of the parent to give his children education suitable to their station in life; and nearly all the states, including Nebraska, enforce this obligation by compulsory laws.

Practically, education of the young is only possible in schools conducted by especially qualified persons who devote themselves thereto. The calling always has been regarded as useful and honorable, essential, indeed, to the public welfare. Mere knowledge of the German language cannot reasonably be regarded as harmful. Heretofore it has been commonly looked upon as helpful and desirable. Plaintiff in error taught this language in school as part of his occupation. His right thus to teach and the right of parents to engage him so to instruct their children, we think, are within the liberty of the amendment.

The challenged statute forbids the teaching in school of any subject except in English; also the teaching of any other language until the pupil has attained and successfully passed the eighth grade, which is not usually accomplished before the age of twelve. The Supreme Court of the state has held that "the so-called ancient or dead languages" are not "within the spirit or the purpose of the act." Latin, Greek, Hebrew are not proscribed; but German, French, Spanish, Italian, and every other alien speech are within the ban. Evidently the Legislature has attempted materially to interfere with the calling of modern language teachers, with the opportunities of pupils to acquire knowledge, and with the power of parents to control the education of their own.

It is said the purpose of the legislation was to promote civic development by inhibiting training and education of the immature in foreign tongues and ideals before they could learn English and acquire American ideals, and "that the English language should be and become the mother tongue of all children reared in this state." It is also affirmed that the foreign born population is very large, that certain communities commonly use foreign words, follow foreign leaders, move in a foreign atmosphere, and that the children are thereby hindered from becoming citizens of the most useful type and the public safety is imperiled.

That the state may do much, go very far, indeed, in order to improve the quality of its citizens, physically, mentally and morally, is clear; but the individual has certain fundamental rights which must be respected. The protection of the Constitution extends to all, to those who speak other languages as well as to those born with English on the tongue. Perhaps it would be highly advantageous if all had ready understanding of our ordinary speech, but this cannot be coerced with methods which conflict with the Constitution—a desirable end cannot be promoted by prohibited means. . . .

The desire of the Legislature to foster a homogeneous people with American ideals prepared readily to understand current discussions of civic matters is easy to appreciate. Unfortunate experiences during the late war and aversion toward every character of truculent adversaries were certainly enough to quicken that aspiration. But the means adopted, we think, exceed the limitations upon the power of the state and conflict with rights assured to plaintiff in error. The interference is plain enough and no adequate reason therefore in time of peace and domestic tranquility has been shown.

The power of the state to compel attendance at some school and to make reasonable regulations for all schools, including a requirement that they shall give instructions in English, is not questioned. Nor has challenge been made of the state's power to prescribe a curriculum for institutions which it supports. Those matters are not within the present controversy. Our concern is with the prohibition approved by the [Nebraska] Supreme Court. . . .

No emergency has arisen which renders knowledge by a child of some language other than English so clearly harmful as to justify its inhibition with the consequent infringement of rights long freely enjoyed. We are constrained to conclude that the statute as applied is arbitrary and without reasonable relation to any end within the competency of the state. As the statute undertakes to interfere only with teaching which involves a modern language, leaving complete freedom as to other matters, there seems no adequate foundation for the suggestion that the purpose was to protect the child's health by limiting his mental activities. It is well known that proficiency in a foreign language seldom comes to one not instructed at an early age, and experience shows that this is not injurious to the health, morals or understanding of the ordinary child. . . .

Questions

1. In what ways did the Supreme Court of Nebraska justify the English-only law?

2. Why does the U.S. Supreme Court see the law as an unreasonable infringement on liberty?

132. Alain Locke, *The New Negro* (1925)

Source: Reprinted with the permission of Scribner, an imprint of Simon & Schuster Adult Publishing Group, from The New Negro: Voices of the Harlem Renaissance *by Alain Locke. Copyright © 1925 by Albert & Charles Boni, Inc. All rights reserved.*

The migration of blacks from South to North, begun in large numbers during World War I, continued during the 1920s. New York's Harlem became famous for "slumming," as groups of whites visited its dance halls, jazz clubs, and speakeasies in search of exotic adventure. The Harlem of the white imagination was a place of primitive passions, free from the puritanical restraints of mainstream American culture. The real Harlem was a community of widespread poverty. But it was also the center of rising racial self-consciousness, a growing awareness of the interconnections between black Americans and persons of African descent elsewhere in the world, and a vibrant black cultural community that established links with New York's artistic mainstream. The term "New Negro," associated in politics with pan-Africanism and the militancy of the Garvey movement, in art meant the rejection of established stereotypes and a search for black values to put in their place. *The New Negro*, a book of essays and literary works edited by Alain Locke, came to symbolize the "Harlem Renaissance."

IN THE LAST decade something beyond the watch and guard of statistics has happened in the life of the American Negro and the three norns who have traditionally presided over the Negro problem have a changeling in their laps. The Sociologist, the Philanthropist, the Race-leader are not unaware of the New Negro, but they are at a loss to account for him. He simply cannot be swathed in their formulæ. For the younger generation is vibrant with a new psychology; the new spirit is awake in the masses, and under the very eyes of the professional observers is transforming what has been a perennial problem into the progressive phases of contemporary Negro life.

• • •

With this renewed self-respect and self-dependence, the life of the Negro community is bound to enter a new dynamic phase, the buoyancy from within compensating for whatever pressure there may be of conditions from without. The migrant masses, shifting from countryside to city, hurdle several generations of experience at a leap, but more important, the same thing happens spiritually in the life-attitudes and self-expression of the Young Negro, in his poetry, his art, his education and his new outlook, with the additional advantage, of course, of the poise and greater certainty of knowing what it is all about. From this comes the promise and warrant of a new leadership. As one of them has discerningly put it:

> We have tomorrow
> Bright before us
> Like a flame.
>
> Yesterday, a night-gone thing
> A sun-down name.
>
> And dawn today
> Broad arch above the road we came.
> We march!

• • •

The day of "aunties," "uncles" and "mammies" is equally gone. Uncle Tom and Sambo have passed on, and even the "Colonel" and "George" play barnstorm roles from which they escape with relief when the public spotlight is off. The popular melodrama has about played itself out, and it is time to scrap the fictions, garret the bogeys and settle down to a realistic facing of facts.

First we must observe some of the changes which since the traditional lines of opinion were drawn have rendered these quite obsolete. A main change has been, of course, that shifting of the Negro population which has made the Negro problem no longer exclusively or even predominantly Southern.

• • •

Here in Manhattan is not merely the largest Negro community in the world, but the first concentration in history of so many diverse elements of Negro life. It has attracted the African, the West Indian, the Negro American; has brought together the Negro of the North and the Negro of the South; the man from the city and the man from the town and village; the peasant, the student, the business man, the professional man, artist, poet, musician, adventurer and worker, preacher and criminal, exploiter and social outcast. Each group has come with its own separate motives and for its own special ends, but their greatest experience has been the finding of one another. Proscription and prejudice have thrown these dissimilar elements into a common area of contact and interaction. Within this area, race sympathy and unity have determined a further fusing of sentiment and experience. So what began in terms of segregation becomes more and more, as its elements mix and react, the laboratory of a great race-welding. Hitherto, it must be admitted that American Negroes have been a race more in name than in fact, or to be exact, more in sentiment than in experience. The chief bond between them has been that of a common condition rather than a common consciousness; a problem in common rather than a life in common. In Harlem, Negro life is seizing upon its first chances for group expression and self-determination. It is—or promises at least to be—a race capital. That is why our comparison is taken with those nascent centers of folk-expression and self-determination which are playing a creative part in the world to-day. Without pretense to their political significance, Harlem has the same role to play for the New Negro as Dublin has had for the New Ireland or Prague for the New Czechoslovakia.

• • •

[Two new] interests are racial but in a new and enlarged way. One is the consciousness of acting as the advance-guard of the African peoples in their contact with Twentieth Century civilization; the other, the sense of a mission of rehabilitating the race in world esteem from that loss of prestige for which the fate and conditions of slavery have so largely been responsible. Harlem, as we shall see, is the center of both these movements; she is the home of the Negro's "Zionism." The pulse of the Negro world has begun to beat in Harlem. A Negro newspaper carrying news material in English, French and Spanish, gathered from all quarters of America, the West Indies and Africa has maintained itself in Harlem for over five years. Two important magazines, both edited from New York, maintain their news and circulation consistently on a cosmopolitan scale. Under American auspices and backing, three pan-African congresses have been held abroad for the discussion of common interests, colonial questions and the future co-operative development of Africa. In terms of the race question as a world problem, the Negro mind has leapt, so to speak, upon the parapets of prejudice and extended its cramped horizons. In so doing it has linked up with the growing group consciousness of the dark peoples and is gradually learning their common interests. As one of our writers has recently put it: "It is imperative that we understand the white world in its relations to the non-white world." As with the Jew, persecution is making the Negro international.

As a world phenomenon this wider race consciousness is a different thing from the much asserted rising tide of color. Its inevitable causes are not of our making. The consequences are not necessarily damaging to the best interests of civilization. Whether it actually brings into being new Armadas of conflict or argosies of cultural exchange and enlightenment can only be decided by the attitude of the dominant races in an era of critical change. With the American Negro, his new internationalism is primarily an effort to recapture contact with the scattered peoples of African derivation. Garveyism may be a transient, if spectacular, phenomenon, but the possible role of the American Negro in the future development of Africa is one of the most constructive and universally helpful missions that any modern people can lay claim to.

• • •

Questions

1. What does Locke mean when he writes, "the day of 'aunties,' 'uncles' and 'mammies' " is gone?

2. Why does Locke consider Harlem a true "race capital" for blacks?

133. Freedom and the Modern World (1928)

Source: Walton H. Hamilton, "Freedom and Economic Necessity," in Horace M. Kallen, ed., Freedom in the Modern World *(New York, 1928), pp. 25–33.*

In 1927, the New School for Social Research in New York City organized a series of lectures on the theme of Freedom in the Modern World. The lectures painted a depressing portrait of American freedom. "The idea of freedom," declared economist Walton H. Hamilton, had become "an intellectual instrument for looking backward." The free exchange of ideas, he claimed, had not recovered from the crisis of World War I. A definition of "freedom" reigned supreme that celebrated the unimpeded reign of economic enterprise yet tolerated the surveillance of private life and individual conscience. Walton called upon Americans to realize that institutions like government can enhance freedom as well as restricting it.

THE IDEAL OF freedom is the holy grail of social progress. It is the blessed state towards which we would have our changing culture move, yet it is forever just out of reach. We cannot set down the ends of our strivings, we cannot consider wherein our institutions need mending, we cannot contrive ways and means for improving the condition of mankind without using some such dynamic word as freedom. Yet, for all our knowledge and understanding, we can no more define freedom than we can realize it. It is a general term the core of which is an opportunity for man to make the most of himself in the fragment of the world about him. When translated into the reality of here and now, or of then and there, or of presently and over yonder, it becomes a multitude of particulars which have been and may be put together in endless permutations. What it is, what it means, what it promises vary with the circumstances of society, the institutions under which we live, and the thoughts which variously lie within our several heads.

There are, in fact, as many freedoms as there are persons to declaim its greatness or to invoke it in the name of humanity.

• • •

It is this capacity of the word for variety in meaning that endows freedom with a hazardous promise. The word suggests opportunities for individual attainment not yet realized; its broad confine has a place which the constructive imagination and the conscious strivings of man can fill with institutions which develop human capacities and give them more ample scope. But the chance at a greater freedom is beset with hazards which are inseparable from the use of the term. For the circumstance which has been crowded into the word, the particulars which have gone into its making, the specific ends and issues which it calls up in the mind narrow its meaning and restrict its use. Men are prone to see the desirable in terms of the historical, to reargue outworn questions, to fight again over issues long ago settled. The word invites maintenance of freedom if the adversary can be pictured as a military dictator, a monarch, or a pope; it commits to an attack if the cause can be paraded as against arbitrary taxation, the interference with trade, chattel slavery, or the pleasure of an irresponsible king. It is, in fact, a summons to a struggle like those which have already been fought in its name. What has been is specific, what may come to pass is not yet so; if the idea of freedom is to find constructive use, it must be emancipated from the particular content which makes it an intellectual instrument for looking backward.

If freedom is to be put to constructive use, the word must be freed from its negative connotation. It must employ institutions rather than escape them. As it has come down to us, the word liberty has been closely associated with a struggle against autocratic power in high places.

• • •

As a result there has grown up a theory that the individual and the institution—unlike as they are—are complementary and antithetical; that individual freedom is to wax with the waning of political authority; that an abridgment of the sovereignty of church or state means an enlargement of the sovereignty of man.

• • •

However useful such a negative freedom is for an attack upon the lords of earth who attempt formally to rule mankind from Olympus, it fails to serve the constructive thought of today.

• • •

Beyond church and state, there are many institutions which may abridge, deny, or enlarge the individual's freedom. The organization of family life gives the child's potentialities their first start towards capacities. The educational system may or may not "improve" the growing mind; but, in its true sense of controlled exposure, it gives or denies to the developing person a chance to find out what he can and what he cannot do. Likewise it furnishes opportunities for practice in the liberal art of personal choice. The law, which in a world full of a number of tangled things has an organic growth that transcends legislation, gives at least a crude form to human activities, and sets rough limits within which the individual must order his life. The press, the institutions for recreation and culture and parade, the organization of the frivolities of life, all have their places as factors in the making of the individual. One and all, in accordance with their characters and qualities, they give or withhold the stuff out of which personal freedom is made.

Not the least among the institutions which give or withhold the chance of freedom is the economic system. For many decades the industrial order has been advertised as a great cooperative enterprise carried on by a scheme of voluntary agreements among free individuals. Liberty of contract has been made the be-all and the end-all of personal freedom; buying and selling has been regarded as a process by which individuals have voluntarily kept industrial activity going; the domain of business has been defended against control from without in the name of freedom. Yet the economic system is as much a scheme of human arrangements as is the church or the state; its control over what individuals are and what they do is just as continuous and just as compelling.

Questions

1. Why does Walton emphasize the impossibility of arriving at a single definition of "freedom"?

2. How does Walton feel that institutions and laws can increase an individual's freedom?

CHAPTER 21

The New Deal, 1932–1940

134. Letter to Secretary of Labor Frances Perkins (1937)

Source: Gerald Markowitz and David Rosner, ed., "Slaves of the Depression": Workers' Letters about Life on the Job (Ithaca, N.Y., 1987), pp. 103–04.

The election of Franklin D. Roosevelt as president in 1932 did much to rekindle hope among the victims of the Great Depression, the worst economic disaster in American history. Throughout the 1930s, ordinary Americans, one of whom referred to the downtrodden as "slaves of the depression," wrote poignant letters to federal officials describing the oppressive working conditions of those who retained their jobs and the difficulty of finding work for the unemployed. They wrote of the threat of starvation, the impossibility of obtaining medical care when ill, and the abuses of dictatorial employers and supervisors. One such letter, addressed to Secretary of Labor Frances Perkins, described the "terrible and inhuman condition" of workers in the sugar fields of Louisiana.

PLAQUEMINE, LOUISIANA, JULY 27, 1937

Dear Miss Perkins:

I am writing to you because I think you are pretty square to the average laboring man. but I am wondering if anyone has told you of the cruel and terrible condition that exist in this part of the country or the so called sugar cane belt in Louisiana. I am sure that it hasn't made any progress or improvement since slavery days and to many people here that toil the soil or saw mills as laboring men I am sure slavery days were much better for the black slaves had their meals for sure three times a day and medical attention at that. but if an American nowadays had that much he is a communist I am speaking of the labor not the ones that the government give a sugar bounty too but the real forgotten people for the ones the government give the sugar bounty too are the ones that really don't need it for those same people that has drawn the sugar bonus for two years has never gave an extra penny to their white and black slaves labor. I will now make an effort to give you an idea of the terrible inhuman condition.

I will first give you the idea of the sugar cane tenants and plantations poor laboring people. The bell rings at 2 a.m. in the morning when all should really be sleeping at rest. they work in the summer until 9 or 10 a.m. the reason they knock them off from the heat is not because of killing the labor from heat but they are afraid it kills the mule not the slave. Their wages runs from 90¢ to $1.10 per day. Their average days per week runs from three to four days a week in other words people that are living in so called United States have to live on the about $4.00 per week standing of living in a so called American Community which is way below the Chinese standard of living for the Chinese at least have a cheaper food and clothing living but here one has to pay dear for food and clothing because these sugar cane slave owners *not* only give inhuman wages but the ones that work for them have to buy to their stores, which sells from 50 per cent to 60 per cent higher than the stores in town still these same people that are worst than the old time slave owners or yelling and hollering for more sugar protection, why should they get more when they don't pay their white and black slaves more. It is true they give the white and black slaves a place to live on. But Miss Perkins if you were to see these places they live on you'd swear that this is not our so call rich America with it high standing of living for I am sure that the lowest places in China or Mexico or Africa has better places to live in. These Southern Senators which are backed by the big shots will tell you it is cheaper to live in the South but have you investigated their living condition. Sometimes I don't wonder why some of these people don't be really communism but they are true Americans only they are living in such a low standing of living that one wouldn't believe they are living in the good old U.S.A.

Now regarding the saw mills of this town and other towns in this section but most particular this town they pay slightly more than the plantation but they get it back by charging more for food & clothing which they have to buy in their stores.

I am writing you this hoping that you will try to read it and understand the situation which if you think is not true you can send an investigator in this section of Louisiana that has American freedom of speech for some hasn't that speech in our so called free America and if you can get in touch with people who are not concern about it I am sure you will see that I am right and I do hope that you are kind enough to give this your carefully attention and I am sure that President Roosevelt nor Mrs. Roosevelt nor you would like to see this terrible and inhuman condition go on worst now then old slavery days for I know you people believe in the real American standing of living.

Again I will call your attention if you don't believe of the slave wages condition in this lost part of U.S. investigate and you will find out. Thanking you for humanity sake.

R.J.

Questions

1. Why does the writer feel that Secretary of Labor Perkins will give the letter a sympathetic reading?

2. Why does the writer refer to "our so called free America"?

135. John Steinbeck, *The Harvest Gypsies* (1936)

Source: Copyright © *1936 by* **The San Francisco News.** *Reprinted by permission of Heyday Books, Berkeley, California.*

The 1930s had a devastating impact on American agriculture. The Great Depression, coupled with a prolonged drought and dust storms in the nation's heartland spurred an exodus of displaced farmers to nearby cities or to the promised land of California. John Steinbeck's novel *The Grapes of Wrath* (1939) and a popular film based on the book captured their plight, tracing a dispossessed family's trek from Oklahoma to California. Before the book appeared, Steinbeck had written a series of newspaper articles based on interviews with the migrants, later gathered in a book, *The Harvest Gypsies.*

THUS, IN CALIFORNIA we find a curious attitude toward a group that makes our agriculture successful. The migrants are needed, and they are hated. Arriving in a district they find the dislike always meted out by the resident to the foreigner, the outlander. This hatred of the stranger occurs in the whole range of human history, from the most primitive village form to our own highly organized industrial farming. The migrants are hated for the following reasons, that they are ignorant and dirty people, that they are carriers of disease, that they increase the necessity for police and the tax bill for schooling in a community, and that if they are allowed to organize they can, simply by refusing to work, wipe out the season's crops. They are never received into a community nor into the life of a community. Wanderers in fact, they are never allowed to feel at home in the communities that demand their services.

Let us see what kind of people they are, where they come from, and the routes of their wanderings. In the past they have been of several races, encouraged to come and often imported as cheap labor; Chinese in the early period, then Filipinos, Japanese and Mexicans.

These were foreigners, and as such they were ostracized and segregated and herded about.

If they attempted to organize they were deported or arrested, and having no advocates they were never able to get a hearing for their problems. But in recent years the foreign migrants have begun to organize, and at this danger signal they have been deported in great numbers, for there was a new reservoir from which a great quantity of cheap labor could be obtained.

The drought in the middle west has driven the agricultural populations of Oklahoma, Nebraska and parts of Kansas and Texas westward. Their lands are destroyed and they can never go back to them. Thousands of them are crossing the borders in ancient rattling automobiles, destitute and hungry and homeless, ready to accept any pay so that they may eat and feed their children. And this is a new thing in migrant labor, for the foreign workers were usually imported without their children and everything that remains of their old life with them.

They arrive in California usually having used up every resource to get here, even to the selling of the poor blankets and utensils and tools on the way to buy gasoline. They arrive bewildered and beaten and usually in a state of semi-starvation, with only one necessity to face immediately, and that is to find work at any wage in order that the family may eat.

And there is only one field in California that can receive them. Ineligible for relief, they must become migratory field workers. . . .

The earlier foreign migrants have invariably been drawn from a peon class. This is not the case with the new migrants. They are small farmers who have lost their farms, or farm hands who have lived with the family in the old American way. They are men who have worked hard on their own farms and have felt the pride of possessing and living in close touch with the land. They are resourceful and intelligent Americans who have gone through the hell of the drought, have seen their lands wither and die and the top soil blow away; and this, to a man who has owned his land, is a curious and terrible pain. . . .

And there is another difference between their old life and the new. They have come from the little farm districts where democracy was not only possible but inevitable, where popular government, whether practiced in the Grange, in church organization or in local government, was the responsibility of every man. And they have come into the country where, because of the movement necessary to make a living, they are not allowed any vote whatever, but are rather considered a properly unprivileged class.

... As one little boy in a squatters' camp said, "When they need us they call us migrants, and when we've picked their crop, we're bums and we got to get out."

Questions

1. How do the migrants of the 1930s differ from previous waves of migrant laborers who emigrated to California?

2. What does Steinbeck see as the impact of the farm migration on American democracy?

136. Labor's Great Upheaval (1936)

Source: John L. Lewis, "Industrial Democracy in Steel," Radio Address, July 6, 1936, in New Deal Thought, *Howard Zinn, ed., pp. 204–11.*

The most striking development of the mid-1930s was the mobilization of millions of workers in mass production industries that had successfully resisted unionization. Previous depressions had devastated the labor movement. Unlike in the past, however, the federal government now seemed to be on the side of labor, as reflected in the Wagner Act of 1935, which granted workers the legal right to form unions.

In 1935, labor leaders dissatisfied with the American Federation of Labor's policy of organizing workers along traditional craft lines called for the creation of unions that united all workers in a specific industry. They formed the Committee for Industrial Organization, which set out to create unions in the main bastions of the American economy. In 1936, in the midst of the battle to organize the steel industry, John L. Lewis, the head of the United Mine Workers, delivered a radio address explaining in militant language labor's vision. In 1937, U.S. Steel, the country's most important single business firm, agreed to recognize the new steel workers' union.

I SALUTE THE hosts of labor who listen. I greet my fellow Americans. My voice tonight will be the voice of millions of men and women employed in America's industries, heretofore unorganized, economically exploited and inarticulate. I speak for the Committee for Industrial Organization, which has honored me with its chairmanship and with which are associated twelve great National and International Unions. These unions have a membership in excess of one million persons, who to a greater or lesser degree enjoy the privileges of self-organization and collective bargaining.

They reflect adequately the sentiment, hopes and aspirations of those thirty million additional Americans employed in the complex processes of our domestic economy who heretofore have been denied by industry and finance the privilege of collective organization and collective participation in the arbitrary fixation of their economic status.

Let him doubt who will that tonight I portray the ceaseless yearning of their hearts and the ambitions of their minds. Let him who will, be he economic tyrant or sordid mercenary, pit his strength against this mighty upsurge of human sentiment now being crystallized in the hearts of thirty millions of workers who clamor for the establishment of industrial democracy and for participation in its tangible fruits. He is a mad man or a fool who believes that this river of human sentiment, flowing as it does from the hearts of these thirty millions, who with their dependents constitute two-thirds of the population of the United States of America, can be dammed or impounded by the erection of arbitrary barriers of restraint. Such barriers, whether they be instrumentalities of corporate control, financial intrigue or judicial interdict, will burst asunder and inevitably destroy the pernicious forces which attempt to create them.

• • •

It is idle to moralize over the abstract relations between an employer and his employee. This is an issue between an industry clearly organized on its management side and the 500,000 men upon whose toil the whole structure depends. The question is whether these men shall have freedom of organization for the purpose of protecting their interest in this colossal economic organism.

• • •

Interference and coercion of employees trying to organize, comes from the economic advantages held by the employer. In the steel industry it is manifested in an elaborate system of spies, and in a studied discharge of those who advocate any form of organization displeasing to the management. It is shown by confining all yearning for organization to make-believe company unions, controlled and dominated by the management itself. This coercion is finally shown in the implied threat of a blacklist which attends the announcement of a joint and common policy for all the steel corporations of this country.

Why shouldn't organized labor throw its influence into this unequal situation? What chance have the steel workers to form a free and independent organization without the aid of organized labor? What opportunity will they have to bargain collectively through representatives of their own choosing except by the formation of an organization free from management control?

• • •

Although the industry has produced thousands of millionaires, and hundreds of multi-millionaires among bankers, promoters, so-called financiers, and steel executives, it has never throughout the past thirty-five years paid a bare subsistence wage, not to mention a living wage, to the great mass of its workers.

• • •

Organized labor in America accepts the challenge of the omnipresent overlords of steel to fight for the prize of economic freedom and industrial democracy. The issue involves the security of every man or woman who works for a living by hand or by brain. The issue cuts across every major economic, social and political problem now pressing with incalculable weight upon the 130 millions of people of this nation. It is an issue of whether the working population of this country shall have a voice in determining their destiny or whether they shall serve as indentured servants for a financial and economic dictatorship which would shamelessly exploit our natural resources and debase the soul and destroy the pride of a free people. On such an issue there can be no compromise for labor or for a thoughtful citizenship.

I call upon the workers in the iron and steel industry who are listening to me tonight to throw off their shackles of servitude and join the union of their industry. I call upon the workers in the textile, lumber, rubber, automotive and other unorganized industries to join with their comrades in the steel industry and forge for themselves the modern instruments of labor wherewith to demand and secure participation in the increased wealth and increased productive efficiency of modern industrial America.

The more than a million members of the twelve great National and International Unions associated with the Committee for Industrial Organization will counsel you and aid you in your individual and collective efforts to establish yourselves as free men and women in every economic, social and political sense. I unhesitatingly place the values represented by thirty million human beings engaged in industry and their sixty million dependents as being above and superior in every moral consideration to the five billions of inanimate dollars represented by the resources of the American Iron and Steel Institute or to the additional billions of inanimate dollars that perforce may be allied with the empire of steel in the impending struggle which the Institute, in the brutality of its arrogance, seeks to make inevitable.

Questions

1. Why does Lewis contrast the "values" represented by the labor movement with those of the steel industry?

2. What does Lewis mean by enabling workers to "establish yourselves as free men and women in every economic, social and political sense"?

—————————

137. Franklin D. Roosevelt on Economic Freedom (1936)

Source: Acceptance of the renomination for the presidency, Democratic National Convention, Philadelphia, June 27, 1936, in Samuel I. Rosenman, ed., The Public Papers and Addresses of Franklin Delano Roosevelt *(New York, 1938–1950), Vol. 5, pp. 230–40.*

Along with being a superb politician, Franklin D. Roosevelt was a master of political communication. He worked to reclaim the word "freedom" from conservatives, and made it a rallying cry for the New Deal. Throughout the 1930s, he consistently linked freedom with economic security and identified economic inequality as its greatest enemy. In his speech accepting renomination, Roosevelt launched a blistering attack against "economic royalists." Throughout the campaign, FDR insisted that the threat posed to economic freedom by the "new despotism" of large corporations was the main issue of the election. Roosevelt won a landslide reelection, with over 60 percent of the popular vote.

—————————

I CANNOT, WITH candor, tell you that all is well with the world. Clouds of suspicion, tides of ill-will and intolerance gather darkly in many places. In our own land we enjoy indeed a fullness of life greater than that of most Nations. But the rush of modern civilization itself has raised for us new difficulties, new problems which must be solved if we are to preserve to the United States the political and economic freedom for which Washington and Jefferson planned and fought.

Philadelphia is a good city in which to write American history. This is fitting ground on which to reaffirm the faith of our fathers; to pledge ourselves to restore to the people a wider freedom; to give to 1936 as the founders gave to 1776—an American way of life.

That very word freedom, in itself and of necessity, suggests freedom from some restraining power. In 1776 we sought freedom from the tyranny of a political autocracy—from the eighteenth century royalists who held special privileges from the crown. It was to perpetuate their privilege that they governed without the consent of the governed; that they denied the right of free assembly and free speech; that they restricted the worship of God; that they put the average man's property and the average man's life in pawn to the mercenaries of dynastic power; that they regimented the people.

And so it was to win freedom from the tyranny of political autocracy that the American Revolution was fought. That victory gave the business of governing into the hands of the average man, who won the right with his neighbors to make and order his own destiny through his own Government. Political tyranny was wiped out at Philadelphia on July 4, 1776.

Since that struggle, however, man's inventive genius released new forces in our land which reordered the lives of our people. The age of machinery, of railroads; of steam and electricity; the telegraph and the radio; mass production, mass distribution—all of these combined to bring forward a new civilization and with it a new problem for those who sought to remain free.

For out of this modern civilization economic royalists carved new dynasties. New kingdoms were built upon concentration of control over material things. Through new uses of corporations, banks and securities, new machinery of industry and agriculture, of labor and capital—all undreamed of by the fathers—the whole structure of modern life was impressed into this royal service.

There was no place among this royalty for our many thousands of small business men and merchants who sought to make a worthy use of the American system of initiative and profit. They were no more free than the worker or the farmer. Even honest and progressive-minded men of wealth, aware of their obligation to their generation, could never know just where they fitted into this dynastic scheme of things.

It was natural and perhaps human that the privileged princes of these new economic dynasties, thirsting for power, reached out for control over Government itself. They created a new despotism and wrapped it in the robes of legal sanction. In its service new mercenaries sought to regiment the people, their labor, and their property. And as a result the average man once more confronts the problem that faced the Minute Man.

The hours men and women worked, the wages they received, the conditions of their labor—these had passed beyond the control of the people, and were imposed by this new industrial dictatorship. The savings of the average family, the capital of the small business man, the investments set aside for old age—other people's money—these were tools which the new economic royalty used to dig itself in.

Those who tilled the soil no longer reaped the rewards which were their right. The small measure of their gains was decreed by men in distant cities.

Throughout the Nation, opportunity was limited by monopoly. Individual initiative was crushed in the cogs of a great machine. The field open for free business was more and more restricted. Private enterprise, indeed, became too private. It became privileged enterprise, not free enterprise.

An old English judge once said: "Necessitous men are not free men." Liberty requires opportunity to make a living—a living decent according to the standard of the time, a living which gives man not only enough to live by, but something to live for.

For too many of us the political equality we once had won was meaningless in the face of economic inequality. A small group had concentrated into their own hands an almost complete control over other people's property, other people's money, other people's labor—

other people's lives. For too many of us life was no longer free; liberty no longer real; men could no longer follow the pursuit of happiness.

Against economic tyranny such as this, the American citizen could appeal only to the organized power of Government. The collapse of 1929 showed up the despotism for what it was. The election of 1932 was the people's mandate to end it. Under that mandate it is being ended.

The royalists of the economic order have conceded that political freedom was the business of the Government, but they have maintained that economic slavery was nobody's business. They granted that the Government could protect the citizen in his right to vote, but they denied that the Government could do anything to protect the citizen in his right to work and his right to live.

Today we stand committed to the proposition that freedom is no half-and-half affair. If the average citizen is guaranteed equal opportunity in the polling place, he must have equal opportunity in the market place.

These economic royalists complain that we seek to overthrow the institutions of America. What they really complain of is that we seek to take away their power. Our allegiance to American institutions requires the overthrow of this kind of power. In vain they seek to hide behind the Flag and the Constitution. In their blindness they forget what the Flag and the Constitution stand for. Now, as always, they stand for democracy, not tyranny; for freedom, not subjection; and against a dictatorship by mob rule and the overprivileged alike.

The brave and clear platform adopted by this Convention, to which I heartily subscribe, sets forth that Government in a modern civilization has certain inescapable obligations to its citizens, among which are protection of the family and the home, the establishment of a democracy of opportunity, and aid to those overtaken by disaster.

• • •

I believe in my heart that only our success can stir their ancient hope. They begin to know that here in America we are waging a great and successful war. It is not alone a war against want and destitution and economic demoralization. It is more than that; it is a war for the survival of democracy. We are fighting to save a great and precious form of government for ourselves and for the world.

Questions

1. What does Roosevelt mean when he quotes an English judge as saying, "Necessitous [needy] men are not free men"?

2. What forces does Roosevelt feel endanger the freedoms of Americans?

138. Herbert Hoover on the New Deal and Liberty (1936)

Source: Herbert Hoover: On the New Deal and Liberty, Official Report of the Proceedings of the 21st Republican National Convention, *1936, pp. 115–19, 122–24. Reprinted with permission of the Republican National Committee.*

Even as Roosevelt invoked the word to uphold the New Deal, "liberty"—in the sense of freedom from powerful government—became the fighting slogan of his opponents. As the 1930s progressed, opponents of the New Deal invoked the language of liberty with greater and greater passion. Freedom, they claimed, meant unrestrained economic opportunity for the enterprising individual. In a speech at the Republican National Convention of 1936, former President Hoover accused his successor of endangering "fundamental American liberties." Roosevelt, he charged, was either operating out of sheer opportunism, with no coherent purpose of policy, or was conspiring to impose "European ideas" on the United States. The election, he continued, in strident language that reflected how wide the gap between the parties had become, was a "holy crusade for liberty" that would "determine the future" of freedom in the United States.

IN THIS ROOM rests the greatest responsibility that has come to a body of Americans in three generations. In the lesser sense this is a convention of a great political party. But in the larger sense it is a convention of Americans to determine the fate of those ideals for which this nation was founded. That far transcends all partisanship.

There are elemental currents which make or break the fate of nations. There is a moral purpose in the universe. Those forces which affect the vitality and the soul of a people will control its destinies. The sum of years of public service in these currents is the overwhelming conviction of their transcendent importance over the more transitory, even though difficult, issues of national life.

I have given about four years to research into the New Deal, trying to determine what its ultimate objectives were, what sort of a system it is imposing on this country.

To some people it appears to be a strange interlude in American history in that it has no philosophy, that it is sheer opportunism, that it is a muddle of a spoils system, of emotional economics, of reckless adventure, of unctuous claims to a monopoly of human sympathy, of greed for power, of a desire for popular acclaim and an aspiration to make the front pages of the newspapers. That is the most charitable view.

To other people it appears to be a cold-blooded attempt by starry-eyed boys to infect the American people by a mixture of European ideas, flavored with our native predilection to get something for nothing.

You can choose either one you like best. But the first is the road of chaos which leads to the second. Both of these roads lead over the same grim precipice that is the crippling and possibly the destruction of the freedom of men.

• • •

We have seen these gigantic expenditures and this torrent of waste pile up a national debt which two generations cannot repay. One time I told a Democratic Congress that "you cannot spend yourselves into prosperity." You recall that advice did not take then. It hasn't taken yet. Billions have been spent to prime the economic pump. It did employ a horde of paid officials upon the pump handle. We have seen the frantic attempts to find new taxes on the rich. Yet three-quarters of the bill will be sent to the average man and the poor. He and his wife and his grandchildren will be giving a quarter of all their working days to pay taxes. Freedom to work for himself is changed into a slavery of work for the follies of government.

We have seen an explosive inflation of bank credits by this government borrowing. We have seen varied steps toward currency inflation that have already enriched the speculator and deprived the poor. If this is to continue the end result is the tears and anguish of universal bankruptcy and distress. No democracy in history has survived its final stages.

We have seen the building up of a horde of political officials, we have seen the pressures upon the helpless and destitute to trade political support for relief. Both are a pollution of the very fountains of liberty.

We have seen the most elemental violation of economic law and experience. The New Deal forgets it is solely by production of more goods and more varieties of goods and services that we advance the living and security of men. If we constantly decrease costs and prices and keep up earnings the production of plenty will be more and more widely distributed. These laws may be restitched in new phrases so that they are the very shoes of human progress. We had so triumphed in this long climb of mankind toward plenty that we had reached Mount Pisgah where we looked over the promised land of abolished poverty. Then men began to quarrel over the division of the goods. The depression produced by war destruction temporarily checked our march toward the promised land.

• • •

Great calamities have come to the whole world. These forces have reached into every calling and every cottage. They have brought tragedy and suffering to millions of firesides. I have great sympathy for those who honestly reach for short cuts to the immensity of our problems. While design of the structure of betterment for the common man must be inspired by the human heart, it can only be achieved by the intellect. It can only be builded by using the mould of justice, by laying brick upon brick from the materials of scientific research; by the painstaking sifting of truth from the collection of fact and experience. Any other mould is distorted; any other bricks are without straw; any other foundations are sand. That great structure of human progress can be built only by free men and women.

The gravest task which confronts the party is to regenerate these freedoms.

• • •

Fundamental American liberties are at stake. Is the Republican party ready for the issue? Are you willing to cast your all upon the issue, or would you falter and look back? Will you, for expediency's sake, also offer will-o'-the-wisps which beguile the people? Or have you determined to enter in a holy crusade for liberty which shall determine the future and the perpetuity for a nation of free men? That star shell fired today over the no man's land of world despair would illuminate the world with hope.

Questions

1. Why does Hoover believe that the future of freedom is at stake in the election of 1936?

2. How does his definition of freedom differ from that of Roosevelt?

139. Norman Cousins, "Will Women Lose Their Jobs?" (1939)

Source: Norman Cousins, "Will Women Lose Their Jobs?" Current History and Forum *Vol. 51 (September 1939), pp. 14–18, 63.*

Mass unemployment during the 1930s persuaded many Americans that women were taking jobs that would otherwise go to men. The federal government prohibited both members of a married couple from holding government jobs and many states and localities prohibited the hiring of women whose husbands earned a "living wage." In the excerpt that follows, the writer Norman Cousins commented on the movement to reduce or eliminate women's presence in the workforce and the various arguments, economic and moral, that lay behind it.

HERE IS THE latest depression cure-all, results guaranteed by its supporters:

"There are approximately 10,000,000 people out of work in the United States today. There are also 10,000,000 or more women, married and single, who are job-holders. Simply fire the women, who shouldn't be working anyway, and hire the men. Presto! No unemployment. No relief rolls. No depression."

This is the general idea behind the greatest assault on women's rights in two decades. Its supporters include not only the something-for-nothing groups which can always be depended upon to support chain-letter movements and share-the-wealth plans, but a large section of public opinion—as yet unacquainted with all the facts—which finds it hard to resist the supposed logic of millions of unemployed men replacing millions of employed women. Impetus to the drive—at least psychologically—is lent by the fact that the payrolls of many communities and private organizations are open only to males.

The first move toward the complete defeminizing of public and private jobs is discrimination against the married woman. Having thus inserted its foot in the door, the oust-women campaign seeks eventually to enter and hang up the verboten [German for "forbidden"] sign to all women, married or single, employed or seeking employment....

Of such concern is this trend to the nation's women leaders that it has been called the greatest issue to affect women since their victorious fight for suffrage. In its recent convention at Kansas City, the National Federation of Business and Professional Women's Clubs announced a frontal attack on what it considers the most serious problem it has faced in twenty years. In the eyes of Federation leaders the legislation already introduced is a portent of even more widespread attacks to come....

There are, of course, many familiar "moral" arguments against the working wife: woman's place is in the home, the management of which is enough work for any person; her first allegiance is to the bearing and raising of children; there is a direct relationship between the increase of women in business and the declining birth rate....

The Women's Bureau of the Department of Labor reports that in recent years the majority of married women at work have been working not because of a desire for a career or for economic independence but because of the need to provide or supplement the family income....

Analysis of these figures prompts the Department of Labor to point out that competition in industry is between one man and another, rather than between men and women. At most, not more than 1,000,000 jobs now held by women could pass to men. And of the 3,000,000-odd jobs held by women who admittedly are married, probably no more than 300,000 could be satisfactorily or willingly filled by males. This would "create" new jobs for only 3 per cent of the men now out of work.

Fundamentally, the unemployment of men is not caused by women who hold jobs but by the infirmities of the economic structure itself. Nor is the depression an affliction visited exclusively upon the male; the woman must bear her part of the burden, as more than 2,000,000 unemployed women can attest....

In answer to all of which the oust-women-from-jobs group may say that, yes, we are living in changing times and that, indeed, this is an emergency. And that, they may add, is precisely why extreme measures are needed and justified. Millions of men, many of them with families, are out of work. Most of them would be satisfied with salaries now paid to women. The ouster should begin with the working married woman because she should be dependent upon the man. After that, single women should be withdrawn from jobs. And who will look after them? Well, someone will; someone always does. Besides, unemployment with women is a matter of relative hardship at worst. But with men—especially family men—the hardship is absolute and complete. The state should have the right to step in and, for the greater benefit of all, say who shall work and who shall not.

An intriguing but hardly a practical thought. Because the more you study the figures of the various occupations which would be involved in the taking over of women's jobs by men, the more preposterous the scheme becomes. Imagine an average day in an America without working women:

John Citizen arrives at his office to be greeted by a male receptionist, a male switchboard operator and a male private secretary who opens his mail, arranges his appointments and takes dictation. At lunch his favorite waitress is missing, her place taken by a young man. At three o'clock he visits his dentist and is greeted by a male nurse. At four-thirty Mrs. Citizen calls to complain about Harry, who has taken the place of the part-time maid, and who refuses to wash the baby's clothes.

At the dinner table, Mary, who has just entered kindergarten, complains about Mr. Mann, the new teacher. Mrs. Citizen resents the personal questions asked by the new male salesclerk when she went shopping for underwear. She also resents the husky baritone voice that moans "Number, please," every time she picks up the phone.

Ridiculous? Certainly. But this is what a general purge of all women in industry would mean. It is impossible to carry through a large-scale replacement of one large bloc of labor for another unless there is an identity of functions all along the line. Approximately 3,500,000 men out of work are manual laborers. Which places vacated by women can they take? Approximately 3,100,000 women are employed as domestics. Which men want to take their places? There are about 920,000 salesgirls, whose replacement by men in most cases would be ludicrous....

But even outside the economic sphere, arguments against the working wife reveal weakness. There is much talk about the mother's place in the home, very little about the fact that the home has changed. Housekeeping for the average family today is no longer a full-time job. We are no longer living in the days when families numbered a dozen or more, and, what with cooking, baking, canning, washing, spinning, sewing and mending, woman's work was never done. The average American family today numbers three children or less, who are away from home at least five hours a day. Inexpensive, modern gadgets simplify what were once long, tedious household tasks. In short, the home has changed from a producing to a consuming unit.

This change is reflected not only in employment of married women but in the growth of social and church work, and in the spread of adult education, of culture and entertainment groups. In these circumstances, it is difficult to blame the married woman who is not content to remain a semi-idle dependent, but who seeks in business an outlet for her talents and energies. Dr. Richard Cabot, of Boston, recently noted that many of his nervous patients were women suffering for want of serious occupational interest.

Nazi Germany thought it could casually disregard these important questions when it decided to oust its 900,000 women workers from industrial and governmental life. For years Germany had been looked upon as the foremost example of a nation in which, to the benefit of the state, equal rights for women were scrupulously upheld. The Nazi regime waved the women out of their jobs and herded them back to the home, where they were told to bear children.

However as Clifford Kirkpatrick revealed in *Nazi Germany: Its*

Women and Family Life, the Nazi conception of woman as a biological instrument soon changed when it was realized that no such large bloc of labor could be displaced—or even replaced—without severely upsetting the national economy. "The 'sacred' mothers went back to the machine," observed Dr. Kirkpatrick, "and the employment of women even increased." ...

... [I]n the final analysis this question of women and jobs will be fought out on the issue of equal rights and opportunities for men and women alike.

Questions

1. Why does Cousins consider the effort to replace employed women with men "the greatest assault on women's rights in two decades"?

2. Why does he consider the proposal impractical?

140. Frank H. Hill on the Indian New Deal (1935)

Source: Frank E. Hill, "A New Pattern of Life for the Indian," New York Times Magazine (July 14, 1935), pp. 10, 22.

The New Deal marked the most radical shift in Indian policy in the nation's history. Under Commissioner of Indian Affairs John Collier, the administration launched an "Indian New Deal," which ended the policy of forced assimilation and allowed Indians unprecedented cultural autonomy. It replaced boarding schools meant to eradicate the tribal heritage of Indian children with schools on reservations and dramatically increased spending on Indian health. Federal authorities once again recognized Indians' right to govern their own affairs.

In 1935, the journalist Frank E. Hill presented a glowing description of the Indian New Deal among the Navajo, the nation's largest tribe. He stressed the benefits of the new policy for Indians, but did not mention that the Navajo strongly protested against a federal soil conservation program that required them to reduce their herds of livestock—an indication that their sovereignty was far from absolute.

MORE THAN A mile above the sea level, on a plateau of the American Southwest, two hundred and fifty men are building a new capitol. It is not the capitol of a State. Its stone walls rise in shapes that are strange to most Americans; its name—Nee Alneeng—falls with a strange accent. Nee Alneeng belongs to a world far from Manhattan and Main Street. It is an Indian world, and the capitol belongs to the Navajo, now the largest of the North American tribes.

This little centre is symbolic of a new way of life among the Navajo: in fact, a new way of life for the 340,000 Indians of the United States. A year ago the Wheeler-Howard Act gave to the tribes the right to decide whether they would accept important privileges in education, self-determination and self-government. A popular vote was asked; the essential question was: "Do you want to help save yourselves?" . . .

Thus the Wheeler-Howard Act embodies an Indian policy far different from that pursued in the past. The Federal Government could have conferred self-government upon the American Indian without asking him if he wanted it. To understand why he was asked, one must take a brief but discriminating glance at American history as it has affected the Red man. . . .

The third stage may be said to have begun with the growing conviction among thoughtful Americans that Indian life had latent strength and important cultural values and that the Indian if given the right opportunities could do what the government had failed to do: he could arrange a place for himself and his customs in this modern America. The appointment of John Collier as Commissioner of Indian Affairs in April, 1933, brought into power a leader of this trend of opinion. . . .

Mr. Collier, slight, almost scholarly in appearance, at his desk in

Washington describes what the administration is trying to do for the Indian and why he believes the new policy to be enlightened.

"In the past," he says, "the government tried to encourage economic independence and initiative by the allotment system, giving each Indian a portion of land and the right to dispose of it. As a result, of the 138,000,000 acres which Indians possessed in 1887 they have lost all but 47,000,000 acres, and the lost area includes the land that was the most valuable. Further, the government sought to give the Indian the schooling of the whites, teaching him to despise his old customs and habits as barbaric. Through this experiment the Indian lost much of his understanding of his own culture and received no usable substitute. In many areas such efforts to change the Indian have broken him economically and spiritually.

"We have proposed in opposition to such a policy to recognize and respect the Indian as he is. We think he must be so accepted before he can be assisted to become something else, if that is desirable. It is objected that we are proposing to make a 'blanket Indian' of him again. That is nonsense. But if he happens to be a blanket Indian we think he should not be ashamed of it. We believe further that while he needs protection and assistance in important ways, these aids should be extended with the idea of enabling him to help himself. We are sure that he can and will do this. But he must have the opportunity to do it in his own way. This is what we have been trying to extend to him. It is an opportunity that he has not had since he entered the reservations, where he has been discouraged from thinking and acting for himself.

"... Our design is to plow up the Indian soul, to make the Indian again the master of his own mind. If this fails, everything fails; if it succeeds, we believe the Indian will do the rest." ...

The people whom the commissioner is trying to reanimate, and to incite to this crusade for self-survival, are in one sense heterogeneous. There is no typical Indian but rather a hundred different types. These are scattered. The 230 tribes that comprise the race are to be found here and there in twenty-two States. They are of many different stocks physically and they speak dozens of different languages.

Their cultures vary, and so does the degree to which they have adopted the white man's ways....

Underneath all their differences lie identical, unifying instincts, habits, aptitudes and spiritual feelings. Fine qualities are to be observed in almost any Indian group: artistic cleverness, tenacity, courage, dignity, and a decent pride. Under the parochial control of the past, with its effort to make the Indian a white man, these qualities have shown but little. They have come out best where the Indian, as in the Southwest, has lived his own life....

The new policy has already started a renaissance in Indian arts. Young Indians are painting murals on the walls of school houses and government buildings. They are studying the ancient pottery of their tribes in museums, and devising new designs and textures in their workshops. The young people are flocking to the ceremonial dances, which for a time they had avoided. This cultural revival goes hand in hand with an interest in self-government and economic independence. In Mr. Collier's opinion, it is equally valuable.

"The Indian," he says, "can use white technologies and remain an Indian. Modernity and white Americanism are not identical. If the Indian life is a good life, then we should be proud and glad to have this different and native culture going on by the side of ours. Anything less than to let Indian culture live on would be a crime against the earth itself. The destruction of a pueblo is a barbarous thing. America is coming to understand this, and to know that in helping the Indian to save himself we are helping to save something that is precious to us as well as to him."

Questions

1. How does Hill describe the motivations for the Indian New Deal?

2. What benefits does he believe the new federal policy brings to the Indians?

141. W. E. B. Du Bois, "A Negro Nation within a Nation" (1935)

Source: W. E. B. Du Bois, "A Negro Nation within a Nation," Current History *(June 1935), pp. 265–70. Reprinted with permission from* Current History *magazine (June 1935). © 2007 Current History, Inc.*

As the "last hired and first fired," African-Americans were hit hardest by the Depression. Half of the families in Harlem received public assistance during the 1930s. But many New Deal programs were either administered in an extremely discriminatory manner, or like Social Security, excluded most blacks from benefits at the insistence of white supremacist southern representatives who controlled key committees in Congress.

During the 1930s, W. E. B. Du Bois abandoned his earlier goal of racial integration as unrealistic for the foreseeable future. He now concluded that blacks must recognize themselves as "a nation within a nation." He called on blacks to organize for economic survival by building an independent, cooperative economy within their segregated communities, and gain control of their own separate schools. Du Bois's shifting position illustrated how the Depression had propelled economic survival to the top of the black agenda and how, despite the social changes of the 1930s, the goal of racial integration remained as remote as ever.

IN THIS BROADER and more intelligent democracy we can hope for progressive softening of the asperities and anomalies of race prejudice, but we cannot hope for its early and complete disappearance. Above all, the doubt, deep-planted in the American mind, as to the Negro's ability and efficiency as worker, artisan and administrator will fade but slowly. Thus, with increased democratic control of industry and capital, the place of the Negro will be increasingly a matter of human choice, of willingness to recognize ability across the barriers of race, of putting fit Negroes in places of power and authority by public opinion. At present, on the railroads, in manufacturing, in the telephone, telegraph and radio business, and in the larger divisions of trade, it is only under exceptional circumstances that any Negro no matter what his ability, gets an opportunity for position and power. Only in those lines where individual enterprise still counts, as in some of the professions, in a few of the trades, in a few branches of retail business and in artistic careers, can the Negro expect a narrow opening.

Negroes and other colored folk nevertheless, exist in larger and growing numbers. Slavery, prostitution to white men, theft of their labor and goods have not killed them and cannot kill them. They are growing in intelligence and dissatisfaction. They occupy strategic positions, within nations and beside nations, amid valuable raw material and on the highways of future expansion. They will survive, but on what terms and conditions? On this point a new school of Negro thought is arising. It believes in the ultimate uniting of mankind and in a unified American nation, with economic classes and racial barriers leveled, but it believes this is an ideal and is to be realized only by such intensified class and race consciousness as will bring irresistible force rather than mere humanitarian appeals to bear on the motives and actions of men.

The peculiar position of Negroes in America offers an opportunity. Negroes today cast probably 2,000,000 votes in a total of 40,000,000, and their vote will increase. This gives them, particularly in northern cities, and at critical times, a chance to hold a very considerable balance of power, and the mere threat of this being used intelligently and with determination may often mean much. The consuming power of 2,800,000 Negro families has recently been estimated at $166,000,000 a month—a tremendous power when intelligently directed. Their manpower as laborers probably equals that of Mexico or Yugoslavia. Their illiteracy is much lower than that of Spain or Italy. Their estimated per capita wealth about equals that of Japan.

For a nation with this start in culture and efficiency to sit down and await the salvation of a white God is idiotic. With the use of their political power, their power as consumers, and their brainpower, added to that chance of personal appeal which proximity and neighborhood always give to human beings, Negroes can develop in the United States an economic nation within a nation, able to work through inner cooperation, to found its own institutions, to educate its genius, and at the same time, without mob violence or extremes of race hatred, to keep in helpful touch and cooperate with the mass of the nation. This has happened more often than most people realize, in the case of groups not so obviously separated from the mass of people as are American Negroes. It must happen in our case, or there is no hope for the Negro in America.

Any movement toward such a program is today hindered by the absurd Negro philosophy of Scatter, Suppress, Wait, Escape. There are even many of our educated young leaders who think that because the Negro problem is not in evidence where there are few or no Negroes, this indicates a way out! They think that the problem of race can be settled by ignoring it and suppressing all reference to it. They think that we have only to wait in silence for the white people to settle the problem for us; and finally and predominantly, they think that the problem of twelve million Negro people, mostly poor, ignorant workers, is going to be settled by having their more educated and wealthy classes gradually and continually escape from their race into the mass of the American people, leaving the rest to sink, suffer and die.

Proponents of this program claim, with much reason, that the plight of the masses is not the fault of the emerging classes. For the slavery and exploitation that reduced Negroes to their present level or at any rate hindered them from rising, the white world is to blame. Since the age-long process of raising a group is through the escape of its upper class into welcome fellowship with risen peoples, the Negro intelligentsia would submerge itself if it bent its back to the task of lifting the mass of people. There is logic in this answer, but futile logic.

If the leading Negro classes cannot assume and bear the uplift of their own proletariat, they are doomed for all time. It is not a case of ethics; it is a plain case of necessity. The method by which this may be done is, first, for the American Negro to achieve a new economic solidarity.

There exists today a chance for the Negroes to organize a cooperative state within their own group. By letting Negro farmers feed Negro artisans, and Negro technicians guide Negro home industries, and Negro thinkers plan this integration of cooperation, while Negro artists dramatize and beautify the struggle, economic independence can be achieved. To doubt that this is possible is to doubt the essential humanity and the quality of brains of the American Negro.

No sooner is this proposed than a great fear sweeps over older Negroes. They cry "No segregation"—no further yielding to prejudice and race separation. Yet any planning for the benefit of American Negroes on the part of a Negro intelligentsia is going to involve organized and deliberate self-segregation. There are plenty of people in the United States who would be only too willing to use such a plan as a way to increase existing legal and customary segregation between the races. This threat which many Negroes see is no mere mirage. What of it? It must be faced.

If the economic and cultural salvation of the American Negro calls for an increase in segregation and prejudice, then that must come. American Negroes must plan for their economic future and the social survival of their fellows in the firm belief that this means in a real sense the survival of colored folk in the world and the building of a full humanity instead of a petty white tyranny. Control of their own education, which is the logical and inevitable end of separate schools, would not be an unmixed ill; it might prove a supreme good. Negro schools once meant poor schools. They need not today; they must not tomorrow. Separate Negro sections will increase race antagonism, but they will also increase economic cooperation, organized self-defense and necessary self-confidence.

Questions

1. Why does Du Bois believe that the situation of American blacks was as "critical" in the 1930s as at any previous point in the nation's past?

2. Why does he feel that economic "self-segregation" offers a more viable strategy for blacks than continued pressure for racial integration.

CHAPTER 22

Fighting for the Four Freedoms: World War II, 1941–1945

142. Franklin D. Roosevelt on the Four Freedoms (1941)

Source: Annual Message to Congress, January 6, 1941, in Samuel I. Rosenman, ed., The Public Papers and Addresses of Franklin Delano Roosevelt *(New York, 1938–1950), Vol. 9, p. 672.*

As in other American wars, freedom became a rallying cry and language of national unity during World War II. Even before the United States entered the war President Roosevelt outlined to Congress his vision of a future world order founded on the "essential human freedoms": freedom of speech, freedom of worship, freedom from want, and freedom from fear. The Four Freedoms became Roosevelt's favorite statement of Allied aims. Freedom from fear meant not only a longing for peace but a more general desire for security in a world that appeared to be out of control. Freedom of speech and religion scarcely required detailed explanation. Freedom from want was the most controversial of the four. To FDR, it meant economic security; to his critics, the phrase conjured up images of socialism or of Americans living off the largesse of the government.

IN THE FUTURE days, which we seek to make secure, we look forward to a world founded upon four essential human freedoms.

The first is freedom of speech and expression—everywhere in the world.

The second is freedom of every person to worship God in his own way—everywhere in the world.

The third is freedom from want—which, translated into world terms, means economic understandings which will secure to every nation a healthy peacetime life for its inhabitants—everywhere in the world.

The fourth is freedom from fear—which, translated into world terms, means a world-wide reduction of armaments to such a point and in such a thorough fashion that no nation will be in a position to commit an act of physical aggression against any neighbor—anywhere in the world.

That is no vision of a distant millennium. It is a definite basis for a kind of world attainable in our own time and generation. That kind of world is the very antithesis of the so-called new order of tyranny which the dictators seek to create with the crash of a bomb.

To that new order we oppose the greater conception—the moral order. A good society is able to face schemes of world domination and foreign revolutions alike without fear.

Since the beginning of our American history, we have been engaged in change—in a perpetual peaceful revolution—a revolution which goes on steadily, quietly adjusting itself to changing conditions—without the concentration camp or the quick-lime in the ditch. The world order which we seek is the cooperation of free countries, working together in a friendly, civilized society.

This nation has placed its destiny in the hands and heads and hearts of its millions of free men and women; and its faith in freedom under the guidance of God. Freedom means the supremacy of human rights everywhere. Our support goes to those who struggle to gain those rights or keep them. Our strength is our unity of purpose.

To that high concept there can be no end save victory.

Questions

1. How do the Four Freedoms reflect Americans' experiences during the 1930s?

2. Roosevelt himself added the phrase "everywhere in the world" to the first draft of this speech. Why do you think he did so?

143. Henry R. Luce, *The American Century* (1941)

Source: Henry R. Luce, The American Century, *Copyright © 1941, pp. 22–31.*

Even before the United States entered World War II, it had become clear that the nation would play a far more active role in international affairs than in the past. One of the most celebrated blueprints for the postwar world was written in 1941 by Henry Luce, the publisher of *Life* and *Time* magazines. In *The American Century*, Luce sought to mobilize the American people for both the coming war and an era of postwar world leadership. Americans, Luce's book insisted, must embrace the role history had thrust upon them as the world's most powerful nation. After the war, American power and American values would underpin a previously unimaginable prosperity—"the abundant life," Luce called it—produced by free economic enterprise.

Luce's essay anticipated important aspects of the postwar world. But some saw the term "American Century" as a call not for future international cooperation, but for an American empire.

IN THE FIELD of national policy, the fundamental trouble with America has been, and is, that whereas their nation became in the Twentieth Century the most powerful and the most vital nation in the world, nevertheless Americans were unable to accommodate themselves spiritually and practically to that fact. Hence they have failed to play their part as a world power—a failure which has had disastrous consequences for themselves and for all mankind. And the cure is this: to accept wholeheartedly our duty and our opportunity as the most powerful and vital nation in the world and in consequence to exert upon the world the full impact of our influence, for such purposes as we see fit and by such means as we see fit.

• • •

This Twentieth Century is baffling, difficult, paradoxical, revolutionary. But by now, at the cost of much pain and many hopes deferred, we know a good deal about it. And we ought to accommodate our outlook to this knowledge so dearly bought. For example, any true conception of our world of the Twentieth Century must surely include a vivid awareness of at least these four propositions.

First: our world of 2,000,000,000 human beings is for the first time in history one world, fundamentally indivisible. Second: modern man hates war and feels intuitively that, in its present scale and frequency, it may even be fatal to his species. Third: our world, again for the first time in human history, is capable of producing all the material needs of the entire human family. Fourth: the world of the Twentieth Century, if it is to come to life in any nobility of health and vigor, must be to a significant degree an American Century.

As to the first and second: in postulating the indivisibility of the contemporary world, one does not necessarily imagine that anything like a world state—a parliament of men—must be brought about in this century. Nor need we assume that war can be abolished. All that it is necessary to feel—and to feel deeply—is that terrific forces of magnetic attraction and repulsion will operate as between every large group of human beings on this planet. Large sections of the human family may be effectively organized into opposition to each other. Tyrannies may require a large amount of living space. But Freedom requires and will require far greater living space than Tyranny. Peace cannot endure unless it prevails over a very large part of the world. Justice will come near to losing all meaning in the minds of men unless Justice can have approximately the same fundamental meanings in many lands and among many peoples.

As to the third point—the promise of adequate production for all mankind, the "more abundant life"—be it noted that this is characteristically an American promise. It is a promise easily made, here and elsewhere, by demagogues and proponents of all manner of slick schemes and "planned economies." What we must insist on is that the abundant life is predicated on Freedom—on the Freedom which has created its possibility—on a vision of Freedom under Law. Without Freedom, there will be no abundant life. With Freedom, there can be.

And finally there is the belief—shared let us remember by most men living—that the Twentieth Century must be to a significant degree an American Century. This knowledge calls us to action now.

• • •

As America enters dynamically upon the world scene, we need most of all to seek and to bring forth a vision of America as a world power which is authentically American and which can inspire us to live and work and fight with vigor and enthusiasm. And as we come now to the great test, it may yet turn out that in all our trials and tribulations of spirit during the first part of this century we as a people have been painfully apprehending the meaning of our time and now in this moment of testing there may come clear at last the vision which will guide us to the authentic creation of the Twentieth Century—our Century.

Questions

1. What does Luce mean when he writes, "Freedom requires and will require far greater living space than Tyranny"?

2. How do you interpret the phrase, "an American Century"?

144. Henry A. Wallace on "The Century of the Common Man" (1942)

Source: "Speech at the Free World Association, May 8, 1942," in Henry A. Wallace, The Price of Free World Victory, ed. Russell Lord (New York, 1942), pp. 11–17.

Many Americans who deplored the bombastic tone of Luce's call for an American Century welcomed the response offered by Vice President Henry Wallace. In a 1942 speech, Wallace outlined a different postwar vision. In contrast to Luce's American Century, a world of business dominance no less than American power, Wallace predicted that the war would usher in a "century of the common man." The "march of freedom," said Wallace, would continue in the postwar world. That world, however, would be marked by international cooperation, not any single power's rule. Governments acting to "humanize" capitalism and redistribute economic resources would eliminate hunger, illiteracy, and poverty.

Luce and Wallace both invoked the idea of freedom. Luce offered a confident vision of worldwide free enterprise, while Wallace anticipated a global New Deal. But they had one thing in common—a new conception of America's role in the world, tied to continued international involvement, the promise of economic abundance, and the idea that the American experience should serve as a model for all other nations.

―――

THE MARCH OF freedom of the past 150 years has been a long-drawn-out people's revolution. In this Great Revolution of the people, there were the American Revolution of 1775, the French Revolution of 1792, the Latin-American revolutions of the Bolivarian era, the German Revolution of 1848, and the Russian Revolution of 1918. Each spoke for the common man in terms of blood on the battlefield. Some went to excess. But the significant thing is that the people groped their way to the light. More of them learned to think and work together.

• • •

The people are on the march toward even fuller freedom than the most fortunate peoples of the earth have hitherto enjoyed. No Nazi counter-revolution will stop it. The common man will smoke the Hitler stooges out into the open in the United States, in Latin America, and in India. He will destroy their influence. No Lavals, no Mussolinis will be tolerated in a Free World.

The people in their millennial and revolutionary march toward manifesting here on earth the dignity that is in every human soul, holds as its credo the Four Freedoms enunciated by President Roosevelt in his message to Congress on January 6, 1941. These Four Freedoms are the very core of the revolution for which the United States have taken their stand. We who live in the United States may think there is nothing very revolutionary about freedom of religion, freedom of expression, and freedom from the fear of secret police. But when we begin to think about the significance of freedom from want for the average man, then we know that the revolution of the past 150 years has not been completed, either here in the United States or in any other nation in the world. We know that this revolution can not stop until freedom from want has actually been attained.

• • •

Some have spoken of the "American Century." I say that the century on which we are entering—the century which will come of this war—can be and must be the century of the common man. Perhaps it will be America's opportunity to suggest the freedoms and duties by which the common man must live. Everywhere the common man must learn to build his own industries with his own hands in a practical fashion. Everywhere the common man must learn to increase his productivity so that he and his children can eventually pay to the world community all that they have received. No nation will have the God-given right to exploit other nations. Older nations will have the privilege to help younger nations get started on the path to industrialization, but there must be neither military nor economic imperialism. The methods of the nineteenth century will not work in the people's century which is now about to begin. India,

China, and Latin America have a tremendous stake in the people's century. As their masses learn to read and write, and as they become productive mechanics, their standard of living will double and treble. Modern science, when devoted whole-heartedly to the general welfare, has in it potentialities of which we do not yet dream.

• • •

When the time of peace comes, the citizen will again have a duty, the supreme duty of sacrificing the lesser interest for the greater interest of the general welfare. Those who write the peace must think of the whole world. There can be no privileged peoples. We ourselves in the United States are no more a master race than the Nazis. And we can not perpetuate economic warfare without planting the seeds of military warfare. We must use our power at the peace table to build an economic peace that is just, charitable and enduring.

Questions

1. How does Wallace's vision of the postwar world differ from Henry Luce's?

2. What does Wallace seem to refer to when he declares that there will be "no privileged peoples" in the postwar world?

145. F. A. Hayek, *The Road to Serfdom* (1944)

Source: F. A. Hayek, The Road to Serfdom, *pp. 16–30. Copyright © 1944 The University of Chicago Press. Reprinted by permission of The University of Chicago Press and the Estate of F. A. Hayek.*

Henry Wallace's description of the world after the war seemed to suggest that government planning was the key to economic abundance. But, as the war drew to a close, a surprise best-seller by Friedrich A. Hayek, a previously obscure Austrian-born economist, offered a vigorous argument that economic planning endangered freedom. In *The Road to Serfdom*, Hayek claimed that even the best-intentioned government efforts to direct the economy posed a threat to individual liberty. He condemned Western political and intellectual leaders for abandoning the traditional "liberal" idea of limited government in favor of an illusory definition of freedom as government action to plan the economy and redistribute resources to the less fortunate. Coming at a time when the miracles of war production had reinvigorated the reputation of capitalism, seriously tarnished by the Great Depression, Hayek offered a new intellectual justification for opponents of active government. In equating fascism, socialism, and the New Deal and identifying economic planning with a loss of freedom, he helped lay the foundation for the rise of modern conservatism and a revival of laissez-faire economic thought.

FOR AT LEAST twenty-five years before the specter of totalitarianism became a real threat, we had progressively been moving away from the basic ideas on which Western civilization has been built. That this movement on which we have entered with such high hopes and ambitions should have brought us face to face with the totalitarian horror has come as a profound shock to this generation, which still refuses to connect the two facts. Yet this development merely confirms the warnings of the fathers of the liberal philosophy which we still profess. We have progressively abandoned that freedom in economic affairs without which personal and political freedom has never existed in the past. Although we had been warned by some of the greatest political thinkers of the nineteenth century, by De Tocqueville and Lord Acton, that socialism means slavery, we have steadily moved in the direction of socialism. And now that we have seen a new form of slavery arise before our eyes, we have so completely forgotten the warning that it scarcely occurs to us that the two things may be connected.

• • •

Because of the growing impatience with the slow advance of liberal policy, the just irritation with those who used liberal phraseology in defense of antisocial privileges, and the boundless ambition seemingly justified by the material improvements already achieved, it came to pass that toward the turn of the century the belief in the basic tenets of liberalism was more and more relinquished. What had been achieved came to be regarded as a secure and imperishable possession, acquired once and for all. The eyes of the people became fixed on the new demands, the rapid satisfaction of which seemed to be barred by the adherence to the old principles. It became more and more widely accepted that further advance could be expected not along the old lines within the general framework which had made past progress possible but only by a complete remodeling of society. It was no longer a question of adding to or improving the existing machinery but of completely scrapping and replacing it. And, as the hope of the new generation came to be centered on something completely new, interest in and understanding of the functioning of the existing society rapidly declined; and, with the decline of the understanding of the way in which the free system worked, our awareness of what depended on its existence also decreased.

This is not the place to discuss how this change in outlook was fostered by the uncritical transfer to the problem of society of habits of thought engendered by the preoccupation with technological problems, the habits of thought of the natural scientist and the engineer, and how these at the same time tended to discredit the results of the past study of society which did not conform to their prejudices and to impose ideals of organization on a sphere to which they are not appropriate. All we are here concerned to show is how completely, though gradually and by almost imperceptible steps, our attitude toward society has changed. What at every stage of this process of change had appeared a difference of degree only has in its cumulative effect already brought about a fundamental difference between the older liberal attitude toward society and the present approach to social problems. The change amounts to a complete reversal of the trend we have sketched, an entire abandonment of the individualist tradition which has created Western civilization.

According to the views now dominant, the question is no longer how we can make the best use of the spontaneous forces found in a free society. We have in effect undertaken to dispense with the forces which produced unforeseen results and to replace the impersonal and anonymous mechanism of the market by collective and "conscious" direction of all social forces to deliberately chosen goals. The difference cannot be better illustrated than by the extreme position taken in a widely acclaimed book on whose program of so-called "planning for freedom" we shall have to comment yet more than once. "We have never had to set up and direct," writes Dr. Karl Mannheim, "the entire system of nature as we are forced to do today with society. . . . Mankind is tending more and more to regulate the whole of its social life, although it has never attempted to create a second nature."

• • •

The subtle change in meaning to which the word "freedom" was subjected in order that this argument should sound plausible is important. To the great apostles of political freedom the word had meant freedom from coercion, freedom from the arbitrary power of other men, release from the ties which left the individual no choice but obedience to the orders of a superior to whom he was attached. The new freedom promised, however, was to be freedom from necessity, release from the compulsion of the circumstances which inevitably limit the range of choice of all of us, although for some very much more than for others. Before man could be truly free, the "despotism of physical want" had to be broken, the "restraints of the economic system" relaxed.

Freedom in this sense is, of course, merely another name for power or wealth. Yet, although the promises of this new freedom were often coupled with irresponsible promises of a great increase in material wealth in a socialist society, it was not from such an absolute conquest of the niggardliness of nature that economic freedom was expected. What the promise really amounted to was that the great existing disparities in the range of choice of different people were to disappear. The demand for the new freedom was thus only another name for the old demand for an equal distribution of wealth. But the new name gave the socialists another word in common with the liberals, and they exploited it to the full. And, although the word was used in a different sense by the two groups, few people noticed this and still fewer asked themselves whether the two kinds of freedom promised could really be combined.

• • •

Questions

1. What does Hayek see as the essence of freedom?

2. How does his outlook differ from President Roosevelt's idea of freedom from want?

146. World War II and Mexican-Americans (1945)

Source: "Editorial," LULAC News. Vol. 12 (October 1945), pp. 5–6.

Founded in 1929, the League of United Latin American Citizens (LULAC) campaigned for equal treatment for Americans of Latino descent and their full integration into American life. Some half a million Mexican-Americans served in the armed forces during World War II, but Latinos continued to face widespread discrimination. An editorial in the LULAC newsletter soon after the war ended drew upon military service to condemn anti-Latino prejudice. Its aggressive language reflected the rising demand for equal rights sparked by the war experience among many minority groups.

"WE DO NOT serve Mexicans here." "You will have to get out as no Mexicans are allowed." "Your uniform and service ribbons mean nothing here. We still do not allow Mexicans."

These, and many other stronger-worded ones, are the embarrassing and humiliating retorts given our returning veterans of Latin American descent and their families. They may all be worded differently, and whereas some are toned with hate and loathness while others are toned with sympathy and remorse, still the implication remains that these so-called "Mexicans" are considered unworthy of equality, regardless of birthright or service. This situation is ironic indeed, in view of the fact that these same "Mexicans" have just finished helping this country to defeat countries to the east and west who would impose upon the world a superior people, a superior culture.

Why this hate, this prejudice, this tendency to discriminate against a people whose only fault seems to be that they are heirs of a culture older than any known "American Culture," to find themselves a part of a land and people they have helped to build and to defend, to find themselves a part of a minority group whose acquired passive nature keeps them from boldly demanding those rights and privileges which are rightfully theirs? Can it be the result of difference in race, nationality, language, loyalty, intelligence or ability?

There is no difference in race. Latin Americans, or so-called "Mexicans," are Caucasian or white. There are only three races: the Caucasian, the Negroid, and the Mongoloid. Racial characteristics place the Latin American among the white. Who dares contradict nature? There is no difference in nationality. These "Mexicans" were born and bred in this country and are just as American as Jones or Smith. In fact, the ancestors of these "Mexicans" were here before those of Jones or Smith decided to take up abode. Difference in language? No. These "Mexicans" speak English. Accented, perhaps, in some cases, but English all over the United States seems to be accented. That these "Mexicans" can speak Spanish is not a detriment, it is an asset. After all, there are not too many people in this country who can boast a knowledge of the most widely spoken languages in the world. Difference in loyalty? How can that be when all revere the same stars and stripes, when they don the same service uniforms for the same principles? Difference in intelligence and ability? Impossible. . . .

We could go on and on naming erroneously imagined differences to be used as a basis for this hate and find each one false. This condition is not a case of difference; it is a case of ignorance. Yes, ignorance. Odd indeed to find this banal state of mind in a country of such enlightment and progress. But then, ignorance is like a disease that is contagious, but contagious only for those who wish to suffer from it. Ignorance, bigotry, prejudice, and intolerance all down through the centuries have tried to crush intelligence with cruelty, reason with brutality, and spirituality with madness. This quartet of banalities constitutes the curse of the world. Ignorance is the parent of the other three.

Yes, ignorance broods hate and all its resultant actions of jealousy, misunderstandings, erroneous opinions, and premeditated feelings of discord and confusion. In this particular case of unjustified failure to foment a fraternal feeling between two groups of Americans, it is an ignorance of facts that poisons the atmosphere. An ignorance of the cultural contributions of Americans of Latin American descent to the still young American Culture; an ignorance of the blood, sweat, and efforts given to this country for its betterment; an ignorance of the sufferings withstood and the lives given to preserve this country free and independent through its various periods of strife and conflict; and finally, an ignorance of a sense of appreciation for a long, profitable, and loyal association with a group of Americans whose voice cries out in desperate supplication:

> We have proved ourselves true and loyal Americans by every trial and test that has confronted us; now give us social, political, and economic equality and the opportunity to practice and enjoy that equality. We ask for it not as a favor, but as a delegated right guaranteed by our Constitution, and as a reward for faithful service.

Questions

1. What are the implications of explaining prejudice and discrimination as arising from ignorance rather than economic self-interest?

2. Why does the editorial insist on identifying Latinos as white?

147. A. Philip Randolph, "Why We Should March" (1942)

Source: A. Philip Randolph, "Why We Should March," Survey Graphic, *Vol. 31 (November 1942), pp. 488–89.*

The war years witnessed the birth of the modern civil rights movement. Angered by the almost complete exclusion of African-Americans from jobs in the rapidly expanding war industries, black labor leader A. Philip Randolph, in July 1941, called for a March on Washington. Its demands included access to defense employment, an end to segregation, and a national antilynching law.

The prospect of thousands of angry blacks descending on Washington, remarked one official, "scared the government half to death." To persuade Randolph to call off the march, Roosevelt issued Executive Order 8802, which banned discrimination in defense jobs and established a Fair Employment Practices Commission (FEPC) to monitor compliance. This was the first federal agency since Reconstruction to campaign for equal opportunity for black Americans. In 1942, to prod the FEPC into action, Randolph repeated his call for mass protests. Randolph also played a key role in organizing the March on Washington of August 1963.

———

THOUGH I HAVE found no Negroes who want to see the United Nations lose this war, I have found many who, before the war ends, want to see the stuffing knocked out of white supremacy and of empire over subject peoples. American Negroes, involved as we are in the general issues of the conflict, are confronted not with a choice but with the challenge both to win democracy for ourselves at home and to help win the war for democracy the world over.

There is no escape from the horns of this dilemma. There ought not to be escape. For if the war for democracy is not won abroad, the fight for democracy cannot be won at home. If this war cannot be won for the white peoples, it will not be won for the darker races.

Conversely, if freedom and equality are not vouchsafed the peoples of color, the war for democracy will not be won. Unless this double-barreled thesis is accepted and applied, the darker races will never wholeheartedly fight for the victory of the United Nations. That is why those familiar with the thinking of the American Negro have sensed his lack of enthusiasm, whether among the educated or uneducated, rich or poor, professional or nonprofessional, religious or secular, rural or urban, north, south, east or west.

That is why questions are being raised by Negroes in church, labor union and fraternal society; in poolroom, barbershop, schoolroom, hospital, hair-dressing parlor; on college campus, railroad, and bus. One can hear such questions asked as these: What have Negroes to fight for? What's the difference between Hitler and that "cracker" Talmadge of Georgia? Why has a man got to be Jim-Crowed to die for democracy? If you haven't got democracy yourself, how can you carry it to somebody else?

What are the reasons for this state of mind? The answer is: discrimination, segregation, Jim Crow. Witness the navy, the army, the air corps; and also government services at Washington. In many parts of the South, Negroes in Uncle Sam's uniform are being put upon, mobbed, sometimes even shot down by civilian and military police, and on occasion lynched. Vested political interests in race prejudice are so deeply entrenched that to them winning the war against Hitler is secondary to preventing Negroes from winning democracy for themselves. This is worth many divisions to Hitler and Hirohito. While labor, business, and farm are subjected to ceilings and floors and not allowed to carry on as usual, these interests trade in the dangerous business of race hate as usual.

When the defense program began and billions of the taxpayers' money were appropriated for guns, ships, tanks and bombs, Negroes presented themselves for work only to be given the cold shoulder. North as well as South, and despite their qualifications, Negroes were denied skilled employment. Not until their wrath and indignation took the form of a proposed protest march on Washington, scheduled for July 1, 1941, did things begin to move in the form of defense jobs for Negroes. The march was postponed by the timely issuance (June 25, 1941) of the famous Executive Order No. 8802 by President Roosevelt. But this order and the President's Committee on Fair Employment Practice, established thereunder, have as yet only scratched the surface by way of eliminating discriminations on account of race or color in war industry. Both management and labor unions in too many places and in too many ways are still drawing the color line.

It is to meet this situation squarely with direct action that the March on Washington Movement launched its present program of protest mass meetings....

The March on Washington Movement is essentially a movement of the people. It is all Negro and pro-Negro, but not for that reason anti-white or anti-Semitic, or anti-Catholic, or anti-foreign, or anti-labor. Its major weapon is the non-violent demonstration of Negro mass power. Negro leadership has united back of its drive for jobs and justice....

By fighting for their rights now, American Negroes are helping to make America a moral and spiritual arsenal of democracy. Their fight against the poll tax, against lynch law, segregation, and Jim Crow, their fight for economic, political, and social equality, thus becomes part of the global war for freedom.

Questions

1. Why does Randolph view World War II as a "double-barreled" conflict?

2. What does Randolph see as the major violations of African-Americans' freedom?

148. Justice Robert A. Jackson, Dissent in *Korematsu v. United States* (1944)

Source: **Korematsu v. United States, *323 U.S. 214 (1944).***

Unlike in World War I, the federal government during the Second World War actively promoted a pluralist vision of the United States as a place where persons of all races, religions, and national origins could enjoy freedom equally. The great exception to this new emphasis on tolerance was the experience of Japanese-Americans. The military in February 1942 persuaded FDR to order the expulsion of all persons of Japanese descent from the West Coast. Authorities removed over 110,000 men, women, and children, nearly two thirds of them American citizens, to internment camps far from their homes.

In 1944, the Supreme Court denied the appeal of Fred Korematsu, who had been arrested for refusing to present himself for internment. Speaking for a 6–3 majority, Justice Hugo Black upheld the constitutionality of the internment policy, insisting that an order applying only to persons of Japanese descent was not based on race. As Justice Robert Jackson pointed out in his dissent, Korematsu was not accused of any crime. He condemned the majority for justifying a massive violation of civil liberties. In 1988, Congress apologized for internment and provided compensation to surviving victims.

KOREMATSU WAS BORN on our soil, of parents born in Japan. The Constitution makes him a citizen of the United States by nativity and a citizen of California by residence. No claim is made that he is not loyal to this country. There is no suggestion that apart from the matter involved here he is not law-abiding and well disposed. Korematsu, however, has been convicted of an act not commonly a crime. It consists merely of being present in the state whereof he is a citizen, near the place where he was born, and where all his life he has lived.

Even more unusual is the series of military orders which made this conduct a crime. They forbid such a one to remain, and they also

forbid him to leave. They were so drawn that the only way Korematsu could avoid violation was to give himself up to the military
authority. This meant submission to custody, examination, and
transportation out of the territory, to be followed by indeterminate
confinement in detention camps.

A citizen's presence in the locality, however, was made a crime
only if his parents were of Japanese birth. Had Korematsu been one
of four—the others being, say, a German alien enemy, an Italian
alien enemy, and a citizen of American-born ancestors convicted of
treason but out on parole—only Korematsu's presence would have
violated the order. The difference between their innocence and his
crime would result, not from anything he did, said, or thought different than they but only in that he was born of different racial
stock.

Now, if any fundamental assumption underlies our system, it is
that guilt is personal and not inheritable. Even if all of one's an-
tecedents had been convicted of treason, the Constitution forbids its
penalties to be visited upon him, for it provides that "no attainder of
treason shall work corruption of blood or forfeiture except during
the life of the person attained." But here is an attempt to make an
otherwise innocent act a crime merely because this prisoner is the
son of parents as to whom he had no choice and belongs to a race
from which there is no way to resign. If Congress in peacetime legislation should enact such a criminal law, I should suppose this Court
would refuse to enforce it.

But the "law" which this prisoner is convicted of disregarding is
not found in an act of Congress but in a military order. Neither the
act of Congress nor the executive order of the President, nor both
together, would afford a basis for this conviction. It rests on the orders of General DeWitt. And it is said that if the military commander
had reasonable military grounds for promulgating the orders, they
are constitutional and become law, and the Court is required to enforce them. There are several reasons why I cannot subscribe to this
doctrine.

It would be impracticable and dangerous idealism to expect or insist that each specific military command in an area of probable operations will conform to conventional tests of constitutionality. When an area is so beset that it must be put under military control at all, the paramount consideration is that its measures be successful rather than legal. The armed services must protect a society, not merely its Constitution. The very essence of the military job is to marshal physical force, to remove every obstacle to its effectiveness, to give it every strategic advantage. Defense measures will not, and often should not, be held within the limits that bind civil authority in peace. No court can require such a commander in such circumstances to act as a reasonable man; he may be unreasonably cautious and exacting. Perhaps he should be. But a commander in temporarily focusing the life of a community on defense is carrying out a military program; he is not making law in the sense the courts know the term. He issues orders, and they may have a certain authority as military commands, although they may be very bad as constitutional law.

But if we cannot confine military expedients by the Constitution, neither would I distort the Constitution to approve all that the military may deem expedient. That is what the Court appears to be doing, whether consciously or not. I cannot say, from any evidence before me, that the orders of General DeWitt were not reasonably expedient military precautions, nor could I say that they were. But even if they were permissible military procedures, I deny that it follows that they are constitutional. If, as the Court holds, it does follow, then we may as well say that any military order will be constitutional and have done with it.

• • •

A military order, however unconstitutional, is not apt to last longer than the military emergency. Even during that period a succeeding commander may revoke it all. But once a judicial opinion rationalizes such an order to show that it conforms to the Constitution, or rather rationalizes the Constitution to show that the Constitution sanctions such an order, the Court for all time has validated the principle of racial discrimination in criminal procedure and of transplanting American citizens. The principle then lies about like a loaded weapon ready for the hand of any authority that can bring forward a plausible claim of an urgent need. Every repetition imbeds that principle more deeply in our law and thinking and expands it to new purposes. All who observe the work of courts are familiar with what Judge Cardozo described as "the tendency of a principle to expand itself to the limit of its logic." A military commander may overstep the bounds of constitutionality and it is an incident. But if we review and approve, that passing incident becomes the doctrine of the Constitution. There it has a generative power of its own, and all that it creates will be in its own image. Nothing better illustrates this danger than does the Court's opinion in this case.

• • •

I should hold that a civil court cannot be made to enforce an order which violates constitutional limitations even if it is a reasonable exercise of military authority. The courts can exercise only the judicial power, can apply only law, and must abide by the Constitution, or they cease to be civil courts and become instruments of military policy.

Questions

1. Why does Jackson believe that even though military authorities have the power to violate constitutional protections in time of war, the courts should not approve their actions?

2. How did the experience of Japanese-Americans differ from that of Americans whose ancestors came from Germany, Italy, or other countries fighting the United States?

CHAPTER 23

The United States and the Cold War, 1945–1953

149. The Truman Doctrine (1947)

Source: "Special Message to the Congress on Greece and Turkey, March 12, 1947," Public Papers of the Presidents of the United States, Harry S. Truman, 1947 *(Washington, D.C., 1963), pp. 176–80.*

In March 1947, in a speech announcing what came to be known as the Truman Doctrine, President Harry S Truman officially embraced the containment of Soviet communism as the foundation of American foreign policy. The immediate occasion was a request for military and financial aid from Greece, a monarchy threatened by a communist-led rebellion, and Turkey, from which the Soviets were demanding joint control of the straits linking the Black Sea and the Mediterranean. Neither were models of democracy. To rally popular backing, Truman appealed to his strongest rhetorical argument—the defense of freedom. Twenty-four times in the eighteen-minute speech, Truman used the words "free" or "freedom." The Truman Doctrine created the language through which most Americans came to understand the postwar world. The speech set a precedent for American assistance to anticommunist regimes throughout the world, no matter how undemocratic, and for the creation of a set of global military alliances directed against the Soviet Union.

THE GRAVITY OF the situation which confronts the world today necessitates my appearance before a joint session of the Congress.

The foreign policy and the national security of this country are involved.

One aspect of the present situation, which I present to you at this time for your consideration and decision, concerns Greece and Turkey.

The United States has received from the Greek Government an urgent appeal for financial and economic assistance. Preliminary reports from the American Economic Mission now in Greece and reports from the American Ambassador in Greece corroborate the statement of the Greek Government that assistance is imperative if Greece is to survive as a free nation.

I do not believe that the American people and the Congress wish to turn a deaf ear to the appeal of the Greek Government.

• • •

The very existence of the Greek state is today threatened by the terrorist activities of several thousand armed men, led by Communists, who defy the government's authority at a number of points, particularly along the northern boundaries. A Commission appointed by the United Nations Security Council is at present investigating disturbed conditions in northern Greece and alleged border violations along the frontier between Greece on the one hand and Albania, Bulgaria, and Yugoslavia on the other.

Meanwhile, the Greek Government is unable to cope with the situation. The Greek army is small and poorly equipped. It needs supplies and equipment if it is to restore authority to the government throughout Greek territory.

• • •

We have considered how the United Nations might assist in this crisis. But the situation is an urgent one requiring immediate action, and the United Nations and its related organizations are not in a position to extend help of the kind that is required.

• • •

The Greek Government has been operating in an atmosphere of chaos and extremism. It has made mistakes. The extension of aid by this country does not mean that the United States condones everything that the Greek Government has done or will do. We have condemned in the past, and we condemn now, extremist measures of the right or the left. We have in the past advised tolerance, and we advise tolerance now.

Greece's neighbor, Turkey, also deserves our attention.

The future of Turkey as an independent and economically sound state is clearly no less important to the freedom-loving peoples of the world than the future of Greece. The circumstances in which Turkey finds itself today are considerably different from those of Greece. Turkey has been spared the disasters that have beset Greece. And during the war, the United States and Great Britain furnished Turkey with material aid.

Nevertheless, Turkey now needs our support.

• • •

At the present moment in world history nearly every nation must choose between alternative ways of life. The choice is too often not a free one.

One way of life is based upon the will of the majority, and is distinguished by free institutions, representative government, free elections, guarantees of individual liberty, freedom of speech and religion, and freedom from political oppression.

The second way of life is based upon the will of a minority forcibly imposed upon the majority. It relies upon terror and oppression, a controlled press and radio, fixed elections, and the suppression of personal freedoms.

I believe that it must be the policy of the United States to support free peoples who are resisting attempted subjugation by armed minorities or by outside pressures.

I believe that we must assist free peoples to work out their own destinies in their own way.

• • •

The free peoples of the world look to us for support in maintaining their freedoms.

If we falter in our leadership, we may endanger the peace of the world—and we shall surely endanger the welfare of this Nation.

Great responsibilities have been placed upon us by the swift movement of events.

I am confident that the Congress will face these responsibilities squarely.

Questions

1. Why does Truman insist that the question of assisting Greece and Turkey involves a choice between "alternative ways of life"?

2. How does he define freedom in the postwar world?

150. NSC 68 and the Ideological Cold War (1950)

Source: U.S. Department of State, **Foreign Relations of the United States,** *1950 (Washington, D.C., 1976–1980), Vol. 1, pp. 237–41.*

In the years immediately following the Truman Doctrine speech, the Cold War rapidly accelerated. In the wake of Soviet-American confrontations over southern and eastern Europe and Berlin, the coming to power of a communist government in China in 1949, and Soviet success in developing an atom bomb, the National Security Council (NSC) in 1950 approved a call for the United States to pursue a global crusade against communism. Drafted by State Department official Paul Nitze and known as NSC 68, this manifesto contained a lengthy exposition of the nature of "the free society" and claimed that the Soviet Union, motivated by a "fanatic faith," sought nothing less than worldwide domination and the elimination of freedom across the globe. Although NSC 68 was not made public until many years after it was written, it circulated widely in government circles. One of the most important policy statements of the early Cold War, it helped to spur a dramatic increase in American military spending. Its description of the Cold War as an epic struggle between "the idea of freedom" and the "idea of slavery under the grim oligarchy of the Kremlin" powerfully shaped the way a generation of American officials understood the world.

WITHIN THE PAST thirty-five years the world has experienced two global wars of tremendous violence. It has witnessed two revolutions—the Russian and the Chinese—of extreme scope and intensity. It has also seen the collapse of five empires—the Ottoman, the Austro-Hungarian, German, Italian, and Japanese—and the drastic decline of two major imperial systems, the British and the French. During the span of one generation, the international distribution of power has been fundamentally altered. For several centuries it had proved impossible for any one nation to gain such preponderant strength that a coalition of other nations could not in time face it with greater strength. The international scene was marked by recurring periods of violence and war, but a system of sovereign and independent states was maintained, over which no state was able to achieve hegemony.

Two complex sets of factors have now basically altered this historical distribution of power. First, the defeat of Germany and Japan and the decline of the British and French Empires have interacted with the development of the United States and the Soviet Union in such a way that power has increasingly gravitated to these two centers. Second, the Soviet Union, unlike previous aspirants to hegemony, is animated by a new fanatic faith, antithetical to our own, and seeks to impose its absolute authority over the rest of the world. Conflict has, therefore, become endemic and is waged, on the part of the Soviet Union, by violent or non-violent methods in accordance with the dictates of expediency. With the development of increasingly terrifying weapons of mass destruction, every individual faces the ever-present possibility of annihilation should the conflict enter the phase of total war.

On the one hand, the people of the world yearn for relief from the anxiety arising from the risk of atomic war. On the other hand, any substantial further extension of the area under the domination of the Kremlin would raise the possibility that no coalition adequate to confront the Kremlin with greater strength could be assembled. It is in this context that this Republic and its citizens in the ascendancy of their strength stand in their deepest peril.

The issues that face us are momentous, involving the fulfillment or destruction not only of this Republic but of civilization itself. They are issues which will not await our deliberations. With conscience and resolution this Government and the people it represents must now take new and fateful decisions.

• • •

The Kremlin regards the United States as the only major threat to the achievement of its fundamental design. There is a basic conflict between the idea of freedom under a government of laws, and the idea of slavery under the grim oligarchy of the Kremlin, which has come to a crisis with the polarization of power described in Section I, and the exclusive possession of atomic weapons by the two protagonists. The idea of freedom, moreover, is peculiarly and intolerably subversive of the idea of slavery. But the converse is not true. The implacable purpose of the slave state to eliminate the challenge of freedom has placed the two great powers at opposite poles. It is this fact which gives the present polarization of power the quality of crisis.

The free society values the individual as an end in himself, requiring of him only that measure of self-discipline and self-restraint which make the rights of each individual compatible with the rights of every other individual. The freedom of the individual has as its counterpart, therefore, the negative responsibility of the individual not to exercise his freedom in ways inconsistent with the freedom of other individuals and the positive responsibility to make constructive use of his freedom in the building of a just society.

From this idea of freedom with responsibility derives the marvelous diversity, the deep tolerance, the lawfulness of the free society. This is the explanation of the strength of free men. It constitutes the integrity and the vitality of a free and democratic system. The free society attempts to create and maintain an environment in which every individual has the opportunity to realize his creative powers. It also explains why the free society tolerates those within it who would use their freedom to destroy it. By the same token, in relations between nations, the prime reliance of the free society is on the strength and appeal of its idea, and it feels no compulsion sooner or later to bring all societies into conformity with it.

For the free society does not fear, it welcomes, diversity. It derives its strength from its hospitality even to antipathetic ideas. It is a market for free trade in ideas, secure in its faith that free men will take the best wares, and grow to a fuller and better realization of their powers in exercising their choice.

The idea of freedom is the most contagious idea in history, more contagious than the idea of submission to authority. For the breadth of freedom cannot be tolerated in a society which has come under the domination of an individual or group of individuals with a will to absolute power. Where the despot holds absolute power—the absolute power of the absolutely powerful will—all other wills must be subjugated in an act of willing submission, a degradation willed by the individual upon himself under the compulsion of a perverted faith. It is the first article of this faith that he finds and can only find the meaning of his existence in serving the ends of the system. The system becomes God, and submission to the will of God becomes submission to the will of the system. It is not enough to yield outwardly to the system—even Gandhian non-violence is not acceptable—for the spirit of resistance and the devotion to a higher authority might then remain, and the individual would not be wholly submissive.

• • •

Thus unwillingly our free society finds itself mortally challenged by the Soviet system. No other value system is so wholly irreconcilable with ours, so implacable in its purpose to destroy ours, so capable of turning to its own uses the most dangerous and divisive trends in our own society, no other so skillfully and powerfully evokes the elements of irrationality in human nature everywhere, and no other has the support of a great and growing center of military power.

Questions

1. Why does NSC 68 view the Soviet Union as different from other great powers?

2. What does it see as the essential elements of the "free society"?

151. Walter Lippmann, a Critique of Containment (1947)

Source: Walter Lippmann, "A Critique of Containment," pp. 21–25 from The Cold War: A Study in U.S. Foreign Policy *by Walter Lippmann. Copyright 1947 by Walter Lippmann. Copyright renewed © 1975 by Walter Lippmann. Reprinted by permission of HarperCollins Publishers.*

Not all Americans happily embraced the Cold War. As a number of contemporary critics, few of them sympathetic to Soviet communism, pointed out, casting the Cold War in terms of a worldwide battle between freedom and slavery made it impossible to view international crises on a case-by-case basis or to determine which genuinely involved either freedom or American interests.

In a penetrating critique of Truman's policies, as expounded by diplomat George Kennan in an article signed "X", Walter Lippmann, one of the nation's most prominent journalists, objected to turning foreign policy into an ideological crusade. To view every challenge to the status quo as part of a contest with the Soviet Union, Lippmann correctly predicted, would require the United States to recruit and subsidize an "array of satellites, clients, dependents and puppets." It would have to intervene continuously in the affairs of nations whose political problems did not arise from

Moscow and could not be easily understood in terms of the battle between freedom and slavery. It would be a serious mistake, Lippmann warned, for the United States to align itself against the movement for colonial independence in the name of anticommunism—a warning amply borne out during the Vietnam War.

THE POLICY OF containment, which Mr. X recommends, demands the employment of American economic, political, and in the last analysis, American military power at "sectors" in the interior of Europe and Asia. This requires, as I have pointed out, ground forces, that is to say reserves of infantry, which we do not possess.

The United States cannot by its own military power contain the expansive pressure of the Russians "at every point where they show signs of encroaching." The United States cannot have ready "unalterable counterforce" consisting of American troops. Therefore, the counterforces which Mr. X requires have to be composed of Chinese, Afghans, Iranians, Turks, Kurds, Arabs, Greeks, Italians, Austrians, of anti-Soviet Poles, Czechoslovaks, Bulgars, Yugoslavs, Albanians, Hungarians, Finns and Germans.

The policy can be implemented only by recruiting, subsidizing and supporting a heterogeneous array of satellites, clients, dependents and puppets. The instrument of the policy of containment is therefore a coalition of disorganized, disunited, feeble or disorderly nations, tribes and factions around the perimeter of the Soviet Union.

To organize a coalition among powerful modern states is, even in time of war and under dire necessity, an enormously difficult thing to do well. To organize a coalition of disunited, feeble and immature states, and to hold it together for a prolonged diplomatic siege, which might last for ten or fifteen years, is, I submit, impossibly difficult.

It would require, however much the real name for it were disavowed, continual and complicated intervention by the United States in the affairs of all the members of the coalition which we were proposing to organize, to protect, to lead and to use. Our diplomatic agents abroad would have to have an almost unerring capacity to judge correctly and quickly which men and which parties were reliable containers. Here at home Congress and the people would have to stand ready to back their judgments as to who should be nominated, who should be subsidized, who should be whitewashed, who should be seen through rose-colored spectacles, who should be made our clients and our allies.

Mr. X offers us the prospect of maintaining such a coalition indefinitely until—eventually—the Soviet power breaks up or mellows because it has been frustrated. It is not a good prospect. Even if we assume, which we ought not, that our diplomatic agents will know how to intervene shrewdly and skillfully all over Asia, the Middle East, and Europe, and even if we assume, which the Department of State cannot, that the American people will back them with a drawing account of blank checks both in money and in military power, still it is not a good prospect. For we must not forget that the Soviet Union, against which this coalition will be directed, will resist and react.

In the complicated contest over this great heterogeneous array of unstable states, the odds are heavily in favor of the Soviets. For if we are to succeed, we must organize our satellites as unified, orderly and reasonably contented nations. The Russians can defeat us by disorganizing states that are already disorganized, by disuniting peoples that are torn with civil strife, and by inciting their discontent which is already very great.

As a matter of fact this borderland in Europe and Asia around the perimeter of the Soviet Union is not a place where Mr. X's "unassailable barriers" can be erected. Satellite states and puppet governments are not good material out of which to construct unassailable barriers. A diplomatic war conducted as this policy demands, that is to say conducted indirectly, means that we must stake our own security and the peace of the world upon satellites, puppets, clients, agents about whom we can know very little. Frequently they will act for their own reasons, and on their own judgments, presenting us with accomplished facts that we did not intend, and with crises for which we are unready. The "unassailable barriers" will present us with an unending series of insoluble dilemmas. We shall have either to disown our puppets, which would be tantamount to appeasement and defeat and the loss of face, or must support them at an incalculable cost on an unintended, unforeseen and perhaps undesirable issue.

Questions

1. Why does Lippmann advise the United States to concentrate its efforts on Europe, not the rest of the world?

2. Why does he feel that the Truman Doctrine is a violation of important American traditions?

152. The Universal Declaration of Human Rights (1948)

Source: Universal Declaration of Human Rights: Adopted and proclaimed by General Assembly resolution 217 A (III) of 10 December 1948. Reprinted with the permission of United Nations Publications.

The atrocities committed during World War II as well as the global language of the Four Freedoms forcefully raised the issue of human rights in the postwar world. In 1948, the U.N. General Assembly approved the Universal Declaration of Human Rights, drafted by a committee chaired by Eleanor Roosevelt, the widow of the late president. The declaration identified a broad range of rights to be enjoyed by all members of the human family, everywhere, including freedom of speech, religious toleration, and protection against arbitrary government, as well as social and economic entitlements like the right to an adequate standard of living and access to housing, education, and medical care. The document had no enforcement mechanism. Some considered it an exercise in empty rhetoric. But the core principle—that a nation's treatment of its own citizens should be subject to outside evaluation—slowly became part of the language in which freedom was discussed.

―――

THE GENERAL ASSEMBLY PROCLAIMS

This universal declaration of human rights as a common standard of achievement for all peoples and all nations, to the end that every individual and every organ of society, keeping this Declaration constantly in mind, shall strive by teaching and education to promote respect for these rights and freedoms and by progressive measures, national and international, to secure their universal and effective recognition and observance, both among the peoples of Member States themselves and among the peoples of territories under their jurisdiction.

Article 1. All human beings are born free and equal in dignity and rights. They are endowed with reason and conscience and should act towards one another in a spirit of brotherhood.

Article 2. Everyone is entitled to all the rights and freedoms set forth in this Declaration, without distinction of any kind, such as race, colour, sex, language, religion, political or other opinion, national or social origin, property, birth or other status.

Furthermore, no distinction shall be made on the basis of the political, jurisdictional or international status of the country or territory to which a person belongs, whether it be independent, trust, non-self-governing or under any other limitation of sovereignty.

Article 3. Everyone has the right to life, liberty and security of person.

Article 4. No one shall be held in slavery or servitude; slavery and the slave trade shall be prohibited in all their forms.

Article 5. No one shall be subjected to torture or to cruel, inhuman or degrading treatment or punishment.

Article 6. Everyone has the right to recognition everywhere as a person before the law.

Article 7. All are equal before the law and are entitled without any discrimination to equal protection of the law. All are entitled to equal protection against any discrimination in violation of this Declaration and against any incitement to such discrimination.

Article 8. Everyone has the right to an effective remedy by the competent national tribunals for acts violating the fundamental rights granted him by the constitution or by law.

Article 9. No one shall be subjected to arbitrary arrest, detention or exile.

Article 10. Everyone is entitled in full equality to a fair and public hearing by an independent and impartial tribunal, in the determination of his rights and obligations and of any criminal charge against him.

Article 11. (1) Everyone charged with a penal offense has the right to be presumed innocent until proved guilty according to law in a public trial at which he has had all the guarantees necessary for his defense.

(2) No one shall be held guilty of any penal offense or of any act or omission which did not constitute a penal offense, under national or international law, at the time when it was committed. Nor shall a heavier penalty be imposed than the one that was applicable at the time the penal offense was committed.

Article 12. No one shall be subject to arbitrary interference with his privacy, family, home or correspondence, nor to attacks upon his honour and reputation. Everyone has the right to the protection of the law against such interference or attacks.

Article 13. (1) Everyone has the right to freedom of movement and residence within the borders of each state.

(2) Everyone has the right to leave any country, including his own, and to return to his country.

Article 14. (1) Everyone has the right to seek and to enjoy in other countries asylum from persecution.

(2) This right may not be invoked in the case of prosecutions genuinely arising from non-political crimes or from acts contrary to the purposes and principles of the United Nations.

Article 15. (1) Everyone has the right to a nationality.

(2) No one shall be arbitrarily deprived of his nationality nor denied the right to change his nationality.

Article 16. (1) Men and women of full age, without any limitation due to race, nationality or religion, have the right to marry and to found a family. They are entitled to equal rights as to marriage, during marriage, and at its dissolution.

(2) Marriage shall be entered into only with the free and full consent of the intending spouses.

(3) The family is the natural and fundamental group unit of society and is entitled to protection by society and the State.

Article 17. (1) Everyone has the right to own property alone as well as in association with others.

(2) No one shall be arbitrarily deprived of his property.

Article 18. Everyone has the right to freedom of thought, conscience and religion; this right includes freedom to change his religion or belief, and freedom, either alone or in community with others and in public or private, to manifest his religion or belief in teaching, practice, worship and observance.

Article 19. Everyone has the right to freedom of opinion and expression; this right includes freedom to hold opinions without interference and to seek, receive and impart information and ideas through any media and regardless of frontiers.

Article 20. (1) Everyone has the right to freedom of peaceful assembly and association.

(2) No one may be compelled to belong to an association.

Article 21. (1) Everyone has the right to take part in the government of his country, directly or through freely chosen representatives.

(2) Everyone has the right of equal access to public service in his country.

(3) The will of the people shall be the basis of the authority of government; this will shall be expressed in periodic and genuine elections which shall be by universal and equal suffrage and shall be held by secret vote or by equivalent free voting procedures.

Article 22. Everyone, as a member of society, has the right to social security and is entitled to realization, through national effort and international co-operation and in accordance with the organization and resources of each State, of the economic, social and cultural rights indispensable for his dignity and the free development of his personality.

Article 23. (1) Everyone has the right to work, to free choice of employment, to just and favourable conditions of work and to protection against unemployment.

(2) Everyone, without any discrimination, has the right to equal pay for equal work.

(3) Everyone who works has the right to just and favourable remuneration ensuring for himself and his family an existence worthy of human dignity, and supplemented, if necessary, by other means of social protection.

(4) Everyone has the right to form and to join trade unions for protection of his interests.

Article 24. Everyone has the right to rest and leisure, including reasonable limitation of working hours and periodic holidays with pay.

Article 25. (1) Everyone has the right to a standard of living adequate for the health and well-being of himself and his family, including food, clothing, housing and medical care and necessary social services, and the right to security in the event of unemployment, sickness, disability, widowhood, old age or other lack of livelihood in circumstances beyond his control.

(2) Motherhood and childhood are entitled to special care and assistance. All children, whether born in or out of wedlock, shall enjoy the same social protection.

Article 26. (1) Everyone has the right to education. Education shall be free, at least in the elementary and fundamental states. Elementary education shall be compulsory. Technical and professional education shall be made generally available and higher education shall be equally accessible to all on the basis of merit.

(2) Education shall be directed to the full development of the human personality and to the strengthening of respect for human rights and fundamental freedoms. It shall promote understanding, tolerance and friendship among all nations, racial or religious groups, and shall further the activities of the United Nations for the maintenance of peace.

(3) Parents shall have a prior right to choose the kind of education that shall be given to their children.

Article 27. (1) Everyone has the right freely to participate in the cultural life of the community, to enjoy the arts and to share in scientific advancement and its benefits.

(2) Everyone has the right to the protection of the moral and material interests resulting from any scientific, literary or artistic production of which he is the author.

Article 28. Everyone is entitled to a social and international order in which the rights and freedoms set forth in this Declaration can be fully realized.

Article 29. (1) Everyone has duties to the community in which alone the free and full development of his personality is possible.

(2) In the exercise of his rights and freedoms, everyone shall be subject only to such limitations as are determined by law solely for the purpose of securing due recognition and respect for the rights and freedoms of others and of meeting the just requirements of morality, public order and the general welfare in a democratic society.

(3) These rights and freedoms may in no case be exercised contrary to the purposes and principles of the United Nations.

Article 30. Nothing in this Declaration may be interpreted as implying for any State, group or person any right to engage in any activity or to perform any act aimed at the destruction of any of the rights and freedoms set forth herein.

Questions

1. Why is a declaration with no enforcement mechanism nonetheless considered significant?

2. How fully, in your opinion, does the United States today live up to the standards set forth in the Universal Declaration of Human Rights?

153. President's Commission on Civil Rights, *To Secure These Rights* (1947)

Source: To Secure These Rights: The Report of the President's Commission on Civil Rights *(Washington, D.C., 1947), pp. 99–103, 139–48.*

In the years immediately following World War II, the status of black Americans enjoyed a prominence in national affairs unmatched since Reconstruction. In October 1947, a Commission on Civil Rights appointed by President Truman issued *To Secure These Rights*, one of the most devastating indictments ever published of racial inequality in America. It outlined the deprivation of rights in areas like employment, housing, and the vote and the widespread occurrence of police brutality against blacks. It called on the federal government to assume the responsibility for ensuring equal civil rights for all Americans. The commission insisted that racial inequality posed a moral challenge to the nation because it conflicted with "the American heritage of freedom." The impact of racism on America's conduct of the Cold War was not far from its mind. The treatment of black Americans, the commission noted, enabled the Soviets to claim that "our nation is a consistent oppressor of underprivileged people," a reputation that could prove disastrous in the battle for the allegiance of peoples throughout the world.

THE NATIONAL GOVERNMENT of the United States must take the lead in safeguarding the civil rights of all Americans. We believe that this is one of the most important observations that can be made about the civil rights problem in our country today. We agree with words used by the President, in an address at the Lincoln Memorial in Washington in June, 1947:

> We must make the Federal Government a friendly, vigilant defender of the rights and equalities of all Americans... Our National Government must show the way.

It is essential that our rights be preserved against the tyrannical actions of public officers. Our forefathers saw the need for such protection when they gave us the Bill of Rights as a safeguard against arbitrary government. But this is not enough today. We need more than protection of our rights against government; we need protection of our rights against private persons or groups, seeking to undermine them.

• • •

There are several reasons why we believe the federal government must play a leading role in our efforts as a nation to improve our civil rights record.

First, many of the most serious wrongs against individual rights are committed by private persons or by local public officers. In the most flagrant of all such wrongs—lynching—private individuals, aided upon occasion by state or local officials, are the ones who take the law into their own hands and deprive the victim of his life. The very fact that these outrages continue to occur, coupled with the fact that the states have been unable to eliminate them, points clearly to a strong need for federal safeguards.

• • •

The Committee rejects the argument that governmental controls are themselves necessarily threats to liberty. This statement overlooks the fact that freedom in a civilized society is always founded on law enforced by government. Freedom in the absence of law is anarchy.

• • •

Twice before in American history the nation has found it necessary to review the state of its civil rights. The first time was during the 15 years between 1776 and 1791, from the drafting of the Declaration of Independence through the Articles of Confederation experiment to the writing of the Constitution and the Bill of Rights. It was then that the distinctively American heritage was finally distilled from earlier views of liberty. The second time was when the Union was temporarily sundered over the question of whether it could exist "half-slave" and "half-free."

It is our profound conviction that we have come to a time for a third reexamination of the situation, and a sustained drive ahead. Our reasons for believing this are those of conscience, of self-interest, and of survival in a threatening world. Or to put it another way, we have a moral reason, an economic reason, and an international reason for believing that the time for action is now.

THE MORAL REASON

We have considered the American heritage of freedom at some length. We need no further justification for a broad and immediate program than the need to reaffirm our faith in the traditional American morality. The pervasive gap between our aims and what we actually do is creating a kind or moral dry rot which eats away at the emotional and rational bases of democratic beliefs. There are times when the difference between what we preach about civil rights and what we practice is shockingly illustrated by individual outrages. There are times when the whole structure of our ideology is made ridiculous by individual instances. And there are certain continuing, quiet, omnipresent practices which do irreparable damage to our beliefs.

As examples of "moral erosion" there are the consequences of suffrage limitations in the South. The fact that Negroes and many whites have not been allowed to vote in some states has actually sapped the morality underlying universal suffrage. Many men in public and private life do not believe that those who have been kept from voting are capable of self rule. They finally convince themselves that disfranchised people do not really have the right to vote.

Wartime segregation in the armed forces is another instance of how a social pattern may wreak moral havoc. Practically all white officers and enlisted men in all branches of service saw Negro military personnel performing only the most menial functions. They saw Negroes recruited for the common defense treated as men apart and distinct from themselves. As a result, men who might otherwise have maintained the equalitarian morality of their forebears were given reason to look down on their fellow citizens. This has been sharply illustrated by the Army study discussed previously, in which white servicemen expressed great surprise at the excellent performance of Negroes who joined them in the firing line. Even now, very few people know of the successful experiment with integrated combat units. Yet it is important in explaining why some Negro troops did not do well; it is proof that equal treatment can produce equal performance.

It is impossible to decide who suffers the greatest moral damage from our civil rights transgressions, because all of us are hurt. That is certainly true of those who are victimized. Their belief in the basic truth of the American promise is undermined. But they do have the realization, galling as it sometimes is, of being morally in the right. The damage to those who are responsible for these violations of our moral standards may well be greater. They, too, have been reared to honor the command of "free and equal." And all of us must share in the shame at the growth of hypocrisies like the "automatic" marble champion. All of us must endure the cynicism about democratic values which our failures breed.

The United States can no longer countenance these burdens on its common conscience, these inroads on its moral fiber

THE ECONOMIC REASON

One of the principal economic problems facing us and the rest of the world is achieving maximum production and continued prosperity. The loss of a huge, potential market for goods is a direct result of the economic discrimination which is practiced against many of our minority groups. A sort of vicious circle is produced. Discrimination depresses the wages and income of minority groups. As a result, their purchasing power is curtailed and markets are reduced. Reduced markets result in reduced production. This cuts down employment, which of course means lower wages and still fewer job opportunities. Rising fear, prejudice, and insecurity aggravate the very discrimination in employment which sets the vicious circle in motion.

Minority groups are not the sole victims of this economic waste; its impact is inevitably felt by the entire population.

• • •

The International Reason

Our position in the postwar world is so vital to the future that our smallest actions have far-reaching effects. We have come to know that our own security in a highly interdependent world is inextricably tied to the security and well-being of all people and all countries. Our foreign policy is designed to make the United States an enormous, positive influence for peace and progress throughout the world. We have tried to let nothing, not even extreme political differences between ourselves and foreign nations, stand in the way of this goal. But our domestic civil rights shortcomings are a serious obstacle.

We cannot escape the fact that our civil rights record has been an issue in world politics. The world's press and radio are full of it. This Committee has seen a multitude of samples. We and our friends have been, and are, stressing our achievements. Those with competing philosophies have stressed—and are shamelessly distorting—our shortcomings. They have not only tried to create hostility toward us among specific nations, races, and religious groups. They have tried to prove our democracy an empty fraud, and our nation a consistent oppressor of underprivileged people. This may seem ludicrous to Americans, but it is sufficiently important to worry our friends.

• • •

Our achievements in building and maintaining a state dedicated to the fundamentals of freedom have already served as a guide for those seeking the best road from chaos to liberty and prosperity. But it is not indelibly written that democracy will encompass the world. We are convinced that our way of life—the free way of life—holds a promise of hope for all people. We have what is perhaps the greatest responsibility ever placed upon a people to keep this promise alive. Only still greater achievements will do it.

The United States is not so strong, the final triumph of the democratic ideal is not so inevitable that we can ignore what the world thinks of us or our record.

Questions

1. Why does the commission believe that the federal government must take the lead in promoting civil rights?

2. Why does it consider "our domestic civil rights shortcomings" a threat to the triumph of democratic ideals in the Cold War?

154. Joseph R. McCarthy on the Attack (1950)

Source: **Congressional Record,** *81st Congress, 2d Session, pt. 2, pp. 1954–56.*

Soon after the announcement of the Truman Doctrine, the president instituted a loyalty review system in which government employees were required to demonstrate their patriotism without, in many cases, knowing the charges against them. But the individual whose name came to be most closely associated with the anticommunist crusade was Senator Joseph R. McCarthy of Wisconsin. In a speech in West Virginia in February 1950, McCarthy stated that he had a list of 205 communists working for the State Department. The charge was preposterous; and a few days later, when he entered the speech in the *Congressional Record*, McCarthy reduced the number to 57—still a wild and unsubstantiated claim. The demagogic pursuit of communists riding roughshod over civil liberties came to be known by the name McCarthyism.

FIVE YEARS AFTER a world war has been won, men's hearts should anticipate a long peace, and men's minds should be free from the heavy weight that comes with war. But this is not such a period—for this is not a period of peace. This is a time of the "cold war." This is a time when all the world is split into two vast, increasingly hostile armed camps—a time of a great armaments race. . . .

Today we are engaged in a final, all-out battle between communistic atheism and Christianity. The modern champions of communism have selected this as the time. And, ladies and gentlemen, the chips are down—they are truly down. . . .

Ladies, and gentlemen, can there be anyone here tonight who is so blind as to say that the war is not on? Can there be anyone who fails to realize that the Communist world has said, "The time is now"— that this is the time for the show-down between the democratic Christian world and the Communist atheist world?

Unless we face this fact, we shall pay the price that must be paid by those who wait too long.

Six years ago, at the time of the first conference to map out the peace . . . there was within the Soviet orbit 180,000,000 people. Lined up on the antitotalitarian side there were in the world at that time roughly 1,625,000,000 people. Today, only six years later, there are 800,000,000 people under the absolute domination of Soviet Russia— an increase of over 400 percent. On our side, the figure has shrunk to around 500,000,000. In other words, in less than six years the odds have changed from 9 to 1 in our favor to 8 to 5 against us. This indicates the swiftness of the tempo of Communist victories and American defeats in the cold war. . . .

The reason why we find ourselves in a position of impotency is not because our only powerful potential enemy has sent men to invade our shores, but rather because of the traitorous actions of those who have been treated so well by this Nation. It has not been the less fortunate or members of minority groups who have been selling this Nation out, but rather those who have had all the benefits that the wealthiest nation on earth has had to offer—the finest homes, the finest college education, and the finest jobs in Government we can give.

This is glaringly true in the State Department. There the bright young men who are born with silver spoons in their mouths are the ones who have been worst....

In my opinion the State Department, which is one of the most important government departments, is thoroughly infested with Communists.

I have in my hand 57 cases of individuals who would appear to be either card carrying members or certainly loyal to the Communist Party, but who nevertheless are still helping to shape our foreign policy.

One thing to remember in discussing the Communists in our Government is that we are not dealing with spies who get thirty pieces of silver to steal the blueprints of a new weapon. We are dealing with a far more sinister type of activity because it permits the enemy to guide and shape our policy....

Questions

1. What kind of social resentments are evident in McCarthy's speech?

2. What evidence does McCarthy offer to support his claim that communists have infiltrated the State Department?

155. Henry Steele Commager, "Who Is Loyal to America?" (1947)

Source: Henry Steele Commager, "Who Is Loyal to America?" Harper's (September 1947), p. 193. Copyright © 1947 by Harper's Magazine.

Like other wars, the Cold War encouraged the drawing of a sharp line between patriotic Americans and those accused of being disloyal. Dividing the world between liberty and slavery automatically made those who could be linked to communism enemies of freedom, and undeserving of traditional civil liberties. By the early 1950s, the anticommunist crusade had created a pervasive atmosphere of fear. The House Committee on Un-American Activities hauled witnessed before it to answer questions about their political beliefs. States and localities required loyalty oaths of teachers, pharmacists, and members of other professions. Under director J. Edgar Hoover, the FBI developed files on thousands of citizens.

As the historian Henry Steele Commager argued in a 1947 magazine article, the anticommunist crusade promoted a new definition of loyalty. Anything other than "uncritical and unquestioning acceptance of America as it is," wrote Commager, could now be labeled unpatriotic.

———

INCREASINGLY CONGRESS IS concerned with the eradication of disloyalty and the defense of Americanism, and scarcely a day passes that some congressman does not treat us to exhortations and admonitions, impassioned appeals and eloquent declamations,...And scarcely a day passes that the outlines of the new loyalty and the new Americanism are not etched more sharply in public policy.

And this is what is significant—the emergence of new patterns of Americanism and of loyalty, patterns radically different from those which have long been traditional. It is not only the Congress that is busy designing the new patterns. They are outlined in President Truman's recent disloyalty order; in similar orders formulated by the New York City Council and by state and local authorities throughout the country; in the programs of the D.A.R., the American Legion, and similar patriotic organizations; in the editorials of the Hearst and the McCormick-Patterson papers; and in an elaborate series of advertisements sponsored by large corporations and business organizations. In the making is a revival of the red hysteria of the early 1920's, one of the shabbiest chapters in the history of American democracy; and more than a revival, for the new crusade is designed not merely to frustrate Communism but to formulate a positive definition of Americanism, and a positive concept of loyalty.

What is the new loyalty? It is, above all, conformity. It is the uncritical and unquestioning acceptance of America as it is—the political institutions, the social relationships, the economic practices. It rejects inquiry into the race question or socialized medicine, or public housing, or into the wisdom or validity of our foreign policy. It regards as particularly heinous any challenge to what is called "the system of private enterprise," identifying that system with Americanism. It abandons evolution, repudiates the once popular concept of progress, and regards America as a finished product, perfect and complete.

It is, it must be added, easily satisfied. For it wants not intellectual conviction nor spiritual conquest, but mere outward conformity. In matters of loyalty it takes the word for the deed, the gesture for the principle. It is content with the flag salute, and does not pause to consider the warning of our Supreme Court that "a person gets from a symbol the meaning he puts into it, and what is one man's comfort and inspiration is another's jest and scorn." It is satisfied with membership in respectable organizations and, as it assumes that every member of a liberal organization is a Communist, concludes that every member of a conservative one is a true American. It has not yet learned that not everyone who saith Lord, Lord, shall enter into the kingdom of Heaven. It is designed neither to discover real disloyalty nor to foster true loyalty.

• • •

The concept of loyalty as conformity is a false one. It is narrow and restrictive, denies freedom of thought and of conscience, and is irremediably stained by private and selfish considerations.

• • •

What do men know of loyalty who make a mockery of the Declaration of Independence and the Bill of Rights, whose energies are dedicated to stirring up race and class hatreds, who would straitjacket the American spirit? What indeed do they know of America— the America of Sam Adams and Tom Paine, of Jackson's defiance of the Court and Lincoln's celebration of labor, of Thoreau's essay on Civil Disobedience and Emerson's championship of John Brown, of the America of the Fourierists and the Come-Outers, of cranks and fanatics, of socialists and anarchists? Who among American heroes could meet their tests, who would be cleared by their committees? Not Washington, who was a rebel. Not Jefferson, who wrote that all men are created equal and whose motto was "rebellion to tyrants is obedience to God." Not Garrison, who publicly burned the Constitution; or Wendell Philips, who spoke for the underprivileged everywhere and counted himself a philosophical anarchist; not Seward of the Higher Law or Sumner of racial equality. Not Lincoln, who admonished us to have malice toward none, charity for all; or Wilson, who warned that our flag was "a flag of liberty of opinion as well as of political liberty"; or Justice Holmes, who said that our Constitution is an experiment and that while that experiment is being made "we should be eternally vigilant against attempts to check the expression of opinions that we loathe and believe to be fraught with death."

• • •

Who are those who are really disloyal? Those who inflame racial hatreds, who sow religious and class dissensions. Those who subvert the Constitution by violating the freedom of the ballot box. Those who make a mockery of majority rule by the use of the filibuster. Those who impair democracy by denying equal educational facilities. Those who frustrate justice by lynch law or by making a farce of jury trials. Those who deny freedom of speech and of the press and of assembly. Those who press for special favors against the interest of the commonwealth. Those who regard public office as a source of private gain. Those who would exalt the military over the civil. Those who for selfish and private purposes stir up national antagonisms and expose the world to the ruin of war.

Will the House Committee on Un-American Activities interfere with the activities of these? Will Mr. Truman's disloyalty proclamation reach these? Will the current campaigns for Americanism convert these? If past experience is any guide, they will not. What they will do, if they are successful, is to silence criticism, stamp out dissent—or drive it underground. But if our democracy is to flourish it must have criticism, if our government is to function it must have dissent. Only totalitarian governments insist upon conformity and they—as we know—do so at their peril. Without criticism abuses will go unrebuked; without dissent our dynamic system will become static.

Questions

1. What does Commager mean when he writes that the new definition of loyalty is "conformity"?

2. Why does he claim that the new patriotism makes "a mockery of the Declaration of Independence and Bill of Rights"?

CHAPTER 24

An Affluent Society, 1953–1960

156. Richard M. Nixon, "What Freedom Means to Us" (1959)

Source: Vital Speeches of the Day *(September 1, 1959), pp. 677–79.*

In 1958, during a "thaw" in the Cold War, the United States and the Soviet Union agreed to exchange national exhibitions in order to allow citizens of each "superpower" to become acquainted with life in the other. The American National Exhibition opened in Moscow in 1959. It was a showcase of consumer goods and leisure equipment, complete with stereo sets, a movie theater, home appliances, and twenty-two different cars. But the exhibit's message was the equating of freedom and consumerism.

Vice President Richard Nixon opened the exhibition with an address that emphasized the "extraordinarily high standard of living" in the United States, with its 56 million cars and 50 million television sets. The Moscow exhibition became the site of a classic Cold War confrontation over the meaning of freedom—the "kitchen debate" between Nixon and Soviet Premier Nikita Khrushchev. Twice during the first day, Nixon and the Soviet leader engaged in unscripted debate about the merits of capitalism and communism. Overall, the speech and ensuing debate reflected the triumph during the 1950s of a conception of freedom centered on economic abundance and consumer choice within the context of traditional family life.

I AM HONORED on behalf of President Eisenhower to open this American Exhibition in Moscow. Mrs. Nixon and I were among the many thousands of Americans who were privileged to visit the splendid Soviet Exhibition in New York, and we want to take this opportunity to congratulate the people of the U.S.S.R. for the great achievements and progress so magnificently portrayed by your Exhibition.

We, in turn, hope that many thousands of Soviet citizens will take advantage of this opportunity to learn about life in the United States by visiting our Exhibition.

Of course, we both realize that no exhibition can portray a complete picture of all aspects of life in great nations like the U.S.S.R. and the United States.

Among the questions which some might raise with regard to our Exhibition are these: To what extent does this Exhibition accurately present life in the United States as it really is? Can only the wealthy people afford the things exhibited here? What about the inequality, the injustice, the other weaknesses which are supposed to be inevitable in a Capitalist society?

As Mr. Khrushchev often says: "You can't leave a word out of a song." Consequently, in the limited time I have, I would like to try to answer some of these questions so that you may get an accurate picture of what America is really like.

Let me start with some of the things in this Exhibit. You will see a house, a car, a television set—each the newest and most modern of its type we can produce. But can only the rich in the United States afford such things? If this were the case we would have to include in our definition of rich the millions of America's wage earners.

Let us take, for example, our 16 million factory workers. The average weekly wage of a factory worker in America is $90.54. With this income he can buy and afford to own a house, a television set, and a car in the price range of those you will see in this Exhibit. What is more, the great majority of American wage earners have done exactly that.

Putting it another way, there are 44 million families in the United States. Twenty-five million of these families live in houses or apartments that have as much or more floor space than the one you see in this Exhibit. Thirty-one million families own their own homes and the land on which they are built. America's 44 million families own a total of 56 million cars, 50 million television sets and 143 million radio sets. And they buy an average of 9 dresses and suits and 14 pairs of shoes per family per year.

Why do I cite these figures? Not because they indicate that the American people have more automobiles, TV sets, or houses than the people of the U.S.S.R.

In fairness we must recognize that our country industrialized sooner than the Soviet Union. And Americans are happy to note that Mr. Khrushchev has set a goal for the Soviet economy of catching up in the production of consumer goods.

We welcome this kind of competition because when we engage in it, no one loses—everyone wins as the living standards of people throughout the world are raised to higher levels. It also should be pointed out that while we may be ahead of you as far as these items are concerned, you are ahead of us in other fields—for example, in the size of the rockets you have developed for the exploration of outer space.

But what these statistics do dramatically demonstrate is this: That the United States, the world's largest capitalist country, has from the standpoint of distribution of wealth come closest to the ideal of prosperity for all in a classless society.

As our revered Abraham Lincoln said "... We do not propose any war upon capital; we do wish to allow the humblest man an equal chance to get rich with everybody else."

The 67 million American wage earners are not the downtrodden masses depicted by the critics of capitalism in the latter part of the Nineteenth and early part of the Twentieth Centuries. They hold their heads high as they proudly enjoy the highest standard of living of any people in the world's history.

The caricature of capitalism as a predatory, monopolist domi-nated society, is as hopelessly out of date, as far as the United States is concerned, as a wooden plow.

This does not mean that we have solved all of our problems. Many of you have heard about the problem of unemployment in the United States. What is not so well known is that the average period that these unemployed were out of work even during our recent re-cession was less than three months. And during that period the un-employed had an average income from unemployment insurance funds of $131.49 per month. The day has passed in the United States when the unemployed were left to shift for themselves.

The same can be said for the aged, the sick, and others who are un-able to earn enough to provide an adequate standard of living. An ex-panded program of Social Security combined with other government and private programs provides aid and assistance for those who are unable to care for themselves. For example, the average retired couple on Social Security in the United States receives an income of $116 per month apart from the additional amounts they receive from private pensions and savings accounts.

What about the strikes which take place in our economy, the lat-est example of which is the steel strike which is going on? The an-swer is that here we have a firsthand example of how a free economy works. The workers right to join with other workers in a union and to bargain collectively with management is recognized and pro-tected by law. No man or woman in the United States can be forced to work for wages he considers to be inadequate or under conditions he believes are unsatisfactory.

Another problem which causes us concern is that of racial dis-crimination in our country. We are making great progress in solving this problem but we shall never be satisfied until we make the Amer-ican ideal of equality of opportunity a reality for every citizen re-gardless of his race, creed or color.

We have other problems in our society but we are confident that for us our system of government provides the best means for solving them. But the primary reason we believe this is not because we have an economy which builds more than 1 million houses, produces 6 million cars and 6 million television sets per year.

Material progress is important but the very heart of the American ideal is that "man does not live by bread alone." To us, progress without freedom to use a common expression is like "potatoes without fat."

Let me give you some examples of what freedom means to us.

President Eisenhower is one of the most popular men ever to hold that high office in our country. Yet never an hour or a day goes by in which criticism of him and his policies cannot be read in our newspapers, heard on our radio and television, or in the Halls of Congress.

And he would not have it any other way. The fact that our people can and do say anything they want about a government official, the fact that in our elections, as this voting machine in our exhibit illustrates, every voter has a free choice between those who hold public office and those who oppose them makes ours a true peoples' government.

We trust the people. We constantly submit big decisions to the people. Our history convinces us that over the years the people have been right much more often than they have been wrong.

As an indication of the extent of this freedom and of our faith in our own system, forty hours of radio broadcasts from the Soviet Union can be heard without jamming in the United States each day, and over a million and a half copies of Soviet publications are purchased in our country each year.

Let us turn now to freedom of religion. Under our Constitution no church or religion can be supported by the State. An American can either worship in the church of his choice or choose to go to no church at all if he wishes. Acting with this complete freedom of choice, 103 million of our citizens are members of 308 of American churches.

We also cherish the freedom to travel, both within our country and outside the United States. Within our country we live and travel where we please without travel permits, internal passports or police registration. We also travel freely abroad. For example, 11 million Americans will travel to other countries during this year, including 10,000 to the Soviet Union. We look forward to the day when millions of Soviet citizens will travel to ours and other countries in this way.

Time will not permit me to tell you of all of the features of American life, but in summary I think these conclusions can objectively be stated.

The great majority of Americans like our system of government. Much as we like it, however, we would not impose it on anyone else. We believe that people everywhere should have a right to choose the form of government they want.

Questions

1. Why do you think Nixon begins his speech by discussing the American standard of living rather than other manifestations of freedom?

2. What other elements of freedom does Nixon refer to in the speech?

---

157. Clark Kerr, *Industrialism and Industrial Man* (1960)

Source: Clark Kerr, et al.: Excerpt from "Industrialism and Industrial Man." Reprinted by permission of the publisher from Industrialism and Industrial Man: The Problems of Labor and Management in Economic Growth *by Clark Kerr, John T. Dunlop, Frederick H. Harbison, and Charles A. Myers, pp. 40, 42, 44, 294, 295–96, Cambridge Mass.: Harvard University Press, Copyright © 1960 by the President and Fellows of Harvard College.*

The end of World War II was followed by a period of economic expansion, low unemployment, and rising living standards. Between 1946 and 1960, the gross national product more than doubled and ordinary citizens' incomes rose dramatically. In every measurable way—diet, housing, wages, education, recreation—most Americans lived better than their parents and grandparents. In this affluent society, consumerism increasingly replaced economic independence and democratic participation as central definitions of American freedom. A study of modern industrial society published in 1960 by Clark Kerr, the president of the University of California, Berkeley, and three other scholars, reflected the era's outlook. Freedom, they acknowledged, may well have been reduced "in the work place," but society offered a far greater range of "goods and services." Leisure activities, not work or politics, would henceforth be "the happy hunting ground for the independent spirit." And the role of intellectuals was not, as in the past, to criticize society, but to help stabilize it by promoting a "consensus" of ideas and values.

THE INDUSTRIAL SOCIETY is necessarily characterized by a substantial range and scale of activities by the government. In a society of advanced technology there are, by virtue of this technology, a larger number of activities for government; for instance, the need for roads and highways, the provision for airports, the regulation of traffic, radio and television, a result of modern means of communication. Urban development has the same consequences. Technology also creates a more complex problem for a military establishment, extending in many directions the activities of government. The more integrated character of the world increases the activities significant to international relations and hence typically the scope of government activities. The scale of some scientific applications and the capital needs of new technologies tend to increase the scope of public agencies. As income rises, the demand of consumers may be for services largely provided by governments, such as education, parks, roads and health services.

The industrial society and individual freedom, however, are not necessarily to be regarded as antagonists. A high degree of discipline in the work place imposed by a web of rules and a large range of governmental activities is fully consistent with a larger freedom for the individual in greater leisure, a greater range of choice in occupations and place of residence, a greater range of alternatives in goods and services on which to use income, and a very wide range of subgroups or associations in which to choose participation. It is a mistake to regard the industrial society as antithetical to individual freedom by citing ways in which the scope of public and private governments has increased without also noting ways in which the industrial society expands individual freedom.

• • •

The industrial society, as any established society, develops a distinctive consensus which relates individuals and groups to each other and provides a common body of ideas, beliefs, and value judgments integrated into a whole. There must be a consensus to permit the industrial society to function. Various forms of the industrial society may create some distinctive features of an ideology, but all industrialized societies have some common values. In the pure industrial society science and technical knowledge have high values, and those engaged in advancing science and in applying it to industrial processes have high prestige and receive high rewards in the society. The pure industrial society eliminates taboos against technical change, and it places high values on being "modern," "up-to-date," and in "progress" for their own sake.

• • •

The function of making explicit a consensus and of combining discrete beliefs and convictions into a reasonably consistent body of ideas is the task of intellectuals in every society. Industrial society does not uniquely create intellectuals; they exist in all societies in some degree. There are probably more intellectuals, at least potentially, in the industrial society on account of the higher levels of general education, higher income levels, and greater leisure. There are also new patrons to the intellectuals as compared to pre-industrial society. A diversity of markets for intellectuals—the university, enterprise, labor organization, voluntary association, government, and self-employment—tends to displace the old aristocratic patrons. The function of formulating and restating the major values, premises, and consensus of a society from time to time, of sweeping away the old and adopting the new or reconciling the industrial processes with the old order, plays a significant role in industrialization. The intellectuals accordingly are an influential group in the process of the creation and molding of the new industrial society.

• • •

The individual will be in a mixed situation far removed either from that of the independent farmer organizing most aspects of his own life or from that of the Chinese in the commune under total surveillance. In his working life he will be subject to great conformity imposed not only by the enterprise manager but also by the state and by his own occupational association. For most people, any true scope for the independent spirit on the job will be missing. However, the skilled worker, while under rules, does get some control over his job, some chance to organize it as he sees fit, some possession of it. Within the narrow limits of this kind of "job control," the worker will have some freedom. But the productive process tends to regiment. People must perform as expected or it breaks down. This is now and will be increasingly accepted as an immutable fact. The state, the manager, the occupational association are all disciplinary agents. But discipline is often achieved by a measure of persuasion and incentive. The worker will be semi-independent with some choice among jobs, some control of the job, and some scope for the effects of morale; but he will also be confined by labor organizations, pensions, and seniority rules, and all sorts of rules governing the conduct of the job.

Outside his working life the individual may have more freedom under pluralistic industrialism than in most earlier forms of society. Politically he can be given some influence. Society has achieved consensus and it is perhaps less necessary for Big Brother to exercise political control. Nor in this Brave New World need genetic and chemical means be employed to avoid revolt. There will not be any revolt, anyway, except little bureaucratic revolts that can be handled piecemeal. An educated population will want political choice and can be given it. There will also be reasonable choice in the controlled labor market, subject to the confining limits of the occupation, and in the controlled product market.

The great new freedom may come in the leisure of individuals. Higher standards of living, more leisure, more education make this not only possible but almost inevitable. This will be the happy hunting ground for the independent spirit. Along with the bureaucratic conservatism of economic and political life may well go a New Bohemianism in the other aspects of life and partly as a reaction to the confining nature of the productive side of society. There may well come a new search for individuality and a new meaning to liberty. The economic system may be highly ordered and the political system barren ideologically; but the social and recreational and cultural aspects of life diverse and changing.

• • •

Utopia never arrives, but men may well settle for the benefits of a greater scope for freedom in their personal lives at the cost of considerable conformity in their working lives.

• • •

Questions

1. How much scope for individual freedom seems to exist in Kerr's description of "industrial society"?

2. What role does democratic politics seem to play in this vision of society?

158. David E. Lilienthal on Big Business and American Freedom (1952)

Source: From pp. ix, 3–9, 40–41, Big Business: A New Era *by David E. Lilienthal. Copyright 1952, 1953 by David E. Lilienthal. Copyright renewed © 1980 by David E. Lilienthal & 1981 by David E. Lilienthal, Jr. Reprinted by permission of HarperCollins Publishers.*

Even as a few large corporations dominated key sectors of the economy, many Americans retained their traditional deep suspicion of big business, associating it with images of robber barons who manipulated politics, suppressed economic competition, and treated their workers unfairly.

Americans, wrote David Lilienthal, chairman of the Atomic Energy Commission, must abandon their traditional fear that concentrated economic power endangered freedom. Large-scale production was not only necessary to fighting the Cold War but enhanced freedom by multiplying consumer goods. Lilienthal's book was a contribution to what one historian calls the "selling of free enterprise," a concerted effort to persuade Americans that existing economic arrangements provided the surest foundation for individual freedom. By the end of the 1950s, public opinion surveys revealed that over 80 percent of Americans believed that "our freedom depends on the free enterprise system."

I CONCEIVE THE purpose of American economic society not as the production and consumption of so many billions of units of steel, copper, automobiles, refrigerators. The purpose of our economic society and system is to promote freedom for the individual, as one prime essential of happiness and human fulfillment. By freedom I mean essentially *freedom to choose* to the maximum degree possible. Freedom is by no means merely a freedom to vote without coercion. "Did you suppose," asked Walt Whitman, "democracy was only for elections, for politics?"

Freedom of choice in economic matters means freedom to choose between competing ideas or services or goods. It means the maximum freedom to choose one job or one profession or one line of business as against some other. It means a maximum range of choice for the consumer when he spends his dollar. It means a maximum possible area of choice for the man who has saved up capital to invest.

These are economic choices. They are, however, more than economic or business acts. They are the mark of men who are free, as free as in society it is possible or workable for men to be. We call our economic system, quite appropriately, free enterprise. To maintain and nourish the essentials of free enterprise for all our people we must maintain and nourish the freedom of choice that makes the system come into being and flourish.

It is the vital role of Big Business in furthering just this freedom of choice that I emphasize in this book. And yet we still carry around our inherited conviction that Bigness means monopoly, which implies the absence of free choice.

It is natural enough that we should so generally regard *Bigness* and *monopoly* as synonymous. During the first years of this century, when many of us acquired our economic and political ideas, it was so often the case that Bigness and monopoly tended to be the same.

There were periodic curbs put on Big Business through these years. Woodrow Wilson created the Federal Trade Commission. Charles Evans Hughes, writing a great chapter of devoted public service, exposed the evils of big utilities and insurance companies. Louis D. Brandeis, with the power of his great spirit and mind, exposed the "curse of bigness," and it was anything but a pretty picture.

The depression of the thirties brought a resurgence of public condemnation and distrust of size: the Pecora investigation of Wall Street, the Temporary Economic Committee, the constructive and overdue reforms of the abuses of finance and large business during the first seven years of the administrations of Franklin Roosevelt.

The apparent contradictions of my own experience are illustrative of those of almost everyone else. I was brought up, like most men and women of my generation, to be suspicious and distrustful of things that are big. My father and his friends, who were small businessmen, spoke with deep apprehension of the trusts and cheered

Teddy Roosevelt in his Bull Moose campaign; they thought the world
was in a bad way when the first five-and-ten bought out an old individual family business and began the "chain-store" influx in our Indiana town. At home and at school, my generation heard the same
refrain of fear and antagonism and distrust of Bigness—though at
the same time we bragged about things because they were big. And
yet by the time I was forty, I found myself directing the biggest integrated power system in the world, the TVA, which was itself the creation of an old-time trust buster, George Norris, and an outstanding
critic of Bigness, Franklin D. Roosevelt. For over thirteen years I
helped develop, as a unit, a region larger geographically than Great
Britain, that embraced parts of seven Southern states. And, in 1946,
I was made head of the largest industrial monopoly of history, the
Atomic Energy Commission of the United States.

Despite our antagonism, despite handicaps of law and public
opinion, Bigness of units has nevertheless developed rapidly until
today size is a chief and outstanding characteristic of the way we do
business, the way we live. And we like the material fruits of size at
the very same time that we continue to view it with distrust. There is
an apparent contradiction between our deep fears of Bigness and our
need of it, that for a good many years has confused and troubled me.
Can these two be reconciled? More narrowly, can Bigness and competition be reconciled?

The Sherman Antitrust Act has had a profound effect upon the
course of American economic and social development. It was a great
feat of statesmanship, an exhibition of remarkable insight.

But to the extent that it has recently been so construed as to condemn Bigness *per se*, the Sherman Act does not live up to the present
needs of the United States. For basic reasons going to the very dy-
namics of modern industry, it is Bigness that helps keep competition
a flourishing reality today. . . .

It is not, however, with the provisions and interpretations of the
Sherman Act that we laymen should be deeply concerned today, but
with the underlying assumptions, "the picture in the mind," the
philosophy for which that act stands as it is applied to large-scale

undertakings. It is the economic and political philosophy and emotion, affecting its present interpretation, that badly needs reexamination. It is by the new facts of the fifties in contrast to the essential facts about our country as it was a generation or two ago, that we need to judge whether Bigness should today be penalized or encouraged, feared or promoted.

Such a fundamental re-examination is appropriate, is indeed essential and vital, at a time like the present. In such a period of crisis and strain, of heart-searching and anxiety about basic things, we need to examine such an all-pervasive issue as this. If, by that inexplicable process of general public consensus by which Americans determine fundamental issues, we decide that Bigness is our ally, that its risk and dangers are now manageable and with wisdom can be surmounted, if we conclude to end this contradiction between our enjoyment of the fruits of Bigness and the suspicions we visit on it, then we can accelerate our progress toward the goals of America in a way that takes one's breath away to contemplate.

Questions

1. What role does the Cold War play in Lilienthal's defense of Big Business?

2. How does Lilienthal define economic freedom, and how does his definition differ from previous understandings?

---

159. Milton Friedman, *Capitalism and Freedom* (1962)

Source: Milton Friedman, Capitalism and Freedom, *pp. 1–4. Copyright ©
1962 The University of Chicago Press, reprinted with permission.*

During the 1950s and early 1960s, conservative ideas seemed to have been marginalized in American politics. Nonetheless, two groups emerged in these years who, while largely ignored at the time, laid the intellectual foundations for the movement's later rebirth. The "new conservatives" feared that the United States was suffering from moral decay and called for a return to traditional values grounded in the Christian tradition and in timeless notions of good and evil. If men and women did not choose to lead virtuous lives, the government must force them to do so.

A quite different group of conservative thinkers were "libertarians," to whom freedom meant individual autonomy, limited government, and unregulated capitalism. This view found powerful support in the writings of the young economist Milton Friedman. In *Capitalism and Freedom*, he identified the free market as the necessary foundation for individual liberty. He called for turning over to the private sector virtually all government functions and the repeal of minimum wage laws, the graduated income tax, and the Social Security system. Friedman extended the idea of unrestricted free choice into virtually every realm of life. Government, he insisted, should seek to regulate neither the economy nor individual conduct.

IN A MUCH quoted passage in his inaugural address, President Kennedy said, "Ask not what your country can do for you—ask what you can do for your country." It is a striking sign of the temper of our times that the controversy about this passage centered on its origin and not on its content. Neither half of the statement expresses a relation between the citizen and his government that is worthy of the ideals of free men in a free society. The paternalistic "what your country can do for you" implies that government is the patron, the citizen the ward, a view that is at odds with the free man's belief in his own responsibility for his own destiny. The organismic, "what you can do for your country" implies that government is the master or the deity, the citizen, the servant or the votary. To the free man, the country is the collection of individuals who compose it, not something over and above them. He is proud of a common heritage and loyal to common traditions. But he regards government as a means, an instrumentality, neither a grantor of favors and gifts, nor a master or god to be blindly worshipped and served. He recognizes no national goal except as it is the consensus of the goals that the citizens sever-ally serve. He recognizes no national purpose except as it is the con-sensus of the purposes for which the citizens severally strive.

The free man will ask neither what his country can do for him nor what he can do for his country. He will ask rather "What can I and my compatriots do through government" to help us discharge our individual responsibilities, to achieve our several goals and pur-poses, and above all, to protect our freedom? And he will accompany this question with another: How can we keep the government we create from becoming a Frankenstein that will destroy the very free-dom we establish it to protect? Freedom is a rare and delicate plant. Our minds tell us, and history confirms, that the great threat to free-dom is the concentration of power. Government is necessary to preserve our freedom, it is an instrument through which we can ex-ercise our freedom; yet by concentrating power in political hands, it is also a threat to freedom. Even though the men who wield this power initially be of good will and even though they be not cor-rupted by the power they exercise, the power will both attract and form men of a different stamp.

How can we benefit from the promise of government while avoid-ing the threat to freedom? Two broad principles embodied in our Constitution give an answer that has preserved our freedom so far, though they have been violated repeatedly in practice while pro-claimed as precept.

First, the scope of government must be limited. Its major function must be to protect our freedom both from the enemies outside our gates and from our fellow-citizens: to preserve law and order, to en-force private contracts, to foster competitive markets. Beyond this major function, government may enable us at times to accomplish jointly what we would find it more difficult or expensive to accom-plish severally. However, any such use of government is fraught with danger. We should not and cannot avoid using government in this way. But there should be a clear and large balance of advantages before we do. By relying primarily on voluntary co-operation and private enterprise, in both economic and other activities, we can insure that the private sector is a check on the powers of the governmental sector and an effective protection of freedom of speech, of religion, and of thought.

The second broad principle is that government power must be dispersed. If government is to exercise power, better in the county than in the state, better in the state than in Washington. If I do not like what my local community does, be it in sewage disposal, or zoning, or schools, I can move to another local community, and though few may take this step, the mere possibility acts as a check. If I do not like what my state does, I can move to another. If I do not like what Washington imposes, I have few alternatives in this world of jealous nations.

The very difficulty of avoiding the enactments of the federal government is of course the great attraction of centralization to many of its proponents. It will enable them more effectively, they believe, to legislate programs that—as they see it—are in the interest of the public, whether it be the transfer of income from the rich to the poor or from private to governmental purposes. They are in a sense right. But this coin has two sides. The power to do good is also the power to do harm; those who control the power today may not tomorrow; and, more important, what one man regards as good, another may regard as harm. The great tragedy of the drive to centralization, as of the drive to extend the scope of government in general, is that it is mostly led by men of good will who will be the first to rue its consequences.

Questions

1. What does Friedman mean by the United States as a "collection of individuals"?

2. How would you describe Friedman's understanding of freedom?

160. C. Wright Mills on "Cheerful Robots" (1959)

Source: From Sociological Imagination, *pp. 174–75. Copyright © 1963. Reprinted by permission of Oxford University Press, Inc.*

With both major parties embracing the Cold War and social criticism stigmatized as "un-American," political debate in the 1950s took place within extremely narrow limits. Nonetheless, some dissenting voices could be heard. Writers criticized the monotony of modern work, the emptiness of suburban life, and the powerlessness of the individual in a world controlled by giant bureaucracies. More radical in pointing to the problem of unequal power in American society, the sociologist C. Wright Mills challenged the self-satisfied vision of democratic pluralism that dominated mainstream social science in the 1950s. Mills wrote of a "power elite"—an interlocking directorate of corporate leaders, politicians, and military men whose control of government and society had made political democracy obsolete. Such criticism helped to set the stage for the revolts of the 1960s. In the 1950s, however, it failed to dent widespread complacency about the American way of life.

FREEDOM IS NOT merely the chance to do as one pleases; neither is it merely the opportunity to choose between set alternatives. Freedom is, first of all, the chance to formulate the available choices, to argue over them—and then, the opportunity to choose. That is why freedom cannot exist without an enlarged role of human reason in human affairs. Within an individual's biography and within a society's history, the social task of reason is to formulate choices, to enlarge the scope of human decisions in the making of history. The future of human affairs is not merely some set of variables to be predicted. The future is what is to be decided—within the limits, to be sure, of historical possibility. But this possibility is not fixed; in our time the limits seem very broad indeed.

Beyond this, the problem of freedom is the problem of how decisions about the future of human affairs are to be made and who is to make them. Organizationally, it is the problem of a just machinery of decision. Morally, it is the problem of political responsibility. Intellectually, it is the problem of what are now the possible futures of human affairs. But the larger aspects of the problem of freedom today concern not only the nature of history and the structural chance for explicit decisions to make a difference in its course; they concern also the nature of man and the fact that the value of freedom cannot be based upon 'man's basic nature.' The ultimate problem of freedom is the problem of the cheerful robot, and it arises in this form today because today it has become evident to us that *all* men do *not* naturally *want* to be free; that all men are not willing or not able, as the case may be, to exert themselves to acquire the reason that freedom requires.

Under what conditions do men come to *want* to be free and capable of acting freely? Under what conditions are they willing and able to bear the burdens freedom does impose and to see these less as burdens than as gladly undertaken self-transformations? And on the negative side: Can men be made to want to become *cheerful* robots?

In our time, must we not face the possibility that the human mind as a social fact might be deteriorating in quality and cultural level, and yet not many would notice it because of the overwhelming accumulation of technological gadgets? Is not that one meaning of rationality without reason? Of human alienation? Of the absence of any free role for reason in human affairs? The accumulation of gadgets hides these meanings: Those who use these devices do not understand them; those who invent them do not understand much else. That is why we may *not*, without great ambiguity, use technological abundance as the index of human quality and cultural progress.

Questions

1. How does Mills's definition of freedom differ from the idea of freedom as consumer choice?

2. What does Mills mean by "cheerful robots"?

---

161. Allen Ginsberg, "Howl" (1955)

Source: Allen Ginsberg, "what sphinx of cement. . . gone down the American river!" (Moloch section, 34 lines) from "Howl," from Collected Poems 1947–1980 by Allen Ginsberg. Copyright © 1955 by Allen Ginsberg. Reprinted by permission of HarperCollins Publishers.

A different kind of criticism of mainstream culture arose from a group of artists and writers of the 1950s known as the Beats, centered in New York City and San Francisco, as well as college towns like Madison, Wisconsin, and Ann Arbor, Michigan. Rejecting the work ethic, the consumer culture of the suburban middle class, and the militarization of American life by the Cold War, the Beats celebrated impulsive action, immediate pleasure (often enhanced by drugs), and sexual experimentation.

"I saw the best minds of my generation destroyed by madness, starving hysterical naked," wrote the Beat poet Alan Ginsberg in "Howl" (1955), a protest against materialism and conformism. Ginsburg wrote of American life through the image of Moloch, an idol in the Bible to whom parents sacrificed their children. In the poem, Moloch was a symbol of a militaristic, materialistic society that stifled spontaneity and human feeling. "Howl" became a kind of manifesto of the Beat Generation.

What sphinx of cement and aluminum bashed open their skulls and
    ate up their brains and imagination?
Moloch! Solitude! Filth! Ugliness! Ashcans and unobtainable dollars!
    Children screaming under the stairways! Boys sobbing in armies!

Old men weeping in the parks!

Moloch! Moloch! Nightmare of Moloch! Moloch the loveless! Mental Moloch! Moloch the heavy judger of men!

Moloch the incomprehensible prison! Moloch the crossbone soulless jailhouse and Congress of sorrows! Moloch whose buildings are judgment! Moloch the vast stone of war! Moloch the stunned governments!

Moloch whose mind is pure machinery! Moloch whose blood is running money! Moloch whose fingers are ten armies! Moloch whose breast is a cannibal dynamo! Moloch whose ear is a smoking tomb!

Moloch whose eyes are a thousand blind windows! Moloch whose skyscrapers stand in the long streets like endless Jehovahs! Moloch whose factories dream and croak in the fog! Moloch whose smokestacks and antennae crown the cities!

Moloch whose love is endless oil and stone! Moloch whose soul is electricity and banks! Moloch whose poverty is the specter of genius! Moloch whose fate is a cloud of sexless hydrogen! Moloch whose name is the Mind!

Moloch who entered my soul early! Moloch in whom I am a consciousness without a body! Moloch who frightened me out of my natural ecstasy! Moloch whom I abandon! Wake up in Moloch! Light streaming out of the sky!

Moloch! Moloch! Robot apartments! invisible suburbs! skeleton treasuries! blind capitals! demonic industries! spectral nations! invincible mad houses! granite cocks! monstrous bombs!

They broke their backs lifting Moloch to Heaven! Pavements, trees, radios, tons! lifting the city to Heaven which exists and is everywhere about us!

Visions! omens! hallucinations! miracles! ecstasies! gone down the American river!

Questions

1. What images convey Ginsberg's critique of 1950s American life?

2. What kind of alternative, if any, does Ginsberg offer to the materialism and conformism of American society?

---

162. Martin Luther King Jr. and the Montgomery Bus Boycott (1955)

Source: Martin Luther King Jr., "Meeting at Holt Street Church," Reprinted by arrangement with The Heirs to the Estate of Martin Luther King Jr., c/o Writers house as agent for the proprietor, New York, NY. Copyright © 1969 Martin Luther King Jr.; Copyright © renewed 1997 Coretta Scott King.

In December 1955, Rosa Parks, a veteran of local black politics who worked as a tailor's assistant in a Montgomery, Alabama, department store, refused to surrender her seat on a city bus to a white rider, as required by local law. Her arrest sparked a year-long bus boycott. Finally, the Supreme Court ruled segregation in public transportation unconstitutional.

The Montgomery bus boycott launched the movement for racial justice as a nonviolent crusade based in the black churches of the South. It marked the emergence of 26-year-old Martin Luther King Jr., who had recently arrived in the city to become pastor of a Baptist church, as the movement's national symbol. On the night of the first protest meeting, King's speech electrified his audience: "We, the disinherited of this land, we who have been oppressed so long, are tired of going through the long night of captivity. And now we are reaching out for the daybreak of freedom and justice and equality."

MY FRIENDS, WE are certainly very happy to see each of you out this evening. We are here this evening for serious business. (*Audience: Yes*) We are here in a general sense because first and foremost we are American citizens (*That's right*) and we are determined to apply our citizenship to the fullness of its meaning. (*Yeah, That's right*) We are here also because of our love for democracy, (*Yes*) because of our deep-seated belief that democracy transformed from thin paper to thick action (*Yes*) is the greatest form of government on earth. (*That's right*).

But we are here in a specific sense, because of the bus situation in Montgomery. (*Yes*) We are here because we are to get the situation corrected. This situation is not at all new. The problem has existed over endless years. (*That's right*) For many years now Negroes in Montgomery and so many other areas have been inflicted with the paralysis of crippling fears (*Yes*) on buses in our community. (*That's right*) On so many occasions, Negroes have been intimidated and humiliated and impressed—oppressed—because of the sheer fact that they were Negroes. (*That's right*) I don't have time this evening to go into the history of these numerous cases. Many of them now are lost in the thick fog of oblivion, (*Yes*) but at least one stands before us now with glaring dimensions. (*Yes*)

Just the other day, just last Thursday to be exact, one of the finest citizens in Montgomery (*Amen*)—not one of the finest Negro citizens (*That's right*) but one of the finest citizens in Montgomery—was taken from a bus (*Yes*) and carried to jail and arrested (*Yes*) because she refused to get up to give her seat to a white person.

• • •

Mrs. Rosa Parks is a fine person. (*Well, well said*) And since it had to happen I'm happy that it happened to a person like Mrs. Parks, for nobody can doubt the boundless outreach of her integrity! (*Sure enough*) Nobody can doubt the height of her character, (*Yes*) nobody can doubt the depth of her Christian commitment and devotion to the teachings of Jesus. (*All right*) And I'm happy since it had to happen, it happened to a person that nobody can call a disturbing factor in the community. (*All right*) Mrs. Parks is a fine Christian person, unassuming, and yet there is integrity and character there. And just because she refused to get up, she was arrested.

And you know, my friends, there comes a time when people get tired of being trampled over by the iron feet of oppression. [*Thundering applause*] There comes a time, my friends, when people get tired of being plunged across the abyss of humiliation where they experience the bleakness of nagging despair. (*Keep talking*) There comes a time when people get tired of being pushed out of the glittering sunlight of life's July, and left standing amid the piercing chill of an alpine November. (*That's right*) [*Applause*] There comes a time. (*Yes sir, Teach*) [*Applause continues*]

We are here, we are here this evening because we're tired now. (*Yes*) [*Applause*] And I want to say, that we are not here advocating violence. (*No*) We have never done that. (*Repeat that, Repeat that*) [*Applause*] I want it to be known throughout Montgomery and throughout this nation (*Well*) that we are Christian people. (*Yes*) [*Applause*] We believe in the Christian religion. We believe in the teachings of Jesus. (*Well*) The only weapon that we have in our hands this evening is the weapon of protest. (*Yes*) [*Applause*] That's all.

And certainly, certainly, this is the glory of America, with all of its faults. (*Yeah*) This is the glory of our democracy. If we were incarcerated behind the iron curtains of a Communistic nation we couldn't do this. If we were dropped in the dungeon of a totalitarian regime we couldn't do this. (*All right*) But the great glory of American democracy is the right to protest for right. (*That's right*) [*Applause*] My friends, don't let anybody make us feel that we to be compared in our actions with the Ku Klux Klan or with the White Citizens Council. [*Applause*] There will be no crosses burned at any bus stops in Montgomery. (*Well, that's right*) There will be no white persons pulled out of their homes and taken out on some distant road and lynched for not cooperating. [*Applause*] There will be nobody amid, among us who will stand up and defy the Constitution of this nation. [*Applause*] We only assemble here because of our desire to see right exist. [*Applause*] My friends, I want it to be known that we're going to work with grim and bold determination to gain justice on the buses in this city. [*Applause*]

And we are not wrong, we are not wrong in what we are doing.

(*Well*) If we are wrong, the Supreme Court of this nation is wrong. (*Yes sir*) [*Applause*] If we are wrong, the Constitution of the United States is wrong. (*Yes*) [*Applause*] If we are wrong, God Almighty is wrong. (*That's right*) [*Applause*] If we are wrong, Jesus of Nazareth was merely a utopian dreamer that never came down to earth. (*Yes*) [*Applause*] If we are wrong, justice is a lie: (*Yes*) love has no meaning. [*Applause*] And we are determined here in Montgomery to work and fight until justice runs down like water (*Yes*) [*Applause*] and righteousness like a mighty stream. (*Keep talking*) [*Applause*]

We, the disinherited of this land, we who have been oppressed so long, are tired of going through the long night of captivity. And now we are reaching out for the daybreak of freedom and justice and equality. [*Applause*] May I say to you my friends, as I come to a close, and just giving some idea of why we are assembled here, that we must keep—and I want to stress this, in all of our doings, in all of our deliberations here this evening and all of the week and while—whatever we do, we must keep God in the forefront. (*Yeah*) Let us be Christian in all of our actions. (*That's right*) But I want to tell you this evening that it is not enough for us to talk about love, love is one of the pivotal points of the Christian face, faith. There is another side called justice. And justice is really love in calculation. (*All right*) Justice is love correcting that which revolts against love. (*Well*)

The Almighty God himself is not . . . only, . . . the God just standing out saying through Hosea, "I love you, Israel." He's also the God that stands up before the nations and said: "Be still and know that I'm God, (*Yeah*) that if you don't obey me I will break the backbone of your power, (*Yeah*) and slap you out of the orbits of your international and national relationships." (*That's right*) Standing beside love is always justice (*Yeah*) and we are only using the tools of justice. Not only are we using the tools of persuasion but we've come to see that we've got to use the tools of coercion. Not only is this thing a process of education but it is also a process of legislation. [*Applause*]

As we stand and sit here this evening and as we prepare ourselves for what lies ahead, let us go out with a grim and bold determination that we are going to stick together. [*Applause*] We are going to work together. [*Applause*] Right here in Montgomery, when the history books are written in the future, (*Yes*) somebody will have to say, "There lived a race of people, (*Well*) a black people, (*Yes sir*) 'fleecy locks and black complexion,' (*Yes*) a people who had the moral courage to stand up for their rights. [*Applause*] And thereby they injected a new meaning into the veins of history and of civilization." And we're gonna do that. God grant that we will do it before it is too late. (*Oh yeah*) As we proceed with our program let us think of these things. (*Yes*) [*Applause*]

Questions

1. What parts of King's speech received the most enthusiastic reception from his audience?

2. In what ways does King appeal for white support for the boycott?

CHAPTER 25

The Sixties, 1960–1968

163. James Baldwin on Student Radicals (1960)

Source: James Baldwin, "They Can't Turn Back," Mademoiselle, August 1960, pp. 324–25, 351–60. Collected in The Price of the Ticket © 1985 by James Baldwin. Published by St. Martin's. Used by arrangement with the James Baldwin Estate.

On February 1, 1960, four students from North Carolina A. and T., a black college in Greensboro, entered the local Woolworth's department store. After making a few purchases, they sat down at the lunch counter, an area reserved for whites. Told that they could not be served, they remained in their seats until the store closed. More than any other event, the Greensboro sit-in launched the 1960s, a decade of political activism and social change. For the first time in American history, students had become the cutting edge of social change.

In 1960, the writer James Baldwin visited Tallahassee, Florida, to report on student activism there. Baldwin ruminated on the underlying causes of black protests and marveled at the militancy and idealism of the younger generation. To Baldwin, the movement challenged all Americans to rethink whether "we really want to be free" and whether freedom applied to all Americans or only to part of the population.

━━━━━━━

HALEY GOES OFF to give his exam and I walk outside, waiting for my taxi and watching the students. Only a decade and a half divide us, but what changes have occurred in those fifteen years! The world into which I was born must seem as remote to them as the flood. I watch them. Their walk, talk, laughter are as familiar to me as my skin, and yet there is something new about them. They remind me of all the Negro boys and girls I have ever known and they remind me of myself; but, really, I was never like these students. It took many years of vomiting up all the filth I'd been taught about myself, and half-believed, before I was able to walk on the earth as though I had a right to be here.

Well, they didn't have to come the way I came. This is what I've heard Negro parents say, with a kind of indescribable pride and relief, when one of their children graduated or won an award or sailed for Europe: began, in short, to move into the world as a free person. The society into which American Negro children are born has always presented a particular challenge to Negro parents. This society makes it necessary that they establish in the child a force that will cause him to *know* that the world's definition of his place and the means used by the world to make this definition binding are not for a moment to be respected. This means that the parent must prove daily, in his own person, how little the force of the world avails against the force of a person who is determined to be free. Now, this is a cruel challenge, for the force of the world is immense. That is why the vow *My children won't come like I came* is nothing less than a declaration of war, a declaration that has led to innumerable casualties. Generations of Negro children have said, as all the students here have said: "My Daddy taught me never to bow my head to nobody." But sometimes Daddy's head was bowed: frequently Daddy was destroyed.

These students were born at the very moment at which Europe's domination of Africa was ending. I remember, for example, the invasion of Ethiopia and Haile Selassie's vain appeal to the League of Nations, but they remember the Bandung Conference and the establishment of the Republic of Ghana.

Americans keep wondering what has "got into" the students. What has "got into" them is their history in this country. They are not the first Negroes to face mobs: they are merely the first Negroes to frighten the mob more than the mob frightens them. Many Americans may have forgotten, for example, the reign of terror in the 1920's that drove Negroes out of the South. Five hundred thousand moved North in one year. Some of the people who got to the North barely in time to be born are the parents of the students now going to school. This was forty years ago, and not enough has happened—not enough freedom has happened. But these young people are determined to make it happen and make it happen now. They cannot be diverted. It seems to me that they are the only people in this country now who really believe in freedom. Insofar as they can make it real for themselves, they will make it real for all of us. The question with which they present the nation is whether or not we really want to be free. It is because these students remain so closely related to their past that they are able to face with such authority a population ignorant of its history and enslaved by a myth. And by this population I do not mean merely the unhappy people who make up the Southern mobs. I have in mind nearly all Americans.

These students prove unmistakably what most people in this country have yet to discover: that time is real.

Questions

1. How does Baldwin explain the militancy of young blacks?

2. What does Baldwin mean by his last sentence and the phrase, "time is real"?

---

164. The Sharon Statement (1960)

Source: *Young Americans for Freedom, The Sharon Statement,* National Review, *September 24, 1960. Reprinted by permission of Young Americans for Freedom/YAF Foundation.*

The 1960s, today recalled as a decade of radicalism, also had a conservative side. With the founding in 1960 of Young Americans for Freedom (YAF), conservative students emerged as a force in politics. There were striking parallels between the Sharon Statement, issued by ninety young people who gathered at the estate of conservative intellectual William F. Buckley in Sharon, Connecticut, to establish YAF, and the Port Huron Statement of SDS two years later. Both manifestos portrayed youth as the cutting edge of a new radicalism. Both claimed to offer Americans a route to greater freedom. The Sharon Statement summarized beliefs that had circulated among conservatives during the past decade—the free market underpinned "personal freedom," political freedom rested on a free market economy, government must be strictly limited, and "international communism," the gravest threat to liberty, must be destroyed. The young conservatives played a major role in the campaign that won the Republican presidential nomination for conservative Barry Goldwater in 1964.

THE SHARON STATEMENT

Adopted by the Young Americans for Freedom in conference at Sharon, Conn., September 9–11, 1960

In this time of moral and political crisis, it is the responsibility of the youth of America to affirm certain eternal truths.

We, as young conservatives, believe:

That foremost among the transcendent values is the individual's use of his God-given free will, whence derives his right to be free from the restrictions of arbitrary force;

That liberty is indivisible, and that political freedom cannot long exist without economic freedom;

That the purposes of government are to protect these freedoms through the preservation of internal order, the provision of national defense, and the administration of justice;

That when government ventures beyond these rightful functions, it accumulates power which tends to diminish order and liberty;

That the Constitution of the United States is the best arrangement yet devised for empowering government to fulfill its proper role, while restraining it from the concentration and abuse of power;

That the genius of the Constitution—the division of powers—is summed up in the clause which reserves primacy to the several states, or to the people, in those spheres not specifically delegated to the Federal Government;

That the market economy, allocating resources by the free play of supply and demand, is the single economic system compatible with the requirements of personal freedom and constitutional government, and that it is at the same time the most productive supplier of human needs;

That when government interferes with the work of the market economy, it tends to reduce the moral and physical strength of the nation; that when it takes from one man to bestow on another, it diminishes the incentive of the first, the integrity of the second, and the moral autonomy of both;

That we will be free only so long as the national sovereignty of the United States is secure; that history shows periods of freedom are rare, and can exist only when free citizens concertedly defend their rights against all enemies;

That the forces of international Communism are, at present, the greatest single threat to these liberties;

That the United States should stress victory over, rather than coexistence with, this menace; and

That American foreign policy must be judged by this criterion: does it serve the just interests of the United States?

Questions

1. How does the statement differ from the government's policy regarding international communism in 1960?

2. How do the young conservatives understand freedom?

165. Barry Goldwater on "Extremism in the Defense of Liberty" (1964)

*Source: Barry Goldwater, Extremism in the Defense of Liberty, Official
Report of the Proceedings of the 28th Republican National Convention,
1964, pp. 413–19. Reprinted with permission of the Republican National
Committee.*

The presidential campaign of 1964 was a milestone in the rebirth of American conservatism. Four years earlier, the Republican candidate, Senator Barry Goldwater of Arizona, had written *The Conscience of a Conservative*, which demanded a more aggressive conduct of the Cold War and warned against "internal" dangers to freedom, especially the New Deal welfare state. In the Senate, Goldwater voted against the Civil Rights Act of 1964. Attacked as an extremist by Democrats and many moderate Republicans, Goldwater used his acceptance speech at the Republican national convention to outline his conservative vision and warn against the increased power of the national government. Toward the end, he made the explosive statement, "extremism in the defense of liberty is no vice."

Goldwater went down to a disastrous defeat. But his campaign aroused enthusiasm in the rapidly expanding suburbs of southern California and the Southwest. The funds that poured into the Goldwater campaign from the Sun Belt's oilmen and aerospace entrepreneurs established a new financial base for conservatism.

I ACCEPT YOUR nomination with a deep sense of humility. (Applause) I accept, too, the responsibility that goes with it, and I seek your continued help and your continued guidance. My fellow Republicans, our cause is too great for a man to feel worthy of it. Our task would be too great for any man, did he not have with him the hearts and the hands of this great Republican Party, and I promise you tonight that every fiber of my being is consecrated to our cause; that nothing shall be lacking from the struggle that can be brought to it by enthusiasm, by devotion and plain hard work. (Cheers and

Applause) In this world no person, no party, can guarantee anything, but what we can do, and we shall do, is to deserve victory, and victory will be ours. (Applause).

The good Lord raised this mighty Republic to be a home for the brave, and to flourish as the land of the free—not to stagnate in the swampland of collectivism, not to cringe before the bullying of communism. (Loud Applause and Cheers)

Now, my fellow Americans, the tide has been running against freedom. Our people have followed false prophets. We must and we shall return to proven ways—not because they are old, but because they are true. (Applause) We must, and we shall, set the tides running again in the cause of freedom. (Applause) And this Party, with its every action, every word, every breath and every heartbeat has but a single resolve, and that is freedom—freedom made orderly for this Nation by our constitutional government; freedom under a government limited by the laws of nature and of nature's God; freedom—balanced so that order, lacking liberty, will not become a slave of the prison cell; balanced so that liberty, lacking order, will not become the license of the mob and the jungle. (Applause)

Now, we Americans understand freedom. We have earned it, lived for it, and died for it. This nation and its people are freedom's model in a searching world. We can be freedom's missionaries in a doubting world. But, ladies and gentlemen, first we must renew freedom's vision in our own hearts and in our own homes. (Applause)

During four futile years, the administration which we shall replace has distorted and lost that vision. (Applause) It has talked and talked and talked and talked the words of freedom.

• • •

Tonight there is violence in our streets, corruption in our highest offices, aimlessness among our youth, anxiety among our elders and there is a virtual despair among the many who look beyond material success for the inner meaning of their lives. Where examples of morality should be set, the opposite is seen. Small men, seeking great wealth or power, have too often and too long turned even the highest levels of public service into mere personal opportunity. (Applause)

Now, certainly, simple honesty is not too much to demand of men in government. We find it in most. Republicans demand it from everyone. (Applause) They demand it from everyone, no matter how exalted or protected his position might be. (Applause) The growing menace in our country tonight, to personal safety, to life, to limb and property, in homes, in churches, on the playgrounds, and places of business, particularly in our great cities, is the mounting concern, or should be, of every thoughtful citizen in the United States. (Applause)

Security from domestic violence, no less than from foreign aggression, is the most elementary and fundamental purpose of any government, and a government that cannot fulfill that purpose is one that cannot long command the loyalty of its citizens. (Loud Applause) History shows us—demonstrates that nothing—nothing prepares the way for tyranny more than the failure of public offices to keep the streets safe from bullies and marauders. (Applause)

Those who seek absolute power, even though they seek it to do what they regard as good, are simply demanding the right to enforce their own version of heaven on earth. (Applause) And let me remind you, they are the very ones who always create the most hellish tyrannies. (Applause) Absolute power does corrupt, and those who seek it must be suspect and must be opposed. Their mistaken course stems from false notions of equality, ladies and gentlemen. Equality, rightly understood, as our founding fathers understood it, leads to liberty and to the emancipation of creative differences. Wrongly understood, as it has been so tragically in our time, it leads first to conformity and then to despotism. (Loud Applause and Cheers)

We Republicans see in our constitutional form of government the great framework which assures the orderly but dynamic fulfillment of the whole man, and we see the whole man as the great reason for instituting orderly government in the first place.

We see, in private property and in economy based upon and fostering private property, the one way to make government a durable ally of the whole man, rather than his determined enemy. (Applause)

We see, in the sanctity of private property, the only durable foundation for constitutional government in a free society. (Applause) And beyond that, we see, in cherished diversity of ways, diversity of thoughts, of motives and accomplishments. We do not seek to lead anyone's life for him—we seek only to secure his rights and to guarantee him opportunity to strive, with government performing only those needed and constitutionally-sanctioned tasks which cannot otherwise be performed. (Prolonged Applause)

We Republicans seek a government that attends to its inherent responsibilities of maintaining a stable monetary and fiscal climate, encouraging a free and a competitive economy and enforcing law and order.

• • •

The task of preserving and enlarging freedom at home and of safeguarding it from the forces of tyranny abroad is great enough to challenge all our resources and to refire all our strength. (Cheers and Applause) Anyone who joins us in all sincerity, we welcome. (Applause) Those who do not care for our cause, we don't expect to enter our ranks in any case. (Applause) And let our Republicanism, so focused and so dedicated, not be made fuzzy and futile by unthinking and stupid labels.

I would remind you that extremism in the defense of liberty is no vice. (Loud Applause and Cheers) And let me remind you also that moderation in the pursuit of justice is no virtue. (Applause and Cheers)

Questions

1. What evidence does Goldwater give of a decline of "morality" in American life?

2. Why does Goldwater stress the interconnection between "order" and liberty?

166. Lyndon B. Johnson, Commencement Address at Howard University (1965)

Source: "Commencement Address at Howard University, June 4, 1965," **Public Papers of the Presidents of the United States, Lyndon B. Johnson, 1965** *(Washington, D.C., 1966), pp. 635–40.*

By 1965, the civil rights movement had achieved many of its goals, including national laws mandating equal access to all public facilities, banning discrimination in employment, and restoring the right to vote to black southerners. Yet violent outbreaks in black ghettoes, beginning in Watts, the black ghetto of Los Angeles, in 1964, drew attention to the national scope of racial injustice and inequalities in jobs, education, and housing that the dismantling of legal segregation left intact.

Lyndon B. Johnson identified himself more fully with the civil rights movement than any president in American history. He believed that special efforts must be made to counteract the heritage of slavery and segregation. In a speech at all-black Howard University in 1965, Johnson sought to redefine the relationship between freedom and equality.

O UR EARTH IS the home of revolution. In every corner of every continent men charged with hope contend with ancient ways in the pursuit of justice. They reach for the newest of weapons to realize the oldest of dreams, that each may walk in freedom and pride, stretching his talents, enjoying the fruits of the earth.

Our enemies may occasionally seize the day of change, but it is the banner of our revolution they take. And our own future is linked to this process of swift and turbulent change in many lands in the world. But nothing in any country touches us more profoundly, and nothing is more freighted with meaning for our own destiny than the revolution of the Negro American.

In far too many ways American Negroes have been another nation: deprived of freedom, crippled by hatred, the doors of opportunity closed to hope.

In our time change has come to this Nation, too. The American Negro, acting with impressive restraint, has peacefully protested and marched, entered the courtrooms and the seats of government, demanding a justice that has long been denied. The voice of the Negro was the call to action. But it is a tribute to America that, once aroused, the courts and the Congress, the President and most of the people, have been the allies of progress.

• • •

That beginning is freedom; and the barriers to that freedom are tumbling down. Freedom is the right to share, share fully and equally, in American society—to vote, to hold a job, to enter a public place, to go to school. It is the right to be treated in every part of our national life as a person equal in dignity and promise to all others.

But freedom is not enough. You do not wipe away the scars of centuries by saying: Now you are free to go where you want, and do as you desire, and choose the leaders you please.

You do not take a person who, for years, has been hobbled by chains and liberate him, bring him up to the starting line of a race and then say, "you are free to compete with all the others," and still justly believe that you have been completely fair.

Thus it is not enough just to open the gates of opportunity. All our citizens must have the ability to walk through those gates.

This is the next and the more profound stage of the battle for civil rights. We seek not just freedom but opportunity. We seek not just legal equity but human ability, not just equality as a right and a theory but equality as a fact and equality as a result.

For the task is to give 20 million Negroes the same chance as every other American to learn and grow, to work and share in society, to develop their abilities—physical, mental and spiritual, and to pursue their individual happiness.

To this end equal opportunity is essential, but not enough, not enough. Men and women of all races are born with the same range of abilities. But ability is not just the product of birth. Ability is stretched or stunted by the family that you live with, and the neighborhood you live in—by the school you go to and the poverty or the richness of your surroundings. It is the product of a hundred unseen forces playing upon the little infant, the child, and finally the man.

• • •

For the great majority of Negro Americans—the poor, the unemployed, the uprooted, and the dispossessed—there is a much grimmer story. They still, as we meet here tonight, are another nation. Despite the court orders and the laws, despite the legislative victories and the speeches, for them the walls are rising and the gulf is widening.

Here are some of the facts of this American failure.

Thirty-five years ago the rate of unemployment for Negroes and whites was about the same. Tonight the Negro rate is twice as high.

In 1948 the 8 percent unemployment rate for Negro teenage boys was actually less than that of whites. By last year that rate had grown to 23 percent, as against 13 percent for whites unemployed.

Between 1949 and 1959, the income of Negro men relative to white men declined in every section of this country. From 1952 to 1963 the median income of Negro families compared to white actually dropped from 57 percent to 53 percent.

• • •

This is the devastating heritage of long years of slavery; and a century of oppression, hatred, and injustice.

For Negro poverty is not white poverty. Many of its causes and many of its cures are the same. But there are differences—deep, corrosive, obstinate differences—radiating painful roots into the community, and into the family, and the nature of the individual.

These differences are not racial differences. They are solely and simply the consequence of ancient brutality, past injustice, and present prejudice. They are anguishing to observe. For the Negro they are a constant reminder of oppression. For the white they are a constant reminder of guilt. But they must be faced and they must be dealt with and they must be overcome, if we are ever to reach the time when the only difference between Negroes and whites is the color of their skin.

Nor can we find a complete answer in the experience of other American minorities.

Perhaps most important—its influence radiating to every part of life—is the breakdown of the Negro family structure. For this, most of all, white America must accept responsibility. It flows from centuries of oppression and persecution of the Negro man. It flows from the long years of degradation and discrimination, which have attacked his dignity and assaulted his ability to produce for his family.

This, too, is not pleasant to look upon. But it must be faced by those whose serious intent is to improve the life of all Americans.

• • •

The family is the cornerstone of our society. More than any other force it shapes the attitude, the hopes, the ambitions, and the values of the child. And when the family collapses it is the children that are usually damaged. When it happens on a massive scale the community itself is crippled.

So, unless we work to strengthen the family, to create conditions under which most parents will stay together—all the rest: schools, and playgrounds, and public assistance, and private concern, will never be enough to cut completely the circle of despair and deprivation.

Questions

1. What does Johnson mean when he says, "freedom is not enough"?

2. Why does he argue that "Negro poverty" is fundamentally different from "white poverty"?

167. The Port Huron Statement (1962)

Source: *Students for a Democratic Society: The Port Huron Statement, 1964, pp. 3–8. Reprinted by permission of Tom Hayden.*

One of the most influential documents of the 1960s emerged in 1962 from a meeting sponsored by the Students for a Democratic Society (SDS), then a small offshoot of the socialist League for Industrial Democracy. Meeting at Port Huron, Michigan, some sixty college students adopted a document that captured the mood and summarized the beliefs of this generation of student protesters.

But what made the document the guiding spirit of what would soon be called the New Left was its new vision of social change. It spoke of participatory democracy, an idea that suggested a rejection of the elitist strain that had marked liberal thinkers from the Progressives to postwar advocates of economic planning, in which government experts would establish national priorities in the name of the people. Although rarely defined with precision, participatory democracy became a standard by which students judged existing social arrangements—work places, schools, government—and found them wanting. By the mid-1960s, fueled by growing opposition among the young to the country's war in Vietnam, SDS would become the most important vehicle for what was rapidly becoming a full-fledged generational rebellion.

WE ARE PEOPLE of this generation, bred in at least modest comfort, housed now in universities, looking uncomfortably to the world we inherit.

When we were kids the United States was the wealthiest and strongest country in the world; the only one with the atom bomb, the least scarred by modern war, an initiator of the United Nations that we thought would distribute Western influence throughout the world. Freedom and equality for each individual, government of, by, and for the people—these American values we found good, principles by which we could live as men. Many of us began maturing in complacency.

As we grew, however, our comfort was penetrated by events too troubling to dismiss. First, the permeating and victimizing fact of human degradation, symbolized by the Southern struggle against racial bigotry, compelled most of us from silence to activism. Second, the enclosing fact of the Cold War, symbolized by the presence of the Bomb, brought awareness that we ourselves, and our friends, and millions of abstract "others" we knew more directly because of our common peril, might die at any time. We might deliberately ignore, or avoid, or fail to feel all other human problems, but not these two, for these were too immediate and crushing in their impact, too challenging in the demand that we as individuals take the responsibility for encounter and resolution.

While these and other problems either directly oppressed us or rankled our consciences and became our own subjective concerns, we began to see complicated and disturbing paradoxes in our surrounding America. The declaration "all men are created equal..." rang hollow before the facts of Negro life in the South and the big cities of the North. The proclaimed peaceful intentions of the United States contradicted its economic and military investments in the Cold War status quo.

We witnessed, and continue to witness, other paradoxes. With nuclear energy whole cities can easily be powered, yet the dominant nation-states seem more likely to unleash destruction greater than that incurred in all wars of human history. Although our own technology is destroying old and creating new forms of social organization, men still tolerate meaningless work and idleness. While two-thirds of mankind suffers undernourishment, our own upper classes revel amidst superfluous abundance. Although world population is expected to double in forty years, the nations still tolerate anarchy as a major principle of international conduct and uncontrolled exploitation governs the sapping of the earth's physical resources. Although mankind desperately needs revolutionary leadership, America rests in national stalemate, its goals ambiguous and tradition-bound instead of informed and clear, its democratic system apathetic and manipulated rather than "of, by, and for the people."

Not only did tarnish appear on our image of American virtue, not only did disillusion occur when the hypocrisy of American ideals was discovered, but we began to sense that what we had originally seen as the American Golden Age was actually the decline of an era. The worldwide outbreak of revolution against colonialism and imperialism, the entrenchment of totalitarian states, the menace of war, overpopulation, international disorder, supertechnology—these trends were testing the tenacity of our own commitment to democracy and freedom and our abilities to visualize their application to a world in upheaval.

Our work is guided by the sense that we may be the last generation in the experiment with living. But we are a minority—the vast majority of our people regard the temporary equilibriums of our society and world as eternally functional parts. In this is perhaps the outstanding paradox: we ourselves are imbued with urgency, yet the message of our society is that there is no viable alternative to the present. Beneath the reassuring tones of the politicians, beneath the common opinion that America will "muddle through," beneath the stagnation of those who have closed their minds to the future, is the pervading feeling that there simply are no alternatives, that our times have witnessed the exhaustion not only of Utopias, but of any new departures as well. Feeling the press of complexity upon the emptiness of life, people are fearful of the thought that at any moment things might be thrust out of control. They fear change itself, since change might smash whatever invisible framework seems to hold back chaos for them now. For most Americans, all crusades are suspect, threatening. The fact that each individual sees apathy in his fellows perpetuates the common reluctance to organize for change. The dominant institutions are complex enough to blunt the minds of their potential critics, and entrenched enough to swiftly dissipate or entirely repel the energies of protest and reform, thus limiting human expectancies. Then, too, we are a materially improved society, and by our own improvements we seem to have weakened the case for further change.

Some would have us believe that Americans feel contentment amidst prosperity—but might it not better be called a glaze above deeply felt anxieties about their role in the new world? And if these anxieties produce a developed indifference to human affairs, do they not as well produce a yearning to believe there is an alternative to the present, that something *can* be done to change circumstances in the school, the workplaces, the bureaucracies, the government? It is to this latter yearning, at once the spark and engine of change, that we direct our present appeal. The search for truly democratic alternatives to the present, and a commitment to social experimentation with them, is a worthy and fulfilling human enterprise, one which moves us and, we hope, others today. On such a basis do we offer this document of our convictions and analysis: as an effort in understanding and changing the conditions of humanity in the late twentieth century, an effort rooted in the ancient, still unfulfilled conception of man attaining determining influence over his circumstances of life.

Making values explicit—an initial task in establishing alternatives—is an activity that has been devalued and corrupted. The conventional moral terms of the age, the politician moralities— "free world," "people's democracies"—reflect realities poorly, if at all, and seem to function more as ruling myths than as descriptive principles. But neither has our experience in the universities brought us moral enlightenment. Our professors and administrators sacrifice controversy to public relations; their curriculums change more slowly than the living events of the world; their skills and silence are purchased by investors in the arms race; passion is called unscholastic. The questions we might want raised—what is really important? can we live in a different and better way? if we wanted to change society, how would we do it?—are not thought to be questions of a "fruitful, empirical nature," and thus are brushed aside.

· · ·

We regard *men* as infinitely precious and possessed of unfulfilled capacities for reason, freedom, and love. In affirming these principles we are aware of countering perhaps the dominant conceptions of man in the twentieth century: that he is a thing to be manipulated, and that he is inherently incapable of directing his own affairs. We oppose the depersonalization that reduces human beings to the status of things—if anything, the brutalities of the twentieth century teach that means and ends are intimately related, that vague appeals to "posterity" cannot justify the mutilations of the present. We oppose, too, the doctrine of human incompetence because it rests essentially on the modern fact that men have been "competently" manipulated into incompetence—we see little reason why men cannot meet with increasing skill the complexities and responsibilities of their situation, if society is organized not for minority, but for majority, participation in decision-making.

Men have unrealized potential for self-cultivation, self-direction, self-understanding, and creativity. It is this potential that we regard as crucial and to which we appeal, not to the human potentiality for violence, unreason, and submission to authority. The goal of man and society should be human independence: a concern not with image or popularity but with finding a meaning in life that is personally authentic; a quality of mind not compulsively driven by a sense of powerlessness, nor one which unthinkingly adopts status values, nor one which represses all threats to its habits, but one which has full, spontaneous access to present and past experiences, one which easily unites the fragmented parts of personal history, one which openly faces problems which are troubling and unresolved; one with an intuitive awareness of possibilities, an active sense of curiosity, an ability and willingness to learn.

• • •

We would replace power rooted in possession, privilege, or circumstance by power and uniqueness rooted in love, reflectiveness, reason, and creativity. As a *social system* we seek the establishment of a democracy of individual participation, governed by two central aims: that the individual share in those social decisions determining the quality and direction of his life; that society be organized to encourage independence in men and provide the media for their common participation.

In a participatory democracy, the political life would be based in several root principles:

> that decision-making of basic social consequence be carried on by public groupings;
>
> that politics be seen positively, as the art of collectively creating an acceptable pattern of social relations;
>
> that politics has the function of bringing people out of isolation and into community, thus being a necessary, though not sufficient, means of finding meaning in personal life;
>
> that the political order should serve to clarify problems in a way instrumental to their solution; it should provide outlets for the expression of personal grievance and aspiration; opposing views should be organized so as to illuminate choices and facilitate the attainment of goals; channels should be commonly available to relate men to knowledge and to power so that private problems—from bad recreation facilities to personal alienation—are formulated as general issues.

The economic sphere would have as its basis the principles:

> that work should involve incentives worthier than money or survival: It should be educative, not stultifying; creative, not mechanical; self-directed, not manipulated, encouraging independence; a respect for others, a sense of dignity, and a willingness to accept social responsibility, since it is this experience that has crucial influence on habits, perceptions, and individual ethics;
>
> that the economic experience is so personally decisive that the individual must share in its full determination;
>
> that the economy itself is of such social importance that its major resources and means of production should be open to democratic participation and subject to democratic social regulation.

Like the political and economic ones, major social institutions—cultural, educational, rehabilitative, and others—should be generally organized with the well-being and dignity of man as the essential measure of success.

• • •

Questions

1. What features of American society seem most to trouble the authors of the Port Huron Statement?

2. How would you define the phrase, "a democracy of individual participation"?

168. Paul Potter on the Antiwar Movement (1965)

Source: Paul Potter, Speech at Washington Anti-War Demonstration, April 17, 1965, Takin' It to the Streets: A Sixties Reader, Alexander Bloom and Wini Brines, eds., pp. 214–16. Reprinted with permission of Oxford University Press, Inc.

The War in Vietnam divided American society more deeply than any military conflict in the nation's history. Early in 1965, President Lyndon Johnson authorized air strikes against North Vietnam and introduced American ground troops in the south. The cause of freedom, he insisted, was at stake. But as casualties mounted, the Cold War foreign policy consensus began to unravel. To SDS, the war seemed the opposite of participatory democracy, since American involvement had come through secret commitments and elite decision-making, with no real public debate.

In April 1965, SDS called on opponents of American policy in Vietnam to attend a rally in Washington. In his speech, SDS president Paul Potter tried to reclaim the language of freedom from the administration. Potter went on to challenge the entire basis of American foreign policy in the Cold War. He ended by calling for the creation of a "social movement" to demand an end to the war.

VIETNAM, WE MAY say, is a laboratory run by a new breed of gamesmen who approach war as a kind of rational exercise in international power politics. It is the testing ground and staging area for a new American response to the social revolution that is sweeping through the impoverished downtrodden areas of the world. It is the beginning of the American counter-revolution.

• • •

What kind of system is it that allows good men to make those kinds of decisions? What kind of system is it that justifies the United States or any country seizing the destinies of the Vietnamese people and using them callously for its own purpose? What kind of system is it that disenfranchises people in the South, leaves millions upon millions of people throughout the country impoverished and excluded from the mainstream and promise of American society, that creates faceless and terrible bureaucracies and makes those the place where people spend their lives and do their work, that consistently puts material values before human values—and still persists in calling itself free and still persists in finding itself fit to police the world?

• • •

We must name that system. We must name it, describe it, analyze it, understand it and change it. For it is only when that system is changed and brought under control that there can be any hope for stopping the forces that create a war in Vietnam today or a murder in the South tomorrow.

• • •

If the people of this country are to end the war in Vietnam, and to change the institutions which create it; then the people of this country must create a massive social movement—and if that can be built around the issue of Vietnam then that is what we must do.

By a social movement I mean more than petitions or letters of protest, or tacit support of dissident Congressmen; I mean people who are willing to change their lives, who are willing to challenge the system, to take the problem of change seriously. By a social movement I mean an effort that is powerful enough to make the country understand that our problems are not in Vietnam, or China or Brazil or outer space or at the bottom of the ocean, but are here in the United States. What we must do is begin to build a democratic and humane society in which Vietnams are unthinkable, in which human life and initiative are precious.

Questions

1. Why does Potter challenge President Johnson's claim that the War in Vietnam is a defense of freedom?

2. What does he mean by saying, "we must name that system"?

---

169. Betty Friedan, *The Feminine Mystique* (1963)

Source: Betty Friedan, excerpts from "The Problem That Has No Name," from The Feminine Mystique *(New York, 1963), pp. 1–31. Copyright © 1983, 1974, 1973, 1963 by Betty Friedan, used by permission of W. W. Norton & Company, Inc.*

The civil rights revolution, soon followed by the rise of the New Left, inspired other Americans to voice their grievances and claim their rights. Most far-reaching in its impact on American society was the emergence of the "second wave" of feminism.

A key catalyst in the public reawakening of feminist consciousness was the publication in 1963 of Betty Friedan's *The Feminine Mystique*. Her opening chapter, "The Problem That Has No Name," painted a devastating picture of talented, educated women trapped in a world that viewed marriage and motherhood as their primary goals. Somehow, after more than a century of agitation for access to the public sphere, women's lives still centered on the home. The suburban housewife, widely pictured as the embodiment of the American dream, in fact lived lives of "desperation," she wrote. Like the civil rights movement, *The Feminine Mystique* focused attention on the gap between the rhetoric of freedom and the reality that millions of Americans felt deprived of freedom.

THE PROBLEM LAY buried, unspoken, for many years in the minds of American women. It was a strange stirring, a sense of dissatisfaction, a yearning that women suffered in the middle of the twentieth century in the United States. Each suburban wife struggled with it alone. As she made the beds, shopped for groceries, matched slipcover material, ate peanut butter sandwiches with her children, chauffeured Cub, Scouts and Brownies, lay beside her husband at night—she was afraid to ask even of herself the silent question—"Is this all?"

• • •

By the end of the nineteen-fifties, the average marriage age of women in America dropped to 20, and was still dropping, into the teens. Fourteen million girls were engaged by 17. The proportion of women attending college in comparison with men dropping from 47 per cent in 1920 to 35 per cent in 1958. A century, earlier, women had fought for higher education; now girls went to college to get a husband. By the mid-fifties, 60 per cent dropped out of college to marry, or because they were afraid too much education would be a marriage bar. Colleges built dormitories for "married students," but the students were almost always the husbands. A new degree was instituted for the wives—"Ph.T." (Putting Husband Through).

• • •

By the end of the fifties, the United States birthrate was overtaking India's. The birth-control movement, renamed Planned Parenthood, was asked to find a method whereby women who had been advised that a third or fourth baby would be born dead or defective might have it anyhow. Statisticians were especially astounded at the fantastic increase in the number of babies among college women. Where once they had two children, now they had four, five, six. Women who had once wanted careers were now making careers out of having babies. So rejoiced *Life* magazine in a 1956 paean to the movement of American women back to the home.

• • •

The suburban housewife—she was the dream image of the young American women and the envy, it was said, of women all over the world. The American housewife—freed by science and labor-saving appliances from the drudgery, the dangers of childbirth and the ill-nesses of her grandmother. She was healthy, beautiful, educated, con-cerned only about her husband, her children, her home. She had found true feminine fulfillment. As a housewife and mother, she was respected as a full and equal partner to man in his world. She was free to choose automobiles, clothes, appliances, supermarkets; she had everything that women ever dreamed of.

In the fifteen years after World War II, this mystique of feminine fulfillment became the cherished and self-perpetuating core of con-temporary American culture. Millions of women lived their lives in the image of those pretty pictures of the American suburban house-wife, kissing their husbands goodbye in front of the picture window, depositing their stationwagonsful of children at school, and smiling as they ran the new electric waxer over the spotless kitchen floor. They baked their own bread, sewed their own and their children's clothes, kept their new washing machines and dryers running all day. They changed the sheets on the beds twice a week instead of once, took the rug-hooking class in adult education, and pitied their poor frustrated mothers, who had dreamed of having a career. Their only dream was to be perfect wives and mothers; their highest ambition to have five children and a beautiful house, their only fight to get and keep their husbands. They had no thought for the unfeminine prob-lems of the world outside the home; they wanted the men to make the major decisions. They gloried in their role as women, and wrote proudly on the census blank: "Occupation: housewife."

• • •

If the woman had a problem in the 1950's and 1960's, she knew that something must be wrong with her marriage, or with herself. Other women were satisfied with their lives, she thought. What kind of a woman was she if she did not feel this mysterious fulfillment waxing the kitchen floor? She was so ashamed to admit her dissatis-faction that she never knew how many other women shared it.

• • •

But on an April morning in 1959, I heard a mother of four, having coffee with four other mothers in a suburban development fifteen miles from New York, say in a tone of quiet desperation, "the problem." And the others knew, without words, that she was not talking about a problem with her husband, or her children, or her home. Suddenly they realized they all shared the same problem, the problem that has no name. They began, hesitantly, to talk about it. Later, after they had picked up their children at nursery school and taken them home to nap, two of the women cried, in sheer relief, just to know they were not alone.

Gradually I came to realize that the problem that has no name was shared by countless women in America. As a magazine writer I often interviewed women about problems with their children, or their marriages, or their houses, or their communities. But after a while I began to recognize the telltale signs of this other problem. I saw the same signs in suburban ranch houses and split-levels on Long Island and in New Jersey and Westchester County; in colonial houses in a small Massachusetts town; on patios in Memphis; in suburban and city apartments; in living rooms in the Midwest. Sometimes I sensed the problem, not as a reporter, but as a suburban housewife, for during this time I was also bringing up my own three children in Rockland County, New York. I heard echoes of the problem in college dormitories and semi-private maternity wards, at PTA meetings and luncheons of the League of Women Voters, at suburban cocktail parties, in station wagons waiting for trains, and in snatches of conversation overheard at Schrafft's. The groping words I heard from other women, on quiet afternoons when children were at school or on quiet evenings when husbands worked late; I think I understood first as a woman long before I understood their larger social and psychological implications.

Just what was this problem that has no name? What were the words women used when they tried to express it? Sometimes a woman would say "I feel empty somehow ... incomplete." Or she would say, "I feel as if I don't exist." Sometimes she blotted out the feeling with a tranquilizer.

• • •

It is no longer possible to ignore that voice, to dismiss the desperation of so many American women.

• • •

If I am right, the problem that has no name stirring in the minds of so many American women today is not a matter of loss of femininity or too much education, or the demands of domesticity. It is far more important than anyone recognizes. It is the key to these other new and old problems which have been torturing women and their husbands and children, and puzzling their doctors and educators for years. It may well be the key to our future as a nation and a culture. We can no longer ignore that voice within women that says: "I want something more than my husband and my children and my home."

Questions

1. What does Friedan mean by the phrase, "the problem that has no name"?

2. What kinds of women seem to be excluded from Friedan's account of the problem?

---

170. César Chavez, "Letter from Delano" (1969)

Source: César Chavez, "Letter from Delano," Christian Century (April 23, 1969), pp. 539–40.

As in the case of blacks, a movement for legal rights had long flourished among Mexican-Americans. But the mid-1960s saw the flowering of a new militancy challenging the group's second-class economic status. Like Black Power advocates, the movement emphasized pride in both the Mexican past and the new Chicano culture that had arisen in the United States. Unlike the Black Power movement and SDS, it was closely linked to labor struggles.

Beginning in 1965, César Chavez, the son of migrant farm workers and a disciple of Martin Luther King Jr., led a series of nonviolent protests including marches, fasts, and a national boycott of California grapes, to pressure growers to agree to labor contracts with the United Farm Workers Union (UFW). The boycott mobilized Latino communities throughout the Southwest and drew national attention to the pitifully low wages and oppressive working conditions of migrant laborers.

Chavez addressed a "Letter from Delano" to agricultural employers. In it he defended his own movement's aims and tactics. In 1970, the major growers agreed to contracts with the UFW.

DEAR MR. BARR   [President, California Grape and Tree Fruit League]:

I am sad to hear about your accusations in the press that our union movement and table grape boycott have been successful because we have used violence and terror tactics. If what you say is true, I have been a failure and should withdraw from the struggle; but you are left with the awesome moral responsibility, before God and man, to come forward with whatever information you have so that corrective action can begin at once. If for any reason you fail to come forth to substantiate your charges, then you must be held responsible for committing violence against us, albeit violence of the tongue. I am convinced that you as a human being did not mean what you said but rather acted hastily under pressure from the public relations firm that has been hired to try to counteract the tremendous moral force of our movement. How many times we ourselves have felt the need to lash out in anger and bitterness.

Today on Good Friday 1969 we remember the life and the sacrifice of Martin Luther King, Jr., who gave himself totally to the nonviolent struggle for peace and justice. In his "Letter from Birmingham Jail" Dr. King describes better than I could our hopes for the strike and boycott: "Injustice must be exposed, with all the tension its exposure creates, to the light of human conscience and the air of national opinion before it can be cured." For our part I admit that we have seized upon every tactic and strategy consistent with the morality of our cause to expose that injustice and thus to heighten the sensitivity of the American conscience so that farm workers will have without bloodshed their own union and the dignity of bargaining with their agribusiness employers. By lying about the nature of our movement, Mr. Barr, you are working against nonviolent social change. Unwittingly perhaps, you may unleash that other force which our union by discipline and deed, censure and education has sought to avoid, that panacean shortcut: that senseless violence which honors no color, class or neighborhood.

You must understand—I must make you understand—that our membership and the hopes and aspirations of the hundreds of thousands of the poor and dispossessed that have been raised on our account are, above all, human beings, no better and no worse than any other cross-section of human society; we are not saints because we are poor, but by the same measure neither are we immoral. We are men and women who have suffered and endured much, and not only because of our abject poverty but because we have been kept poor. The colors of our skins, the languages of our cultural and native origins, the lack of formal education, the exclusion from the democratic process, the numbers of our slain in recent wars—all these burdens generation after generation have sought to demoralize us, to break our human spirit. But God knows that we are not beasts of burden, agricultural implements or rented slaves; we are men. And mark this well, Mr. Barr, we are men locked in a death struggle against man's inhumanity to man in the industry that you represent. And this struggle itself gives meaning to our life and ennobles our dying.

As your industry has experienced, our strikers here in Delano and those who represent us throughout the world are well trained for this struggle. They have been under the gun, they have been kicked and beaten and herded by dogs, they have been cursed and ridiculed, they have been stripped and chained and jailed, they have been sprayed with the poisons used in the vineyards; but they have been taught not to lie down and die nor to flee in shame, but to resist with every ounce of human endurance and spirit. To resist not with retaliation in kind but to overcome with love and compassion, with ingenuity and creativity, with hard work and longer hours, with stamina and patient tenacity, with truth and public appeal, with friends and allies, with mobility and discipline, with politics and law, and with prayer and fasting. They were not trained in a month or even a year; after all, this new harvest season will mark our fourth full year of strike and even now we continue to plan and prepare for the years to come. Time accomplishes for the poor what money does for the rich.

This is not to pretend that we have everywhere been successful enough or that we have not made mistakes. And while we do not belittle or underestimate our adversaries—for they are the rich and the powerful and they possess the land—we are not afraid nor do we cringe from the confrontation. We welcome it! We have planned for it. We know that our cause is just, that history is a story of social revolution, and that the poor shall inherit the land.

Once again, I appeal to you as the representative of your industry and as a man. I ask you to recognize and bargain with our union before the economic pressure of the boycott and strike takes an irrevocable toll; but if not, I ask you to at least sit down with us to discuss the safeguards necessary to keep our historical struggle free of violence. I make this appeal because as one of the leaders of our nonviolent movement, I know and accept my responsibility for preventing, if possible, the destruction of human life and property. For these reasons and knowing of Gandhi's admonition that fasting is the last resort in place of the sword, during a most critical time in our movement last February 1968 I undertook a 25-day fast. I repeat to you the principle enunciated to the membership at the start of the fast: if to build our union required the deliberate taking of life, either the life of a grower or his child, or the life of a farm worker or his child, then I choose not to see the union built.

Mr. Barr, let me be painfully honest with you. You must understand these things. We advocate militant nonviolence as our means for social revolution and to achieve justice for our people, but we are not blind or deaf to the desperate and moody winds of human frustration, impatience and rage that blow among us. Gandhi himself admitted that if his only choice were cowardice or violence, he would choose violence. Men are not angels, and time and tide wait for no man. Precisely because of these powerful human emotions, we have tried to involve masses of people in their own struggle. Participation and self-determination remain the best experience of freedom, and free men instinctively prefer democratic change and even protect the rights guaranteed to seek it. Only the enslaved in despair have need of violent overthrow.

This letter does not express all that is in my heart, Mr. Barr. But if it says nothing else it says that we do not hate you or rejoice to see your industry destroyed; we hate the agribusiness system that seeks to keep us enslaved, and we shall overcome and change it not by retaliation or bloodshed but by a determined nonviolent struggle carried on by those masses of farm workers who intend to be free and human.

Questions

1. Why does Chavez describe the farm workers movement as a "social revolution"?

2. What would enable the farm workers to be "free and human," the phrase with which Chavez ends his letter?

CHAPTER 26

The Triumph of Conservatism, 1969–1988

171. Redstockings Manifesto (1969)

Source: Redstockings of the Women's Liberation Movement, "The Redstockings Manifesto." Reprinted with the permission of Archives for Action. The Redstockings Manifesto was issued in New York City on July 7, 1969. It first appeared as a mimeographed flyer, designed for distribution at women's liberation events. Further information about the Manifesto and other materials from the 1960's rebirth years of feminism is available from the Redstockings Women's Liberation Archives for Action at www.redstockings.org or P.O. Box 744 Stuyvesant Station, New York, NY 10009.

Like other social movements spawned by the 1960s, the second wave of feminism became more radical as the decade neared its end. Women's rights evolved into women's liberation, which went well beyond a demand for equal rights to propose far-reaching changes in family life and in relations between men and women. Redstockings, a short-lived but influential radical feminist group founded in New York City in 1969, pioneered in the development of "consciousness raising" sessions so that women of varying backgrounds could discuss their experiences and grievances without men being present. They also helped to bring the issue of abortion rights to public attention. Redstockings identified male supremacy as the primary reason for female inequality and called on women to unite against "male privileges." Although Redstockings remained a tiny organization, the 1970s saw the sexual revolution move from the Sixties counterculture into the mainstream of American life.

━━━━━━━━

I. AFTER CENTURIES OF individual and preliminary political struggle, women are uniting to achieve their final liberation from male supremacy. Redstockings is dedicated to building this unity and winning our freedom.

II. Women are an oppressed class. Our oppression is total, affecting every facet of our lives. We are exploited as sex objects, breeders, domestic servants, and cheap labor. We are considered inferior beings, whose only purpose is to enhance men's lives. Our humanity is denied. Our prescribed behavior is enforced by the threat of physical violence.

Because we have lived so intimately with our oppressors, in isolation from each other, we have been kept from seeing our personal suffering as a political condition. This creates the illusion that a woman's relationship with her man is a matter of interplay between two unique personalities, and can be worked out individually. In reality, every such relationship is a *class* relationship, and the conflicts between individual men and women are *political* conflicts that can only be solved collectively.

III. We identify the agents of our oppression as men. Male supremacy is the oldest, most basic form of domination. All other forms of exploitation and oppression (racism, capitalism, imperialism, etc.) are extensions of male supremacy: men dominate women, a few men dominate the rest. All power structures throughout history have been male-dominated and male-oriented. Men have controlled all political, economic and cultural institutions and backed up this control with physical force. They have used their power to keep women in an inferior position. *All men* receive economic, sexual, and psychological benefits from male supremacy. *All men* have oppressed women.

IV. Attempts have been made to shift the burden of responsibility from men to institutions or to women themselves. We condemn these arguments as evasions. Institutions alone do not oppress; they are merely tools of the oppressor. To blame institutions implies that men and women are equally victimized, obscures the fact that men benefit from the subordination of women, and gives men the excuse that they are forced to be oppressors. On the contrary, any man is free to renounce his superior position provided that he is willing to be treated like a woman by other men.

We also reject the idea that women consent to or are to blame for their own oppression. Women's submission is not the result of brainwashing, stupidity, or mental illness but of continual, daily pressure from men. We do not need to change ourselves, but to change men.

The most slanderous evasion of all is that women can oppress men. The basis for this illusion is the isolation of individual relationships from their political context and the tendency of men to see any legitimate challenge to their privileges as persecution.

V. We regard our personal experience, and our feelings about that experience, as the basis for an analysis of our common situation. We cannot rely on existing ideologies as they are all products of male supremacist culture. We question every generalization and accept none that are not confirmed by our experience.

Our chief task at present is to develop female class consciousness through sharing experience and publicly exposing the sexist foundation of all our institutions. Consciousness-raising is not "therapy," which implies the existence of individual solutions and falsely assumes that the male-female relationship is purely personal, but the only method by which we can ensure that our program for liberation is based on the concrete realities of our lives.

The first requirement for raising class consciousness is honesty, in private and in public, with ourselves and other women.

VI. We identify with all women. We define our best interest as that of the poorest, most brutally exploited woman.

We repudiate all economic, racial, educational or status privileges that divide us from other women. We are determined to recognize and eliminate any prejudices we may hold against other women.

We are committed to achieving internal democracy. We will do whatever is necessary to ensure that every woman in our movement has an equal chance to participate, assume responsibility, and develop her political potential.

VII. We call on all our sisters to unite with us in struggle.

We call on all men to give up their male privileges and support women's liberation in the interest of our humanity and their own.

In fighting for our liberation we will always take the side of women against their oppressors. We will not ask what is "revolutionary" or "reformist," only what is good for women.

The time for individual skirmishes has passed. This time we are going all the way.

Questions

1. What does the manifesto mean by its final sentence: "This time we are going all the way"?

2. Why does Redstockings believe that all men are oppressors of women?

172. Barry Commoner, *The Closing Circle* (1971)

Source: From The Closing Circle *by Barry Commoner, copyright © 1971 by Barry Commoner. Used by permission of Alfred A. Knopf, a division of Random House, Inc.*

Another movement born in the 1960s that expanded rapidly in the following decade was environmentalism, which called into question pillars of American life—the equation of progress with endless increases in consumption and the faith that science, technology, and economic growth would advance the social welfare. Concern for preserving the natural environment dated back to the creation of national parks and other conservation efforts during the Progressive era. But the new environmentalism was more activist and youth oriented. *The Closing Circle*, by the biologist Barry Commoner, did much to direct American's attention to the environmental costs of technological development. Commoner insisted that rather than focus on a particular environmental problem, Americans must view the "ecosphere"—the natural system within which people live—as a whole.

Environmentalism attracted the broadest bipartisan support of any of the new social movements. Under Republican President Richard Nixon, Congress during the late 1960s and early 1970s passed a series of measures to protect the environment, including the Clean Air and Clean Water Acts and the Endangered Species Act. On April 22, 1970, in the first Earth Day, some 20 million people, most of them under the age of 30, participated in rallies, concerts, and teach-ins devoted to promoting awareness of dangers to the natural environment.

―――――

THE ENVIRONMENT HAS just been rediscovered by the people who live in it. In the United States the event was celebrated in April 1970, during Earth Week. It was a sudden, noisy awakening. School children cleaned up rubbish; college students organized huge demonstrations; determined citizens recaptured the streets from the automobile, at least for a day. Everyone seemed to be aroused to the environmental danger and eager to do something about it.

They were offered lots of advice. Almost every writer, almost every speaker, on the college campuses, in the streets and on television and radio broadcasts, was ready to fix the blame and pronounce a cure for the environmental crisis.

Some blamed pollution on the rising population.... Some blamed man's innate aggressiveness.... Earth week and the accompanying outburst of publicity, preaching, and prognostication surprised most people, including those of us who had worked for years to generate public recognition of the environmental crisis. What surprised me most were the numerous, confident explanations of the cause and cure of the crisis. For having spent some years in the effort simply to detect and describe the growing list of environmental problems—radioactive fallout, air and water pollution, the deterioration of the soil—and in tracing some of their links to social and political processes, the identification of a single cause and cure seemed a rather bold step....

After the excitement of Earth Week, I tried to find some meaning in the welter of contradictory advice that it produced. It seemed to me that the confusion of Earth Week was a sign that the situation was so complex and ambiguous that people could read into it whatever conclusion, their own beliefs—about human nature, economics, and politics—suggested. Like a Rorschach ink blot, Earth Week mirrored personal conviction more than objective knowledge.

Earth Week convinced me of the urgency of a deeper public understanding of the origins of the environmental crisis and its possible cures. That is what this book is about. It is an effort to find out what the environmental crisis means. Such understanding must begin at the source of life itself: the earth's thin skin of air, water, and soil, and the radiant solar fire that bathes it. Here, several billion years ago, life appeared and was nourished by the earth's substance. As it grew, life evolved, its old forms transforming the earth's skin and new ones adapting to these changes. Living things multiplied in number, variety, and habitat until they formed a global network, becoming deftly enmeshed in the surroundings they had themselves created. This is the ecosphere, the home that life has built for itself on the planet's outer surface.

Any living thing that hopes to live on the earth must fit into the ecosphere or perish. The environmental crisis is a sign that the finely sculptured fit between life and its surroundings has begun to corrode. As the links between one living thing and another, and between all of them and their surroundings, begin to break down, the dynamic interactions that sustain the whole have begun to falter and, in some places, stop.

Why, after millions of years of harmonious co-existance, have the relationships between living things and their earthly surroundings begun to collapse? Where did the fabric of the ecosphere begin to unravel? How far will the process go? How can we stop it and restore the broken links?

Understanding the ecosphere comes hard because, to the modern mind, it is a curiously foreign place. We have become accustomed to think of separate, singular events, each dependent upon a unique, singular cause. But in the ecosphere every effect is also a cause: an animal's waste becomes food for soil bacteria; what bacteria excrete nourishes plants; animals eat the plants. Such ecological cycles are hard to fit into human experience in the age of technology, where machine A always yields product B, and product B, once used, is cast away, having no further meaning for the machine, the product, or the user.

Here is the first great fault in the life of man in the ecosphere. We have broken out of the circle of life, converting its endless cycles into man-made, linear events: oil is taken from the ground, distilled into fuel, burned in an engine, converted thereby into noxious fumes, which are emitted into the air. At the end of the line is smog. Other man-made breaks in the ecosphere's cycle spew out toxic chemicals, sewage, heaps of rubbish—the testimony to our power to tear the ecological fabric that has, for millions of years, sustained the planet's life.

Suddenly we have discovered what we should have known long before: that the ecosphere sustains people and everything that they do; that anything that fails to fit into the ecosphere is a threat to its finely balanced cycles; that wastes are not only unpleasant, not only toxic, but, more meaningfully, evidence that the ecosphere is being driven towards collapse.

If we are to survive, we must understand why this collapse now threatens. Here the issues become far more complex than even the ecosphere. Our assaults on the ecosystem are so powerful, so numerous, so finely interconnected, that although the damage they do is clear, it is very difficult to discover how it was done. By which weapon? In whose hand? Are we driving the ecosphere to destruction simply by our growing numbers? By our greedy accumulation of wealth? Or are the machines which we have built to gain this wealth—the magnificent technology that now feeds us out of neat packages, that clothes us in man-made fibers, that surround us with new chemical creations—at fault?

This book is concerned with these questions. It begins with the ecosphere, the setting in which civilization has done its great—and terrible—deeds. Then it moves to a description of some of the damage we have done to the ecosphere—to the air, the water, the soil. However, by now such horror stories of environmental destruction are familiar, even tiresome. Much less clear is what we need to learn from them, and so I have chosen less to shed tears of our past mistakes than to try to understand them. Most of this book is an effort to discover which human acts have broken the circle of life, and why. I trace the environmental crisis from its overt manifestations in the ecosphere to the ecological stresses which they reflect, to the faults in production technology—and in its scientific background—that generate these stresses, and finally to the economic, social, and political forces which have driven us down this self-destructive course. All this in the hope—and expectation—that once we understand the origins of the environmental crisis, we can begin to manage the huge undertaking of surviving it.

Questions

1. Why does Commoner feel that most explanations of environmental problems are inadequate?

2. What kinds of human actions does he feel endanger the ecosphere?

173. Jimmy Carter on Human Rights (1977)

Source: Address at Commencement Exercises, Notre Dame University, May 22, 1977, **Public Papers of the Presidents of the United States, Jimmy Carter, 1977 (Washington, D.C., 1977), pp. 954–58.**

In the aftermath of the American defeat in the Vietnam War, President Jimmy Carter tried to reorient foreign policy away from Cold War assumptions. In a 1977 address at Notre Dame University, he insisted that foreign policy could not be separated from "questions of justice, equity, and human rights." Implicitly criticizing his predecessors' tendency to ally with Third World dictatorships in order to pursue the policy of containing communism, Carter called for a policy based on democratic principles. Combating poverty in the Third World, preventing the spread of nuclear weapons, and promoting human rights should take priority over what he called "the inordinate fear of communism." Carter sometimes found it impossible to translate rhetoric into action. Nonetheless, he helped to place human rights on the agenda of American foreign policy.

I WANT TO speak to you today about the strands that connect our actions overseas with our essential character as a nation. I believe we can have a foreign policy that is democratic, that is based on fundamental values, and that uses power and influence, which we have, for humane purposes. We can also have a foreign policy that American people both support and, for a change, know about and understand.

I have a quiet confidence in our own political system. Because we know that democracy works, we can reject the arguments of those rulers who deny human rights to their people.

We are confident that democracy's example will be compelling, and so we seek to bring that example closer to those from whom in the past few years we have been separated and who are not yet convinced about the advantages of our kind of life.

We are confident that the democratic methods are the most effective, and so we are not tempted to employ improper tactics here at home or abroad.

We are confident of our own strength, so we can seek substantial mutual reductions in the nuclear arms race.

And we are confident of the good sense of American people, and so we let them share in the process of making foreign policy decisions. We can thus speak with the voices of 215 million, and not just of an isolated handful.

Democracy's great recent successes—in India, Portugal, Spain, Greece—show that our confidence in this system is not misplaced.

Being confident of our own future, we are now free of that inordinate fear of communism which once led us to embrace any dictator who joined us in that fear. I'm glad that that's being changed.

For too many years, we've been willing to adopt the flawed and erroneous principles and tactics of our adversaries, sometimes abandoning our own values for theirs. We've fought fire with fire, never thinking that fire is better quenched with water. This approach failed, with Vietnam the best example of its intellectual and moral poverty. But through failure we have now found our way back to our own principles and values, and we have regained our lost confidence.

By the measure of history, our nation's 200 years are very brief, and our rise to world eminence is briefer still. It dates from 1945, when Europe and the old international order lay in ruins. Before then, America was largely on the periphery of world affairs. But since then, we have inescapably been at the center of world affairs.

Our policy during this period was guided by two principles: a belief that Soviet expansion was almost inevitable but that it must be contained, and the corresponding belief in the importance of an almost exclusive alliance among non-Communist nations on both sides of the Atlantic. That system could not last forever unchanged. Historical trends have weakened its foundation. The unifying threat of conflict with the Soviet Union has become less intensive, even though the competition has become more extensive.

The Vietnamese war produced a profound moral crisis, sapping worldwide faith in our own policy and our system of life, a crisis of confidence made even more grave by the covert pessimism of some of our leaders.

In less than a generation, we've seen the world change dramatically. The daily lives and aspirations of most human beings have been transformed. Colonialism is nearly gone. A new sense of national identity now exists in almost 100 new countries that have been formed in the last generation. Knowledge has become more widespread. Aspirations are higher. As more people have been freed from traditional constraints, more have been determined to achieve, for the first time in their lives, social justice.

The world is still divided by ideological disputes, dominated by regional conflicts, and threatened by danger that we will not resolve the differences of race and wealth without violence or without drawing into combat the major military powers. We can no longer separate the traditional issues of war and peace from the new global questions of justice, equity, and human rights.

It is a new world, but America should not fear it. It is a new world, and we should help to shape it. It is a new world that calls for a new American foreign policy—a policy based on constant decency in its values and on optimism in our historical vision.

• • •

First, we have reaffirmed America's commitment to human rights as a fundamental tenet of our foreign policy. In ancestry, religion, color, place of origin, and cultural background, we Americans are as diverse a nation as the world has even seen. No common mystique of blood or soil unites us. What draws us together, perhaps more than anything else, is a belief in human freedom. We want the world to know that our Nation stands for more than financial prosperity.

This does not mean that we can conduct our foreign policy by rigid moral maxims. We live in a world that is imperfect and which will always be imperfect—a world that is complex and confused and which will always be complex and confused.

• • •

Throughout the world today, in free nations and in totalitarian countries as well, there is a preoccupation with the subject of human freedom, human rights. And I believe it is incumbent on us in this country to keep that discussion, that debate, that contention alive. No other country is as well-qualified as we to set an example. We have our own shortcomings and faults, and we should strive constantly and with courage to make sure that we are legitimately proud of what we have.

• • •

Questions

1. What does Carter refer to when he says that the United States has too often abandoned "democratic methods" in foreign relations in favor of adopting the "tactics of our adversaries"?

2. What are the difficulties of making respect for human rights a major consideration in conducting foreign policy?

---

174. Jerry Falwell, *Listen America* (1980)

Source: From Listen America *by Jerry Falwell, copyright © 1980 by Jerry Falwell. Used by permission of Doubleday, a division of Random House, Inc.*

The rise of religious fundamentalism during the 1970s expanded conservatism's popular base. Evangelical Christians had become more and more alienated from a culture that seemed to them to trivialize religion and promote immorality. They demanded the reversal of Supreme Court decisions banning prayer in public schools, protecting pornography as free speech, and legalizing abortion. Although it spoke of restoring traditional values, the "religious Right" proved remarkably adept at using modern technology, including mass mailings and televised religious programing, to raise funds for their crusade and to spread their message. In 1979, Jerry Falwell, a Virginia minister, created the self-styled Moral Majority, devoted to waging a "war against sin" and electing "pro-life, pro-family, pro-America" candidates to office.

WE MUST REVERSE the trend America finds herself in today. Young people between the ages of twenty-five and forty have been born and reared in a different world than Americans of years past. The television set has been their primary babysitter. From the television set they have learned situation ethics and immorality—they have learned a loss of respect for human life. They have learned to disrespect the family as God has established it. They have been educated in a public-school system that is permeated with secular humanism. They have been taught that the Bible is just another book of literature. They have been taught that there are no absolutes in our world today. They have been introduced to the drug culture. They have been reared by the family and the public school in a society that is greatly void of discipline and character-building. These same young people have been reared under the influence of a government that has taught them socialism and welfarism. They have been taught to believe that the world owes them a living whether they work or not.

I believe that America was built on integrity, on faith in God, and on hard work. I do not believe that anyone has ever been successful in life without being willing to add that last ingredient—diligence or hard work. We now have second- and third-generation welfare recipients. Welfare is not always wrong. There are those who do need welfare, but we have reared a generation that understands neither the dignity nor the importance of work.

Every American who looks at the facts must share a deep concern and burden for our country. We are not unduly concerned when we say that there are some very dark clouds on America's horizon. I am not a pessimist, but it is indeed a time for truth. If Americans will face the truth, our nation can be turned around and can be saved from the evils and the destruction that have fallen upon every other nation that has turned its back on God.

There is no excuse for what is happening in our country. We must, from the highest office in the land right down to the shoe shine boy in the airport, have a return to biblical basics. If the Congress of our United States will take its stand on that which is right and wrong, and if our President, our judiciary system, and our state and local leaders will take their stand on holy living, we can turn this country around.

I personally feel that the home and the family are still held in reverence by the vast majority of the American public. I believe there is still a vast number of Americans who love their country, are patriotic, and are willing to sacrifice for her. I remember the time when it was positive to be patriotic, and as far as I am concerned, it still is. I remember as a boy, when the flag was raised, everyone stood proudly and put his hand upon his heart and pledged allegiance with gratitude. I remember when the band struck up "The Stars and Stripes Forever," we stood and goose pimples would run all over me. I remember when I was in elementary school during World War II, when every report from the other shores meant something to us. We were not out demonstrating against our boys who were dying in Europe and Asia. We were praying for them and thanking God for them and buying war bonds to help pay for the materials and artillery they needed to fight and win and come back.

I believe that Americans want to see this country come back to basics, back to values, back to biblical morality, back to sensibility, and back to patriotism. Americans are looking for leadership and guidance. It is fair to ask the question, "If 84 percent of the American people still believe in morality, why is America having such internal problems?" We must look for the answer to the highest places in every level of government. We have a lack of leadership in America. But Americans have been lax in voting in and out of office the right and the wrong people.

My responsibility as a preacher of the Gospel is one of influence, not of control, and that is the responsibility of each individual citizen. Through the ballot box Americans must provide for strong moral leadership at every level. If our country will get back on the track in sensibility and moral sanity, the crises that I have herein mentioned will work out in the course of time and with God's blessings.

It is now time to take a stand on certain moral issues, and we can only stand if we have leaders. We must stand against the Equal Rights Amendment, the feminist revolution, and the homosexual revolution. We must have a revival in this country. . . . As a preacher of the Gospel, I not only believe in prayer and preaching, I also believe in good citizenship. If a labor union in America has the right to organize and improve its working conditions, then I believe that the churches and the pastors, the priests, and the rabbis of America have a responsibility, not just the right, to see to it that the moral climate and conscience of Americans is such that this nation can be healed inwardly. If it is healed inwardly, then it will heal itself outwardly. . . .

Americans have been silent much too long. We have stood by and watched as American power and influence have been systematically weakened in every sphere of the world.

We are not a perfect nation, but we are still a free nation because we have the blessing of God upon us. We must continue to follow in a path that will ensure that blessing. . . .

Let us never forget that as our Constitution declares, we are endowed by our Creator with certain inalienable rights. It is only as we abide by those laws established by our Creator that He will continue to bless us with these rights. We are endowed our rights to freedom and liberty and the pursuit of happiness by the God who created man to be free and equal.

The hope of reversing the trends of decay in our republic now lies with the Christian public in America. We cannot expect help from the liberals. They certainly are not going to call our nation back to righteousness and neither are the pornographers, the smut peddlers, and those who are corrupting our youth. Moral Americans must be willing to put their reputations, their fortunes, and their very lives on the line for this great nation of ours. Would that we had the courage of our forefathers who knew the great responsibility that freedom carries with it. . . .

Our Founding Fathers separated church and state in function, but never intended to establish a government void of God. As is evidenced by our Constitution, good people in America must exert an influence and provide a conscience and climate of morality in which it is difficult to go wrong, not difficult for people to go right in America.

I am positive in my belief regarding the Constitution that God led in the development of that document, and as a result, we here in America have enjoyed 204 years of unparalleled freedom. The most positive people in the world are people who believe the Bible to be the Word of God. The Bible contains a positive message. It is a message written by 40 men over a period of approximately 1,500 years under divine inspiration. It is God's message of love, redemption, and deliverance for a fallen race. What could be more positive than the message of redemption in the Bible? But God will force Himself upon no man. Each individual American must make His choice....

Americans must no longer linger in ignorance and apathy. We cannot be silent about the sins that are destroying this nation. The choice is ours. We must turn America around or prepare for inevitable destruction. I am listening to the sounds that threaten to take away our liberties in America. And I have listened to God's admonitions and His direction—the only hopes of saving America. Are you listening too?

Questions

1. What does Falwell see as the major threats to moral standards in 1970s America?

2. How does Falwell appear to understand the idea of freedom?

---

175. Phyllis Schlafly, "The Fraud of the Equal Rights Amendment" (1972)

Source: From The Phyllis Schlafly Report, *Vol. 5, February 1972. Reprinted with permission of Phyllis Schlafly.*

One of the first major conservative victories of the 1970s was the defeat of the Equal Rights Amendment (ERA), a proposed change in the Constitution that would have affirmed that "equality of rights under the law" could not be abridged because of sex. This seemingly uncontroversial measure passed Congress in 1972 with little opposition. It soon aroused unexpected protest from those who claimed it would discredit the role of wife and homemaker.

To its supporters, the amendment offered a guarantee of women's right to participate fully in public life. Its foes insisted that women should remain within the divinely appointed roles of wife and mother. They claimed it would subject women to the military draft and let men "off the hook" by denying their responsibility to provide for their wives and children. Phyllis Schlafly, a veteran of anticommunist politics of the 1950s, led the campaign against the ERA. Polls consistently showed that a majority of Americans, male and female, favored the measure. But thanks to the mobilization of conservative women, the amendment failed to achieve ratification by the required thirty-eight states.

IN THE LAST couple of years, a noisy movement has sprung up agitating for "women's rights." Suddenly, everywhere we are afflicted with aggressive females on television talk shows yapping about how mistreated American women are, suggesting that marriage has put us in some kind of "slavery," that housework is menial and degrading, and—perish the thought—that women are discriminated against. New "women's liberation" organizations are popping up, agitating and demonstrating, serving demands on public officials, getting wide press coverage always, and purporting to speak for some 100,000,000 American women.

It's time to set the record straight. The claim that American women are downtrodden and unfairly treated is the fraud of the century. The truth is that American women never had it so good. Why should we lower ourselves to "equal rights" when we already have the status of special privilege?

The proposed Equal Rights Amendment states: "Equality of rights under the law shall not be denied or abridged by the United States or by any state on account of sex." So what's wrong with that? Well, here are a few examples of what's wrong with it.

This Amendment will absolutely and positively make women subject to the draft. Why any woman would support such a ridiculous and un-American proposal as this is beyond comprehension. Why any Congressman who had any regard for his wife, sister, or daughter would support such a proposition is just as hard to understand. Foxholes are bad enough for men, but they certainly are *not* the place for women—and we should reject any proposal which would put them there in the name of "equal rights." ...

Another bad effect of the Equal Rights Amendment is that it will abolish a woman's right to child support and alimony, and substitute what the women's libbers think is a more "equal" policy, that "such decisions should be within the discretion of the Court and should be made on the economic situation and need of the parties in the case."

Under present American laws, the man is *always* required to support his wife and each child he caused to be brought into the world. Why should women abandon these good laws—by trading them for something so nebulous and uncertain as the "discretion of the Court"?

The law now requires a husband to support his wife as best as his financial situation permits, but a wife is not required to support her husband (unless he is about to become a public charge). A husband cannot demand that his wife go to work to help pay for family expenses. He has the duty of financial support under our laws and customs. Why should we abandon these mandatory wife-support and child-support laws so that a wife would have an "equal" obligation to take a job?

By law and custom in America, in case of divorce, the mother always is given custody of her children unless there is overwhelming evidence of mistreatment, neglect or bad character. This is our special privilege because of the high rank that is placed on motherhood in our society. Do women really want to give up this special privilege and lower themselves to "equal rights," so that the mother gets one child and the father gets the other? I think not. ...

What "Women's Lib" Really Means

Many women are under the mistaken impression that "women's lib" means more job employment opportunities for women, equal pay for equal work, appointments of women to high positions, admitting more women to medical schools, and other desirable objectives which all women favor. We all support these purposes, as well as any necessary legislation which would bring them about.

But all this is only a sweet syrup which covers the deadly poison masquerading as "women's lib." The women's libbers are radicals who are waging a total assault on the family, on marriage, and on children.

Questions

1. Why does Schlafly believe that the Equal Rights Amendment will actually harm women?

2. How does Schlafly's picture of the status of American women differ from that of the Redstockings manifesto?

176. James Watt, "Environmentalists: A Threat to the Ecology of the West" (1978)

Source: James Watt, "Enviromentalists: A Threat to the Ecology of the West," speech at the Conservation Foundation, Dallas, May 8, 1978, James G. Watt Papers, American Heritage Center, University of Wyoming.

The rapid growth of the environmentalist movement sparked a conservative reaction. New environmental regulations led to calls for less government intervention in the economy. These were most strident in the West, where measures to protect the environment threatened irrigation projects and private access to public lands. Using the language of freedom from government tyranny, western leaders denounced control of large areas of land by the Bureau of Land Management in Washington, D.C., and insisted that decision-making power over issues like grazing rights, mining development, and whether public lands should be closed to fishing and hunting be given to the states. Conservative westerners like James Watt, later Secretary of the Interior under President Reagan, insisted that environmentalism threatened to prevent the development of the West's energy resources and therefore would damage the national economy as a whole.

―――――――

IN RECENT YEARS, the unique life style of the West has been challenged. The nation has demanded from our states additional supplies of coal, oil and gas, uranium, forest products, and food and fiber.

Because of good leadership and the rugged individualism of our citizens, the states of the West have accommodated the new pressures. We have struggled, and with but a few exceptions, have been able to protect our natural environment while the increased demands have been met. . . .

But now, all this is being threatened.

Today, there is a new political force in the land—a small group of extremists who don't concern themselves with a balanced perspective or a concern about improving the quality of life for mankind—they are called the environmentalists. Unlike the conservationists, they are single-minded and appear to be determined to accomplish their objectives at whatever cost to society. . . .

The energy resources of the West are and will be the cornerstone of our future energy needs. There is no other major domestic energy resource base for the Nation. . . . These energy resources will be developed. The only question remaining is, when? Will it be orderly and phased-in over time with proper environmental safeguards? Or, will it be explosively developed, fired by a political-economic crisis . . . ?

My thesis is that because of the actions being taken by extremists to delay or stop the orderly development of energy resources . . . the Nation is likely to suffer energy shortages and thus severe economic hardship. . . . When this happens, whether triggered by an Arab oil boycott, or slowly through time, the politicians in Washington will seize on the crisis and take whatever energy is necessary to extract energy from the Western states, in order to light and heat the East and to maintain jobs in the Midwest and on the East coast. The cost of taking our energy resources in a crisis atmosphere could be the ravaging of our land and the destruction of our natural resources. . . .

I fear for our ecology in the West and for our lifestyle. When the economic pressures start strangling the Eastern states due to short supplies of energy, their political leadership will come after our resources. In the minds of the affected job holders, no price will be too great (including the destruction of the ecology of the West), to get the necessary energy resources to keep their homes heated and their employment secure. . . .

What is the real motive of these extreme environmentalists? Is it to simply protect the environment? Is it to delay and deny energy development? Is it to weaken America? . . .

I am a concerned Westerner. . . . Today, the extremists—the environmentalists—are fighting this needed orderly development. I fear that our states may be ravaged as a result of the actions of the environmentalists—the greatest threat to the ecology of the West.

Questions

1. What does Watt see as the hidden motive of the environmentalist movement?

2. How does he argue that environmentalism actually threatens the natural environment in the West?

177. Ronald Reagan, Inaugural Address (1981)

Source: Inaugural Address, January 20, 1981, **Public Papers of the Presidents, Ronald Reagan, 1981** *(Washington, D.C., 1982), pp. 1–3.*

Riding a wave of dissatisfaction with the country's economic problems and apparently diminished strength in world affairs, Ronald Reagan was elected president in 1980. An excellent public speaker, Reagan reshaped the nation's agenda and political language more effectively than any other president since Franklin D. Roosevelt. He made conservatism seem progressive, rather than an attempt to turn back the tide of progress. His inaugural address reflected how he made freedom the watchword of what came to be called the Reagan Revolution—an effort to scale back the scope of government, lower taxes, and reinvigorate the Cold War. He ended by invoking the time-honored idea that the United States has a mission to serve as a "beacon" of freedom for people throughout the world.

MR. PRESIDENT, . . . by your gracious cooperation in the transition process, you have shown a watching world that we are a united people pledged to maintaining a political system which guarantees individual liberty to a greater degree than any other, and I thank you and your people for all your help in maintaining the continuity which is the bulwark of our Republic.

The business of our nation goes forward. These United States are confronted with an economic affliction of great proportions. We suffer from the longest and one of the worst sustained inflations in our national history. It distorts our economic decisions, penalizes thrift, and crushes the struggling young and the fixed-income elderly alike. It threatens to shatter the lives of millions of our people.

In this present crisis, government is not the solution to our problem; government is the problem. From time to time we've been tempted to believe that society has become too complex to be managed by self-rule, that government by an elite group is superior to government for, by, and of the people. Well, if no one among us is capable of governing himself, then who among us has the capacity to govern someone else? All of us together, in and out of government, must bear the burden. The solutions we seek must be equitable, with no one group singled out to pay a higher price.

So, as we begin, let us take inventory. We are a nation that has a government—not the other way around. And this makes us special among the nations of the Earth. Our government has no power except that granted it by the people. It is time to check and reverse the growth of government, which shows signs of having grown beyond the consent of the governed.

It is my intention to curb the size and influence of the Federal establishment and to demand recognition of the distinction between the powers granted to the Federal Government and those reserved to the States or to the people. All of us need to be reminded that the Federal Government did not create the States; the States created the Federal Government.

Now, so there will be no misunderstanding, it's not my intention to do away with government. It is rather to make it work—work with us, not over us; to stand by our side, not ride on our back. Government can and must provide opportunity, not smother it; foster productivity, not stifle it.

If we look to the answer as to why for so many years we achieved so much, prospered as no other people on Earth, it was because here in this land we unleashed the energy and individual genius of man to a greater extent than has ever been done before. Freedom and the dignity of the individual have been more available and assured here than in any other place on Earth. The price for this freedom at times has been high, but we have never been unwilling to pay that price.

It is no coincidence that our present troubles parallel and are proportionate to the intervention and intrusion in our lives that result from unnecessary and excessive growth of government. It is time for us to realize that we're too great a nation to limit ourselves to small dreams. We're not, as some would have us believe, doomed to an inevitable decline. I do not believe in a fate that will fall on us no matter what we do. I do believe in a fate that will fall on us if we do nothing. So, with all the creative energy at our command, let us begin an era of national renewal. Let us renew our determination, our courage, and our strength. And let us renew our faith and our hope.

• • •

Well, I believe we, the Americans of today, are ready to act worthy of ourselves, ready to do what must be done to ensure happiness and liberty for ourselves, our children, and our children's children. And as we renew ourselves here in our own land, we will be seen as having greater strength throughout the world. We will again be the exemplar of freedom and a beacon of hope for those who do not now have freedom.

Questions

1. What is Reagan's definition of freedom?

2. What does Reagan mean when he says, "government is not the solution to our problem; government is the problem"?

CHAPTER 27

Globalization and Its Discontents, 1989–2000

178. Declaration for Global Democracy (1999)

Source: Global Exchange: Declaration for Global Democracy, Seattle, 1999. Reprinted by permission of the Global Exchange.

During the 1990s, the country resounded with talk of a new era in human history, with a borderless economy and a "global civilization." The collapse of communism between 1989 and 1991 opened the entire world to the spread of market capitalism and the idea that government should interfere as little as possible with economic activity. Leaders of both parties spoke of an American mission to create a global free market as the path to greater worldwide freedom.

In December 1999, delegates gathered in Seattle for a meeting of the World Trade Organization, a 135-nation group that worked to reduce barriers to international commerce and settle trade disputes. To their astonishment, over 30,000 persons gathered to protest the meeting. A handful of self-proclaimed anarchists embarked on a window-breaking spree at local stores. Most demonstrators were peaceful. The Battle of Seattle placed on the national and international agendas a question that promises to be among the most pressing concerns of the twenty-first century—the relationship between globalization, economic justice, democracy, and freedom.

―――――――――

AS CITIZENS OF global society, recognizing that the World Trade Organization is unjustly dominated by corporate interests and run for the enrichment of the few at the expense of all others, we demand:

1. Representatives from all sectors of society must be included in all levels of trade policy formulations. All global citizens must be democratically represented in the formulation, implementation, and evaluation of all global social and economic policies.

2. The World Trade Organization must immediately halt all meetings and negotiations in order for a full, fair, and public assessment to be conducted of the impacts of the WTO's policies to date.

3. Global trade and investment must not be ends in themselves, but rather the instruments for achieving equitable and sustainable development including protection for workers and the environment.

4. Global trade agreements must not undermine the ability of each nation state or local community to meet its citizens' social, environmental, cultural or economic needs.

5. The World Trade Organization must be replaced by a democratic and transparent body accountable to citizens—not to corporations.

No globalization without representation!

Questions

1. What are the declaration's major complaints about the way globalization is being implemented?

2. How might decision making about globalization be made more democratic?

―――――――――

179. *The Freedom Revolution* (1995)

Source: Dick Armey, "The Freedom Revolution," from The Freedom
Revolution: The New Republican House Majority Leader Tells Why Big
Government Failed, Why Freedom Works, and How We Will Rebuild
America, *Copyright © 1995.*

The congressional elections of 1994 produced one of the most surprising
political turnabouts in American history. With the economy recovering
slowly from the recession and Bill Clinton's first two years in office seemingly lacking in significant accomplishments, voters gave Republicans
control of both houses of Congress for the first time since the 1950s. Republicans called their victory the Freedom Revolution. As one of their
party's congressional leaders, Richard Armey, explained, "no matter what
cause you advocate, you must sell it in the language of freedom." In a book
published a few months after the election, Armey outlined his vision of "a
truly free society."

SO MUCH OF our politics today is a competition over words whose
great prize is Freedom. No matter what cause you advocate, you
must sell it in the language of Freedom. No aspiring tyrant ever declared, "Follow me and I will enslave you!" They all say, "I will make
you free!" Freedom is the universal currency. Even proponents of discredited causes like communism and socialism offer it as an all-
excusing defense: their "isms" began as visions to make men free. It
was, alas, supposed to work out differently. The most sinister symbol
of this was the sign greeting prisoners to Auschwitz: "Work Makes
[You] Free."

The same goes for people enslaved by one or another false idol.
The addict doesn't take his first pill or drink saying to himself, "I'm
having this now in the hope that one day it will make me a miser-
able, dependent wretch respected by no one." He thinks, "This will
help. This will free me from (fill in the blank)." On the label of every
poison man ever concocted for himself is the word "Freedom."

The idealism of a truly free society, it seems to me, lies in the belief that we are all called to do certain work that no one else can do for us. This does not mean every man is out for himself and we are trapped in furious competition for goods like rivals in a state of nature, with minimal government providing a veneer of civility. The most important responsibilities we undertake—marriage, parenthood, vocation—are personal. No one else can shoulder the burden for us, and indeed only in Freedom do we come to realize they are not burdens at all.

Morality and the Market

A few remaining critics still regard the free market as an arena for raw, unbridled self-interest. This charge always leaves me a little bewildered. Yes, capitalism declares that we are free to pursue our own interests. And, yes, often those interests are material. We are partly material beings, so what else can you expect? But that seems to be the only side of the idea that the critics ever see, perhaps reflecting their own narrow view of people.

What these critics don't notice is the humility underlying the idea of individual Freedom. We are not free because we stand at the summit of existence, worshipping nothing beyond our own powers and appetites. We are not free because we have willed it so, because we want and demand Freedom. We have been called to Freedom by God. I think the free market arose from that calling. We feel the stirrings of Freedom in our anger when others presume, under whatever pretext, to give us orders or to divvy up our property. Alone among economic systems, the free market answers the protests of our spirit against wrongful power. It's the only available economic meeting ground of the idealistic and practical worlds, the world of duties and the world of opportunities. Adam Smith could be invoked on this point, or George Gilder, or any number of free-market philosophers, but probably no one has ever quite captured it like Clint Eastwood as the preacher in Pale Rider: "The spirit ain't worth spit without a little sweat now and then."

We are, I believe, beginning to feel for the free market the same reverence we moderns have always had for democracy. There has in the past been something a little grudging in our acceptance of capitalism. We accepted its practical superiority: it worked. It was the source of most everything we have, including the time and luxury to sit back and debate the finer points of public policy. But always, off to the side, scoffers pointed to the crudeness and materialism of it all. But every year, as the free market lifts up more people, produces better technology, creates more cures and conveniences, simplifies our lives, and raises our vision—this old criticism rings more and more hollow. The intellectual "vanguard," it turns out, has been outwitted by the "proletariat." Ordinary people relying on their own powers and their own vision decided to lead a little revolution of their own, proving not only that democracy and capitalism work—they work together.

• • •

To end poverty, reduce out-of-wedlock births, and give poor children hope for the future, we must scrap today's failed welfare system and replace dependency with work, marriage, and personal responsibility. To end crime, we must put police back on the street, reform our justice system, abolish parole, and double the number of prisons. If this sounds like a radical agenda, it is. But it is not an unrealistic agenda. It is no different from the norms that prevailed in America from the founding right up through the fourth decade of this century.

This "Tough Love" option is truly compassionate because it trusts in the inborn abilities of people. It assumes they are capable of handling Freedom's responsibilities and that, to the extent they are not capable, the natural safety-net—family, friends, churches, and charities—will supply, with few exceptions, what is lacking. Indeed, society's safety net will grow stronger when no longer displaced by government largesse.

Questions

1. How does Armey try to reconcile conservatives' commitment to the free market with their concern for fostering moral behavior?

2. How realistic do you consider Armey's proposed solution to the problem of poverty in America?

---

180. The Beijing Declaration on Women (1995)

Source: From The Fourth World Conference on Women. Reprinted with the permission of United Nations Publications.

The Fourth World Conference on Women, held in Beijing in 1995 under the auspices of the United Nations, illustrated the growing centrality of human rights in international discourse, and the growing importance of nongovernmental organizations (NGOs) in promoting human rights. Hillary Clinton, President Clinton's wife, attended and gave a widely quoted address pointing to the problems of adequate health care, access to education, and sexual abuse that afflicted women around the world. Nearly 200 countries sent official delegations, and thousands of representatives of various NGOs also attended. Of course, in so large and heterogeneous a gathering, controversy arose over whether the same rights applied in all societies. But the final declaration outlined an agenda for promoting women's freedom in the twenty-first century.

---

1. WE, THE GOVERNMENTS participating in the Fourth World Conference on Women,

2. Gathered here in Beijing in September 1995, the year of the fiftieth anniversary of the founding of the United Nations,

3. Determined to advance the goals of equality, development and peace for all women everywhere in the interest of all humanity,

4. Acknowledging the voices of all women everywhere and taking note of the diversity of women and their roles and circumstances,

honouring the women who paved the way and inspired by the hope present in the world's youth,

5. Recognize that the status of women has advanced in some important respects in the past decade but that progress has been uneven, inequalities between women and men have persisted and major obstacles remain, with serious consequences for the well-being of all people,

6. Also recognize that this situation is exacerbated by the increasing poverty that is affecting the lives of the majority of the world's people, in particular women and children, with origins in both the national and international domains,

7. Dedicate ourselves unreservedly to addressing these constraints and obstacles and thus enhancing further the advancement and empowerment of women all over the world, and agree that this requires urgent action in the spirit of determination, hope, cooperation and solidarity, now and to carry us forward into the next century.

We reaffirm our commitment to:

8. The equal rights and inherent human dignity of women and men and other purposes and principles enshrined in the Charter of the United Nations, to the Universal Declaration of Human Rights and other international human rights instruments, in particular the Convention on the Elimination of All Forms of Discrimination against Women and the Convention on the Rights of the Child, as well as the Declaration on the Elimination of Violence against Women and the Declaration on the Right to Development;

9. Ensure the full implementation of the human rights of women and of the girl child as an inalienable, integral and indivisible part of all human rights and fundamental freedoms;

• • •

We are convinced that:

13. Women's empowerment and their full participation on the basis of equality in all spheres of society, including participation in the decision-making process and access to power, are fundamental for the achievement of equality, development and peace;

14. Women's rights are human rights;

15. Equal rights, opportunities and access to resources, equal sharing of responsibilities for the family by men and women, and a harmonious partnership between them are critical to their well-being and that of their families as well as to the consolidation of democracy;

16. Eradication of poverty based on sustained economic growth, social development, environmental protection and social justice requires the involvement of women in economic and social development, equal opportunities and the full and equal participation of women and men as agents and beneficiaries of people-centred sustainable development;

17. The explicit recognition and reaffirmation of the right of all women to control all aspects of their health, in particular their own fertility, is basic to their empowerment;

18. Local, national, regional and global peace is attainable and is inextricably linked with the advancement of women, who are a fundamental force for leadership, conflict resolution and the promotion of lasting peace at all levels;

19. It is essential to design, implement and monitor, with the full participation of women, effective, efficient and mutually reinforcing gender-sensitive policies and programmes, including development policies and programmes, at all levels that will foster the empowerment and advancement of women;

20. The participation and contribution of all actors of civil society, particularly women's groups and networks and other non-governmental organizations and community-based organizations, with full respect for their autonomy, in cooperation with Governments, are important to the effective implementation and follow-up of the Platform for Action;

21. The implementation of the Platform for Action requires commitment from Governments and the international community. By making national and international commitments for action, including those made at the Conference, Governments and the international community recognize the need to take priority action for the empowerment and advancement of women.

We are determined to:

• • •

23. Ensure the full enjoyment by women and the girl child of all human rights and fundamental freedoms and take effective action against violations of these rights and freedoms;

24. Take all necessary measures to eliminate all forms of discrimination against women and the girl child and remove all obstacles to gender equality and the advancement and empowerment of women;

25. Encourage men to participate fully in all actions towards equality;

26. Promote women's economic independence, including employment, and eradicate the persistent and increasing burden of poverty on women by addressing the structural causes of poverty through changes in economic structures, ensuring equal access for all women, including those in rural areas, as vital development agents, to productive resources, opportunities and public services;

27. Promote people-centred sustainable development, including sustained economic growth, through the provision of basic education, life-long education, literacy and training, and primary health care for girls and women;

28. Take positive steps to ensure peace for the advancement of women and, recognizing the leading role that women have played in the peace movement, work actively towards general and complete disarmament under strict and effective international control, and support negotiations on the conclusion, without delay, of a universal and multilaterally and effectively verifiable comprehensive nuclear-test-ban treaty which contributes to nuclear disarmament and the prevention of the proliferation of nuclear weapons in all its aspects;

29. Prevent and eliminate all forms of violence against women and girls;

30. Ensure equal access to and equal treatment of women and men in education and health care and enhance women's sexual and reproductive health as well as education;

31. Promote and protect all human rights of women and girls;

32. Intensify efforts to ensure equal enjoyment of all human rights and fundamental freedoms for all women and girls who face multiple barriers to their empowerment and advancement because of such factors as their race, age, language, ethnicity, culture, religion, or disability, or because they are indigenous people;

33. Ensure respect for international law, including humanitarian law, in order to protect women and girls in particular;

34. Develop the fullest potential of girls and women of all ages, ensure their full and equal participation in building a better world for all and enhance their role in the development process.

We are determined to:

35. Ensure women's equal access to economic resources, including land, credit, science and technology, vocational training, information, communication and markets, as a means to further the advancement and empowerment of women and girls, including through the enhancement of their capacities to enjoy the benefits of equal access to these resources, inter alia, by means of international cooperation;

36. Ensure the success of the Platform for Action, which will require a strong commitment on the part of Governments, international organizations and institutions at all levels. We are deeply convinced that economic development, social development and environmental protection are interdependent and mutually reinforcing components of sustainable development, which is the framework for our efforts to achieve a higher quality of life for all people. Equitable social development that recognizes empowering the poor, particularly women living in poverty, to utilize environmental resources sustainably is a necessary foundation for sustainable development. We also recognize that broad-based and sustained economic growth in the context of sustainable development is necessary to sustain social development and social justice. The success of the Platform for Action will also require adequate mobilization of resources at the national and international levels as well as new and additional resources to the developing countries from all available funding mechanisms, including multilateral, bilateral and private sources for the advancement of women; financial resources to strengthen the capacity of national, subregional, regional and international institutions; a commitment to equal rights, equal responsibilities and equal opportunities and to the equal participation of women and men in all national, regional and international bodies and policy-making processes; and the establishment or strengthening of mechanisms at all levels for accountability to the world's women;

• • •

Questions

1. What kinds of rights for women does the declaration emphasize?

2. What changes on the part of men would be required to implement the recommendations of the declaration?

181. Puwat Chaukamnoetkanok, "Triple Identity: My Experience as an Immigrant in America" (1990)

Source: *Puwat Charukamnoetkanok, "Triple Identity: My Experience as an Immigrant in America," from* **Becoming American, Becoming Ethnic: College Students Explore Their Roots,** *Thomas Dublin, editor. Copyright © 1996. Reprinted with permission of the author.*

Because of shifts in immigration, cultural and racial diversity became increasingly visible in the United States during the 1990s. Until the immigration law of 1965, the vast majority of twentieth-century newcomers had hailed from Europe. That law sparked a wholesale shift in immigrants' origins. Between 1965 and 2000, some 20 million immigrants entered the United States. Half came from Latin America and the Caribbean, 35 percent from Asia, and smaller numbers from the Middle East and Africa.

Like all immigrants, those of the late twentieth century faced painful adjustments in the United States. In this autobiographical essay written in 1990, Puwat Chaukamnoetkanok, a student at the State University of New York, Binghamton, who had entered the country from Thailand four years earlier, reflects on his own experiences and compares them to those of his grandfather, who moved from China to Thailand in 1937, at the age of thirteen. Chaukamnoetkanok graduated from college in 1992, attended medical school, and is now a physician.

———

"AMERICA IS THE land of opportunity." Is this a myth or reality? I came to America four years ago with a faith that I would find opportunity here. However, I realize a reality: racism exists and most people will not easily accept immigrants. In the spring of 1990, I took a course, "Immigration and Ethnicity in the United States," in which I learned that I am not alone. Many immigrants encountered similar barriers. My grandparents are also immigrants, and I have learned about their experiences. In this essay, I compare the experiences of my paternal grandparents with my own experiences.

In 1937 my grandfather, whom I call Ar-kong, came to Thailand from Ch'eng-Hai in Teochiu state (in southern China). He was thirteen years old. His mother brought him to meet his father, who was attracted by the economic opportunity of Thailand and had left China to open a jewelry store in Nakornrajsima (my birthplace, northeast of Bangkok). Greatgrandfather had a second wife who was Thai, which was not an uncommon phenomenon for there were many benefits. Because he was far from home, she was his companion. The marriage also served economic purposes; she could speak Thai, which was good for business. However, the two wives were like oil and water, which put the family under pressure. For this reason,

Ar-kong developed a keen sense of self-reliance and independence. He married my grandmother, Ar-ma, the daughter of a rice mill owner. The bridegroom and the bride were eighteen and seventeen years old, respectively. When Ar-kong was twenty-five years old, he opened his own jewelry store, which has been in business ever since.

• • •

Anti-Chinese sentiment reached its pinnacle during World War II, when all aliens (the majority were Chinese) were forced to evacuate the big cities and relocate to the countryside. Soon after their marriage, my grandparents had to move to Bou Yai (a small town near Nakornrajsima). It is interesting to note the similarity of this development and the evacuation of the Japanese from the West Coast of the United States during the same period. National security was the official reason in both cases, but I believe that the desire to undermine the economic prosperity of the evacuees was the real intention. However, the two practices were by no means equivalent; the Chinese in Thailand suffered much less from this experience. They were not subjected to incarceration and could move their businesses with them. Ar-kong helped his father run a new store in Bou Yai, but the business was not as good because there were fewer customers. The evacuation lasted for four years, and during this period my father was born. Then the family moved back to Nakornrajsima.

My grandparents ignored the prejudice they faced. They worked hard, hoping that when they became established economically people would accept them for who they really were—kind, generous, and peaceful persons. I believe they have succeeded.

• • •

Because of my grandparents' willingness to assimilate and the generous attitude of the majority of Thai people, I never experienced an identity crisis in Thailand. To me, having Chinese ancestry was another fact, just like being a male. It was not something to think about. I was born in Thailand, therefore I was Thai. The fact that Chinese and Thai are physically different was never obvious to me—or at least not until I came to America.

In April 1986 I was told that we would go to America. I only knew about America from movies and television shows, and was very eager to see tall buildings and advanced technology. I said goodbye to all my friends, all of whom were envious of me. My uncle brought us—my brothers, my sister, and myself—to meet our parents who had left earlier to look for a house, school, and business. We traveled by Korea Airlines. The plane stopped at Taiwan, Korea, Japan, Hawaii, and finally New York. We rented a house in Elmont for a few months until the closing of the purchase of our house in Valley Stream. When we went to New York City, I saw tall buildings just like in the movies. But I experienced many things that have never been shown accurately by Hollywood.

The major difference between my immigration and my grandparents' is the motivation. Ar-kong migrated from China mainly for economic reasons. My parents' main objective for migrating was the education of their children. This point can be proven by the fact that my parents left their established business behind and have started from scratch in America. Circumstances in China and Thailand prevented my grandfather Ar-kong from providing his son an education. My father left high school to work, and that kept him from reaching his full potential. He had no choice but to follow his father in the jewelry business.

However, both migration experiences are similar in many ways. For the first time in my life, I have learned about prejudice and discrimination. I have been taught to be nice to others, which includes people who are "different" from myself. But I have learned, in America, that not everybody has been taught that way. Many people judge a person only on appearances. I have not yet experienced prejudice directly. Nobody has ever called me by derogatory terms or beaten me because of the color of my skin. But knowing of the existence of racism has affected me just the same. I will not blame the racists, but I cannot keep from feeling sorry for them, for they have lost the opportunity to meet potential friends because they are narrow-minded.

Like my grandparents, I also experience difficulty regarding language. Now I feel very bad for making fun of Ar-ma. I have realized how hard it is to learn another language. An inability to communicate is very frustrating. I become hypersensitive sometimes because I am constantly not sure what people are saying around me. Speaking with a strange accent makes me become self-conscious. There are many times when I feel that it is difficult to articulate my thoughts.

In America, there are many cultural differences that I have to learn. For example there are many occasions where I feel totally lost, as when my friends talk about TV shows before 1986. Many values are different. I, like many children from Asia, have been taught to respect elders, including parents, relatives, and teachers. Needless to say, it is quite different here in America. I do not understand why, since you lose nothing by giving respect. This essay would not have been possible without these marvelous people. I also meet Chinese friends who have never been in Thailand; people who look just like me but are not Thai.

Living in America, I learn about racism and cultural differences, and experience language difficulties. For the first time, I experience an identity crisis. While most immigrants have double identities to deal with, I have three. Am I Chinese, Thai, or American? At times, I am very confused and angry. No matter which identity I choose, I will be different. However, I will never be able to solve this crisis if I care too much about what other people think. I cannot change their thoughts, but I can change mine. Ar-kong and Ar-ma ignored people who were prejudiced against them in Thailand, and I should be able to do the same in America. I do not really have to choose.

I have a unique opportunity to combine the good qualities of each identity into one. This is, of course, easier said than done. But at least now that I know what to do, achieving the goal can be done with less distraction. If I am willing to work hard at it, hopefully some day people will accept me for who I am. America is really a land of opportunity, but as with all good land, hard work and patience are needed to harvest the crops.

Questions

1. What are the most unfamiliar features of American life to the immigrant from Thailand?

2. What does Chaukamnoetkanok see as the main differences between his experience and that of his grandparents?

---

182. Bill Clinton, Remarks at the "America's Millennium" Celebration (1999)

Source: "Remarks at the 'America's Millennium' Celebration," December 31, 1999, **Public Papers of the Presidents, William J. Clinton, 1999** *(Washington, D.C., 2000), pp. 2358–59.*

On the night of December 31, 1999–January 1, 2000, Americans celebrated the advent of a new century and millennium (although strictly speaking, these actually would not begin until one year later). Having survived an impeachment trial in 1999, President Bill Clinton presided over the ceremonies in Washington, D.C. He called on Americans to look back with pride on the remarkable accomplishments of the twentieth century and rededicate themselves to combating poverty and intolerance in the twenty-first. As Clinton's remarks suggested, freedom remained a crucial point of self-definition for Americans at the dawn of the new century.

LADIES AND GENTLEMEN, tonight we celebrate. The change of centuries, the dawning of a new millennium are now just minutes away. We celebrate the past. We have honored America's remarkable achievements, struggles, and triumphs in the twentieth century. We celebrate the future, imagining an even more remarkable twenty-first century.

As we marvel at the changes of the last hundred years, we dream of what changes the next hundred and the next thousand will bring. And as powerful as our memories are, our dreams must be even stronger. For when our memories outweigh our dreams, we become old, and it is the eternal destiny of America to remain forever young, always reaching beyond, always becoming, as our Founders pledged, "a more perfect Union." So we Americans must not fear change. Instead, let us welcome it, embrace it, and create it.

The great story of the twentieth century is the triumph of freedom and free people, a story told in the drama of new immigrants, the struggles for equal rights, the victories over totalitarianism, the stunning advances in economic well-being, in culture, in health, in space and telecommunications, and in building a world in which more than half the people live under governments of their own choosing for the first time in all history. We must never forget the meaning of the twentieth century or the gifts of the Internet, microscopes that envision the infinitesimal, and telescopes that elucidate the infinite, soon-to-be complete blueprint for human life itself.

And they will see that this moment was earned through a passion for creativity. National power may spring from economic and military might, but the greatness of a nation emanates from the life of the mind and the stirrings of the soul. So many of you have contributed to that greatness, and we are all grateful.

In this century, American artists of the page and the canvas, the stage and screen, have drawn from our diverse palate of cultural traditions and given the world a great gift of uniquely American creations with universal and timeless appeal.

The new century and the new millennium will bring a cascade of new triumphs. We see new hope for peace in lands bedeviled by ancient hatreds, new technologies both opening the storehouse of human knowledge for people across the globe and offering the promise of alleviating the poverty that still haunts so many millions of our children. We see scientists rapidly approaching the day when newborns can expect to live well past 100 years, and children will know "cancer" only as a constellation of stars. But by far, my most solemn prayer for this new millennium is that we will find, somehow, the strength and wisdom in our hearts to keep growing together, first, as one America and then, as one people on this ever smaller planet we all call home.

If you look at the glowing diversity of race and background that illuminates America's house on this evening, a vivid illustration, we see that human capacity is distributed equally across the human landscape. I cannot help but think how different America is, how different history is, and how much better, because those of you in this room and those you represent were able to imagine, to invent, to inspire. And by the same token, I cannot help but dream of how much different and how much better our future can be if we can give every child the same chance to live up to his or her God-given potential and to live together as brothers and sisters, celebrating our common humanity and our shared destiny.

This is the future I hope every American will take a moment to imagine on this millennial evening. This is the future I pray we can all join together to build. So I ask you to join me in a toast to yourselves, to the First Lady, and to our shared future. . . .

As we ring in this new year, in a new century, in a new millennium, we must, now and always, echo Dr. King in the words of the old American hymn: "Let freedom ring."

If the story of the twentieth century is the triumph of freedom, what will the story of the twenty-first century be? Let it be the triumph of freedom wisely used, to bring peace to a world in which we honor our differences and, even more, our common humanity. Such a triumph will require great efforts from us all.

It will require us to stand against the forces of hatred and bigotry, terror and destruction. It will require us to continue to prosper, to alleviate poverty, to better balance the demands of work and family, and to serve each of us in our communities. It will require us to take better care of our environment. It will require us to make further breakthroughs in science and technology, to cure dread diseases, heal broken bodies, lengthen life, and unlock secrets from global warming to the black holes in the universe. And perhaps most important, it will require us to share with our fellow Americans and, increasingly, with our fellow citizens of the world the economic benefits of globalization, the political benefits of democracy and human rights, the educational and health benefits of all things modern, from the Internet to the genetic encyclopedia to the mysteries beyond our solar system.

Now, we may not be able to eliminate all hateful intolerance, but we can develop a healthy intolerance of bigotry, oppression, and abject poverty. We may not be able to eliminate all the harsh consequences of globalization, but we can communicate more and travel more and trade more, in a way that lifts the lives of ordinary working families everywhere and the quality of our global environment. We may not be able to eliminate all the failures of government and international institutions, but we can certainly strengthen democracy so all children are prepared for the twenty-first century world and protected from its harshest side effects.

And we can do so much more to work together, to cooperate among ourselves, to seize the problems and the opportunities of this ever small planet we all call home. In short, if we want the story of the twenty-first century to be the triumph of peace and harmony, we must embrace our common humanity and our shared destiny.

Now, we're just moments from that new millennium. Two centuries ago, as the framers where crafting our Constitution, Benjamin Franklin was often seen in Independence Hall looking at a painting of the Sun low on the horizon. When, at long last, the Constitution finally was signed, Mr. Franklin said, "I have often wondered whether that Sun was rising or setting. Today I have the happiness to know it is a rising Sun." Well, two centuries later, we know the Sun will always rise on America, as long as each new generation lights the fire of freedom. Our children are ready. So again, the torch is passed to a new century of young Americans.

Questions

1. Why does Clinton describe the twentieth century as a "triumph of freedom"?

2. In what areas does he seem to believe that freedom is still incomplete?

CHAPTER 28

September 11 and the Next American Century

183. The National Security Strategy of the United States (2002)

Source: The National Security Strategy of the United States *(Washington, D.C., 2002), pp. iv–vi, 15, 29–30.*

In September 2002, one year after the September 11 terrorist attacks, the Bush administration released a document called the National Security Strategy. It outlined a fundamental shift in American foreign policy. The report began with a discussion not of weaponry or military strategy but of freedom. It went on to promise that the United States would "extend the benefits of freedom" by fighting not only "terrorists" but "tyrants" around the world.

The National Security Strategy announced that the United States must maintain an overwhelming preponderance of military power, not allowing any other country to challenge its overall strength or its dominance in any region of the world. To replace the Cold War doctrine of deterrence, which assumed that the certainty of retaliation would prevent attacks on the United States and its allies, the document announced a new foreign policy principle—preemptive war. If the United States believed that a nation posed a possible future threat to its security, it had the right to attack before such a threat materialized.

THE GREAT STRUGGLES of the twentieth century between liberty and totalitarianism ended with a decisive victory for the forces of freedom—and a single sustainable model for national success: freedom, democracy, and free enterprise. In the twenty-first century, only nations that share a commitment to protecting basic human rights and guaranteeing political and economic freedom will be able to unleash the potential of their people and assure their future prosperity. People everywhere want to be able to speak freely; choose who will govern them; worship as they please; educate their children—male and female; own property; and enjoy the benefits of their labor. These values of freedom are right and true for every person, in every society—and the duty of protecting these values against their enemies is the common calling of freedom-loving people across the globe and across the ages.

Today, the United States enjoys a position of unparalleled military strength and great economic and political influence. In keeping with our heritage and principles, we do not use our strength to press for unilateral advantage. We seek instead to create a balance of power that favors human freedom: conditions in which all nations and all societies can choose for themselves the rewards and challenges of political and economic liberty. In a world that is safe, people will be able to make their own lives better. We will defend the peace by fighting terrorists and tyrants. We will preserve the peace by building good relations among the great powers. We will extend the peace by encouraging free and open societies on every continent.

• • •

Freedom is the non-negotiable demand of human dignity; the birthright of every person—in every civilization. Throughout history, freedom has been threatened by war and terror; it has been challenged by the clashing wills of powerful states and the evil designs of tyrants; and it has been tested by widespread poverty and disease. Today, humanity holds in its hands the opportunity to further freedom's triumph over all these foes. The United States welcomes our responsibility to lead in this great mission.

• • •

The United States has long maintained the option of preemptive actions to counter a sufficient threat to our national security. The greater the threat, the greater is the risk of inaction—and the more compelling the case for taking anticipatory action to defend ourselves, even if uncertainty remains as to the time and place of the enemy's attack. To forestall or prevent such hostile acts by our adversaries, the United States will, if necessary, act preemptively.

The United States will not use force in all cases to preempt emerging threats, nor should nations use preemption as a pretext for aggression. Yet in an age where the enemies of civilization openly and actively seek the world's most destructive technologies, the United States cannot remain idle while dangers gather.

• • •

The presence of American forces overseas is one of the most profound symbols of the U.S. commitments to allies and friends. Through our willingness to use force in our own defense and in defense of others, the United States demonstrates its resolve to maintain a balance of power that favors freedom. To contend with uncertainty and to meet the many security challenges we face, the United States will require bases and stations within and beyond Western Europe and Northeast Asia, as well as temporary access arrangements for the long-distance deployment of U.S. forces.

We know from history that deterrence can fail; and we know from experience that some enemies cannot be deterred. The United States must and will maintain the capability to defeat any attempt by an enemy—whether a state or non-state actor—to impose its will on the United States, our allies, or our friends. We will maintain the forces sufficient to support our obligations, and to defend freedom. Our forces will be strong enough to dissuade potential adversaries from pursuing a military build-up in hopes of surpassing, or equaling, the power of the United States.

Questions

1. Why does the document assert that its understanding of freedom is "right and true for every person, in every society"?

2. Why did the doctrine of preemptive war arouse so much opposition in other countries?

---

184. Robert Byrd on the War in Iraq (2003)

Source: Speech of Senator Robert Byrd, February 12, 2003, U.S. Senate.

The first implementation of the principles of the National Security Strategy came in 2003, when the United States invaded and occupied Iraq, overthrowing the dictatorial government of Saddam Hussein. The decision split the western alliance and inspired a massive antiwar movement throughout the world. In February 2003, between 10 and 15 million people across the globe demonstrated against the impending war.

With President Bush still widely popular, few elected officials were willing to criticize him as the country moved toward war. One who did so was Senator Robert Byrd of West Virginia. Byrd condemned his colleagues for refusing even to debate the question. He criticized the idea of an "unprovoked military attack" on another nation and the Bush administration's indifference to worldwide opposition to the impending war. Unable to obtain approval from the United Nations, the United States went to war anyway in March 2003. Within a month, American troops occupied Baghdad. But, as Byrd had warned, securing the peace proved to be extremely difficult.

TO CONTEMPLATE WAR is to think about the most horrible of human experiences. On this February day, as this nation stands at the brink of battle, every American on some level must be contemplating the horrors of war.

Yet, this Chamber is, for the most part, silent—ominously, dreadfully silent. There is no debate, no discussion, no attempt to lay out for the nation the pros and cons of this particular war. There is nothing.

We stand passively mute in the United States Senate, paralyzed by our own uncertainty, seemingly stunned by the sheer turmoil of events. Only on the editorial pages of our newspapers is there much substantive discussion of the prudence or imprudence of engaging in this particular war.

And this is no small conflagration we contemplate. This is no simple attempt to defang a villain. No. This coming battle, if it materializes, represents a turning point in U.S. foreign policy and possibly a turning point in the recent history of the world.

This nation is about to embark upon the first test of a revolutionary doctrine applied in an extraordinary way at an unfortunate time. The doctrine of preemption—the idea that the United States or any other nation can legitimately attack a nation that is not imminently threatening but may be threatening in the future—is a radical new twist on the traditional idea of self defense. It appears to be in contravention of international law and the UN Charter. And it is being tested at a time of world-wide terrorism, making many countries around the globe wonder if they will soon be on our—or some other nation's—hit list. High level Administration figures recently refused to take nuclear weapons off of the table when discussing a possible attack against Iraq. What could be more destabilizing and unwise than this type of uncertainty, particularly in a world where globalism has tied the vital economic and security interests of many nations so closely together? There are huge cracks emerging in our time-honored alliances, and U.S. intentions are suddenly subject to damaging worldwide speculation. Anti-Americanism based on mistrust, misinformation, suspicion, and alarming rhetoric from U.S. leaders is fracturing the once solid alliance against global terrorism which existed after September 11.

Here at home, people are warned of imminent terrorist attacks with little guidance as to when or where such attacks might occur.

Family members are being called to active military duty, with no idea of the duration of their stay or what horrors they may face. Communities are being left with less than adequate police and fire protection. Other essential services are also short-staffed. The mood of the nation is grim. The economy is stumbling. Fuel prices are rising and may soon spike higher.

• • •

Calling heads of state pygmies, labeling whole countries as evil, denigrating powerful European allies as irrelevant—these types of crude insensitivities can do our great nation no good. We may have massive military might, but we cannot fight a global war on terrorism alone. We need the cooperation and friendship of our time-honored allies as well as the newer found friends whom we can attract with our wealth. Our awesome military machine will do us little good if we suffer another devastating attack on our homeland which severely damages our economy. Our military manpower is already stretched thin and we will need the augmenting support of those nations who can supply troop strength, not just sign letters cheering us on.

The war in Afghanistan has cost us $37 billion so far, yet there is evidence that terrorism may already be starting to regain its hold in that region. We have not found bin Laden, and unless we secure the peace in Afghanistan, the dark dens of terrorism may yet again flourish in that remote and devastated land.

Pakistan as well is at risk of destabilizing forces. This Administration has not finished the first war against terrorism and yet it is eager to embark on another conflict with perils much greater than those in Afghanistan. Is our attention span that short? Have we not learned that after winning the war one must always secure the peace?

And yet we hear little about the aftermath of war in Iraq. In the absence of plans, speculation abroad is rife. Will we seize Iraq's oil fields, becoming an occupying power which controls the price and supply of that nation's oil for the foreseeable future? To whom do we propose to hand the reigns of power after Saddam Hussein?

Will our war inflame the Muslim world resulting in devastating attacks on Israel? Will Israel retaliate with its own nuclear arsenal? Will the Jordanian and Saudi Arabian governments be toppled by radicals, bolstered by Iran which has much closer ties to terrorism than Iraq?

Could a disruption of the world's oil supply lead to a world-wide recession? Has our senselessly bellicose language and our callous disregard of the interests and opinions of other nations increased the global race to join the nuclear club and made proliferation an even more lucrative practice for nations which need the income?

• • •

We are truly "sleepwalking through history." In my heart of hearts I pray that this great nation and its good and trusting citizens are not in for a rudest of awakenings.

To engage in war is always to pick a wild card. And war must always be a last resort, not a first choice. I truly must question the judgment of any President who can say that a massive unprovoked military attack on a nation which is over 50% children is "in the highest moral traditions of our country." This war is not necessary at this time. Pressure appears to be having a good result in Iraq. Our mistake was to put ourselves in a corner so quickly. Our challenge is to now find a graceful way out of a box of our own making. Perhaps there is still a way if we allow more time.

Questions

1. Why does Byrd consider the impending attack on Iraq as dangerous and unwarranted?

2. Why does he believe it essential for the United States to obtain the cooperation of other countries?

185. Second Inaugural Address of George W. Bush (2005)

Source: The White House.

In his second inaugural address, in January 2005, Bush outlined a new American goal—"ending tyranny in the world." Striking a more conciliatory tone than during his first administration, he promised that the United States would not try to impose "our style of government" on others and that, in the future, it would seek the advice of allies. He said nothing specific about Iraq but tried to shore up falling support for the war by invoking the ideal of freedom: "the survival of liberty in our land increasingly depends on the success of liberty in other lands." In his first inaugural, in 2001, Bush had used the words "freedom," "free," or "liberty" seven times. In his second, they appeared forty-nine times. Again and again, Bush insisted that the United States stands for the worldwide triumph of freedom.

━━━

AT THIS SECOND gathering, our duties are defined not by the words I use, but by the history we have seen together. For a half century, America defended our own freedom by standing watch on distant borders. After the shipwreck of communism came years of relative quiet, years of repose, years of sabbatical—and then there came a day of fire.

We have seen our vulnerability—and we have seen its deepest source. For as long as whole regions of the world simmer in resentment and tyranny—prone to ideologies that feed hatred and excuse murder—violence will gather, and multiply in destructive power, and cross the most defended borders, and raise a mortal threat. There is only one force of history that can break the reign of hatred and resentment, and expose the pretensions of tyrants, and reward the hopes of the decent and tolerant, and that is the force of human freedom.

We are led, by events and common sense, to one conclusion: The survival of liberty in our land increasingly depends on the success of liberty in other lands. The best hope for peace in our world is the expansion of freedom in all the world.

America's vital interests and our deepest beliefs are now one. From the day of our Founding, we have proclaimed that every man and woman on this earth has rights, and dignity, and matchless value, because they bear the image of the Maker of Heaven and earth. Across the generations we have proclaimed the imperative of self-government, because no one is fit to be a master, and no one deserves to be a slave. Advancing these ideals is the mission that created our Nation. It is the honorable achievement of our fathers. Now it is the urgent requirement of our nation's security, and the calling of our time.

So it is the policy of the United States to seek and support the growth of democratic movements and institutions in every nation and culture, with the ultimate goal of ending tyranny in our world.

This is not primarily the task of arms, though we will defend ourselves and our friends by force of arms when necessary. Freedom, by its nature, must be chosen, and defended by citizens, and sustained by the rule of law and the protection of minorities. And when the soul of a nation finally speaks, the institutions that arise may reflect customs and traditions very different from our own. America will not impose our own style of government on the unwilling. Our goal instead is to help others find their own voice, attain their own freedom, and make their own way. . . .

We will persistently clarify the choice before every ruler and every nation: The moral choice between oppression, which is always wrong, and freedom, which is eternally right. America will not pretend that jailed dissidents prefer their chains, or that women welcome humiliation and servitude, or that any human being aspires to live at the mercy of bullies.

We will encourage reform in other governments by making clear that success in our relations will require the decent treatment of their own people. America's belief in human dignity will guide our policies, yet rights must be more than the grudging concessions of dictators; they are secured by free dissent and the participation of the governed. In the long run, there is no justice without freedom, and there can be no human rights without human liberty. . . .

Today, America speaks anew to the peoples of the world:

All who live in tyranny and hopelessness can know: the United States will not ignore your oppression, or excuse your oppressors. When you stand for your liberty, we will stand with you.

Democratic reformers facing repression, prison, or exile can know: America sees you for who you are: the future leaders of your free country.

The rulers of outlaw regimes can know that we still believe as Abraham Lincoln did: "Those who deny freedom to others deserve it not for themselves; and, under the rule of a just God, cannot long retain it."

The leaders of governments with long habits of control need to know: To serve your people you must learn to trust them. Start on this journey of progress and justice, and America will walk at your side.

And all the allies of the United States can know: we honor your friendship, we rely on your counsel, and we depend on your help. Division among free nations is a primary goal of freedom's enemies. The concerted effort of free nations to promote democracy is a prelude to our enemies' defeat....

We go forward with complete confidence in the eventual triumph of freedom. Not because history runs on the wheels of inevitability; it is human choices that move events. Not because we consider ourselves a chosen nation; God moves and chooses as He wills. We have confidence because freedom is the permanent hope of mankind, the hunger in dark places, the longing of the soul. When our Founders declared a new order of the ages; when soldiers died in wave upon wave for a union based on liberty; when citizens marched in peaceful outrage under the banner "Freedom Now"—they were acting on an ancient hope that is meant to be fulfilled. History has an ebb and flow of justice, but history also has a visible direction, set by liberty and the Author of Liberty.

When the Declaration of Independence was first read in public and the Liberty Bell was sounded in celebration, a witness said, "It rang as if it meant something." In our time it means something still. America, in this young century, proclaims liberty throughout all the world, and to all the inhabitants thereof. Renewed in our strength—

tested, but not weary—we are ready for the greatest achievements in the history of freedom.

May God bless you, and may He watch over the United States of America.

Questions

1. How convincing is Bush's description of a world divided into friends and enemies of freedom?

2. What traditional American ideals does Bush appeal to in this speech?

---

186. Archbishop Roger Mahoney, "Called by God to Help" (2006)

*Source: Roger Mahoney: "Called by God to Help." **The New York Times,** March 22, 2006. Copyright © 2006, The New York Times. Reprinted by permission.*

The influx of immigrants proceeded apace during the first years of the twenty-first century. Alongside legal immigrants, undocumented newcomers made their way to the United States, mostly from Mexico. At the end of 2005, it was estimated, there were 11 million illegal aliens in the United States. With many Americans convinced that the United States had lost control of its borders and that immigration was in part responsible for the stagnation of real wages, the House of Representatives approved a bill making it a felony to be in the country illegally and a crime to offer aid to illegal immigrants. The response was utterly unexpected—a series of massive popular demonstrations by immigrants, legal and illegal, and their supporters, demanding the right to remain in the country as citizens.

At the same time, church groups used to sheltering and feeding the destitute denounced the proposed bill as akin to the Fugitive Slave Law of 1850 for making it a crime to help a suffering human being and vowed to resist it. One eloquent statement of this position came from Roger Mahoney, the

Roman Catholic archbishop of Los Angeles, a city with one of the highest proportions of immigrants, legal and undocumented, in the country. In 2006, Congress failed to agree on any immigration legislation, except for a law authorizing the construction of a fence along hundreds of miles of the border between the United States and Mexico.

I'VE RECEIVED A lot of criticism for stating last month that I would instruct the priests of my archdiocese to disobey a proposed law that would subject them, as well as other church and humanitarian workers, to criminal penalties. The proposed Border Protection, Antiterrorism and Illegal Immigration Control bill, which was approved by the House of Representatives in December and is expected to be taken up by the Senate next week, would among other things subject to five years in prison anyone who "assists" an undocumented immigrant "to remain in the United States."

Some supporters of the bill have even accused the church of encouraging illegal immigration and meddling in politics. But I stand by my statement. Part of the mission of the Roman Catholic Church is to help people in need. It is our Gospel mandate, in which Christ instructs us to clothe the naked, feed the poor and welcome the stranger. Indeed, the Catholic Church, through Catholic Charities agencies around the country, is one of the largest nonprofit providers of social services in the nation, serving both citizens and immigrants.

Providing humanitarian assistance to those in need should not be made a crime, as the House bill decrees. As written, the proposed law is so broad that it would criminalize even minor acts of mercy like offering a meal or administering first aid.

Current law does not require social service agencies to obtain evidence of legal status before rendering aid, nor should it. Denying aid to a fellow human being violates a law with a higher authority than Congress—the law of God.

That does not mean that the Catholic Church encourages or supports illegal immigration. Every day in our parishes, social service

programs, hospitals and schools, we witness the baleful consequences of illegal immigration. Families are separated, workers are
exploited and migrants are left by smugglers to die in the desert. Illegal immigration serves neither the migrant nor the common good.

What the church supports is an overhaul of the immigration system so that legal status and legal channels for migration replace illegal status and illegal immigration. Creating legal structures for
migration protects not only those who migrate but also our nation,
by giving the government the ability to better identify who is in the
country as well as to control who enters it.

Only comprehensive reform of the immigration system, embodied in the principles of another proposal in Congress, the Secure
America and Orderly Immigration bill, will help solve our current
immigration crisis.

Enforcement-only proposals like the Border Protection act take
the country in the opposite direction. Increasing penalties, building
more detention centers and erecting walls along our border with
Mexico, as the act provides, will not solve the problem.

The legislation will not deter migrants who are desperate to survive and support their families from seeking jobs in the United
States. It will only drive them further into the shadows, encourage
the creation of more elaborate smuggling networks and cause hardship and suffering. I hope that the Senate will not take the same
enforcement-only road as the House.

The unspoken truth of the immigration debate is that at the same
time our nation benefits economically from the presence of undocumented workers, we turn a blind eye when they are exploited by employers. They work in industries that are vital to our economy yet
they have little legal protection and no opportunity to contribute
fully to our nation.

While we gladly accept their taxes and sweat, we do not acknowledge or uphold their basic labor rights. At the same time, we scape-
goat them for our social ills and label them as security threats and
criminals to justify the passage of anti-immigrant bills.

This situation affects the dignity of millions of our fellow human beings and makes immigration, ultimately, a moral and ethical issue. That is why the church is compelled to take a stand against harmful legislation and to work toward positive change.

It is my hope that our elected officials will understand this and enact immigration reform that respects our common humanity and reflects the values—fairness, compassion and opportunity—upon which our nation, a nation of immigrants, was built.

Questions

1. Why does Archbishop Mahoney believe that he has a right to disobey the proposed law?

2. How does he believe the question of immigration should be addressed?

187. Anthony Kennedy, Opinion of the Court in *Lawrence v. Texas* (2003)

Source: Opinion of the Court, Lawrence v. Texas *539 U.S. 558 (2003).*

One of the most remarkable Supreme Court decisions of recent years came in 2003 in the case of *Lawrence v. Texas.* A 6–3 majority declared unconstitutional a Texas law making homosexual acts a crime. Written by Justice Anthony Kennedy, the majority opinion overturned the court's 1986 ruling in *Bowers v. Hardwick,* which had upheld a similar Georgia law. But Kennedy went much further than simply voiding a state law that many Americans deemed an invasion of adult privacy. His decision included an exposition on the meaning of freedom at the dawn of the twenty-first century. The decision showed how the struggles for equality by the feminist and gay movements had succeeded in extending the idea of freedom into the most personal realms of life. Kennedy went on to repudiate the conservative view that constitutional interpretation must rest on the "original intent" of the founding fathers or on a narrow reading of the document's text. Instead, he reaffirmed the liberal view of the Constitution as a living document whose protections expand as society changes.

⸻

LIBERTY PROTECTS THE person from unwarranted government intrusions into a dwelling or other private places. In our tradition the State is not omnipresent in the home. And there are other spheres of our lives and existence, outside the home, where the State should not be a dominant presence. Freedom extends beyond spatial bounds. Liberty presumes an autonomy of self that includes freedom of thought, belief, expression, and certain intimate conduct. The instant case involves liberty of the person both in its spatial and more transcendent dimensions.

• • •

Equality of treatment and the due process right to demand respect for conduct protected by the substantive guarantee of liberty are linked in important respects, and a decision on the latter point advances both interests. If protected conduct is made criminal and the law which does so remains unexamined for its substantive validity, its stigma might remain even if it were not enforceable as drawn for equal protection reasons. When homosexual conduct is made criminal by the law of the State, that declaration in and of itself is an invitation to subject homosexual persons to discrimination both in the public and in the private spheres. The central holding of *Bowers* has been brought in question by this case, and it should be addressed. Its continuance as precedent demeans the lives of homosexual persons.

• • •

The petitioners are entitled to respect for their private lives. The State cannot demean their existence or control their destiny by making their private sexual conduct a crime. Their right to liberty under the Due Process Clause gives them the full right to engage in their conduct without intervention of the government. "It is a promise of the Constitution that there is a realm of personal liberty which the government may not enter." *Casey, supra,* at 847. The Texas statute furthers no legitimate state interest which can justify its intrusion into the personal and private life of the individual.

Had those who drew and ratified the Due Process Clauses of the *Fifth Amendment* or the *Fourteenth Amendment* known the components of liberty in its manifold possibilities, they might have been more specific. They did not presume to have this insight. They knew times can blind us to certain truths and later generations can see that laws once thought necessary and proper in fact serve only to oppress. As the Constitution endures, persons in every generation can invoke its principles in their own search for greater freedom.

Questions

1. How does Kennedy understand the meaning of freedom?

2. How does his definition differ from understandings of freedom in previous eras of American history?

188. Sandra Day O'Connor, Opinion of the Court in *Hamdi v. Rumsfeld* (2004)

Source: Opinion of the Court, Hamdi v. Rumsfeld, *542 U.S. 507 (2004).*

In the aftermath of the attacks of 2001, the Bush administration claimed sweeping powers to fight the "war on terrorism," including the right to arrest and hold indefinitely those declared by the president to be enemy combatants. The Supreme Court proved unreceptive to President Bush's claim of authority to suspend constitutional protections of individual liberties. It reaffirmed the rule of law both for American citizens and foreigners held prisoner by the United States.

In *Hamdi v. Rumsfeld,* the court considered the lawsuit of Yasir Hamdi, an American citizen who had moved to Saudi Arabia and been captured in Afghanistan. Hamdi was imprisoned in a military jail in South Carolina without charge or the right to see a lawyer. Writing for the 8–1 majority and quoting previous Supreme Court decisions, Justice Sandra Day O'Connor insisted that Hamdi had a right to a judicial hearing. She also reaffirmed that the courts have the power to oversee the president's actions, even in wartime. Even Justice Antonin Scalia, the court's most prominent conservative, rejected the president's claim of authority to imprison a citizen at will as antithetical to "the very core of liberty."

After claiming in court that Hamdi was so dangerous that he could not even be allowed a hearing, the administration allowed him to return to Saudi Arabia on condition that he relinquish his American citizenship.

STRIKING THE PROPER constitutional balance here is of great importance to the Nation during this period of ongoing combat. But it is equally vital that our calculus not give short shrift to the values that this country holds dear or to the privilege that is American citizenship. It is during our most challenging and uncertain moments that our Nation's commitment to due process is most severely tested; and it is in those times that we must preserve our commitment at home to the principles for which we fight abroad.... ("It would indeed be ironic if, in the name of national defense, we would sanction the subversion of one of those liberties ... which makes the defense of the Nation worthwhile.")

With due recognition of these competing concerns, we believe that ... the process proposed by the Government [fails to strike] the proper constitutional balance when a United States citizen is detained in the United States as an enemy combatant. That is, "the risk of erroneous deprivation" of a detainee's liberty interest is unacceptably high under the Government's proposed rule, ... We therefore hold that a citizen-detainee seeking to challenge his classification as an enemy combatant must receive notice of the factual basis for his classification, and a fair opportunity to rebut the Government's factual assertions before a neutral decisionmaker. These essential constitutional promises may not be eroded....

In so holding, we necessarily reject the Government's assertion that separation of powers principles mandate a heavily circumscribed role for the courts in such circumstances. Indeed, the position that the courts must forgo any examination of the individual case and focus exclusively on the legality of the broader detention scheme cannot be mandated by any reasonable view of separation of powers, as this approach serves only to condense power into a single branch of government. We have long since made clear that a state of war is not a blank check for the President when it comes to the rights of the Nation's citizens.... Whatever power the United States Constitution envisions for the Executive in its exchanges with other nations or with enemy organizations in times of conflict, it most assuredly envisions a role for all three branches when individual liberties are at stake.... Likewise, we have made clear that, unless Congress acts to suspend it, the Great Writ of habeas corpus allows the Judicial Branch to play a necessary role in maintaining this delicate balance of governance, serving as an important judicial check on the Executive's discretion in the realm of detentions.... Thus, while we do not question that our due process assessment must pay keen attention to the particular burdens faced by the Executive in the context of military action, it would turn our system of checks and balances on its head to suggest that a citizen could not make his way to court with a challenge to the factual basis for his detention by his government, simply because the Executive opposes making available such a challenge. Absent suspension of the writ by Congress, a citizen detained as an enemy combatant is entitled to this process.

Questions

1. Why does O'Connor emphasize the "separation of powers" in her decision?

2. How does O'Connor respond to the government's claim that a state of war allows it to suspend traditional liberties?